The Mayo Ind onora

The Mayo Indians of Sonora

A People Who Refuse to Die

N. Ross Crumrine
University of Victoria

WAVELAND
PRESS, INC.
Prospect Heights, Illinois

About the Author . . .

N. Ross Crumrine, professor of anthropology at the University of Victoria, has explored the modern Mayo way of life during two years of residence and various brief visits which have fostered in-depth study of Mayo culture and traditions. His academic background includes undergraduate studies at Northwestern University and graduate studies in anthropology at the Universities of Chicago and Washington culminating in graduate degrees from the University of Arizona. In addition to research among the Mayos, he has done fieldwork on the far north coast of Peru which focuses on the modern ceremonialism of the lower Piura River valley.

Cover: The arrival of the *Pilato* and *Pariserom* to "kill" Christ at a neighboring Mayo church, Good Friday morning.

For information about this book, write or call:

Waveland Press, Inc.
P.O. Box 400
Prospect Heights, Illinois 60070
(312) 634-0081

Printed in the United States of America

7 6 5 4 3 2 1

Contents

Foreword

In the textbooks from which twentieth-century Sonoran Mexican children are taught, the Mayo Indians are always described as peaceful and inclined toward acceptance of "civilization," which of course in the view of the textbook writers means acceptance of Mexican ways. They are dismissed with a few phrases, as if regarded as not having any history, while the textbooks contain a chapter or more devoted entirely to the "Yaqui Wars." Yaquis for years prevented the landlords who governed the state of Sonora during the nineteenth century from absorbing the Yaqui land and people into the hacienda system of peonage, and thus made an unforgettable impact on Sonoran life.

Now, however, it becomes clear that the Mayos, too, have a history, and it is an especially interesting one. The Mayo people were, at the coming of the Spaniards, the most numerous of all the natives of what has been called the greater Southwest, that is, the region of northwestern Mexico and the southwestern U.S., where some fifty human groups now live. According to the missionaries, the Mayos at that time numbered 25,000 along the Mayo River and at least that many more in the Fuerte River Valley to the south.

In this book, Ross Crumrine gives us the first intensive description of the Mayo Indians and shows us how the Mayos, like all people who do not wholly disappear from the human record, have been retelling their history as they go along. This is part of the process of maintaining an identity. Only when a people is no longer concerned to relate current happenings to the picture they have of themselves in the past do they lose their identity and disappear. Thousands of Mayos continue to be interested in building the role in human history which they believe they have played for centuries. They have maintained fundamental elements of that interesting synthesis of native American and medieval Christian ways which they developed in Jesuit communities of the 1600s and 1700s, not by passively preserving the earlier culture synthesis intact, but rather by repeated adaptation to the recurrent profound alterations in their lives. Thus they rework the events of the recent past and the present into a fabric of meaning which gives them a sense of continuity and human dignity.

Mayo history is that of a people who, for various reasons unable to field a fighting force after the 1880s, turned to prophetic vision. They listened, as Crumrine mentions, to the prophet Santa Teresa of Cabora, who predicted the destruction of the Mexicans, which the Mayos passionately wanted but had not been able to bring about by force of arms. Santa Teresa was of immense influence among the Mayos, inspiring many disciples who preached her vision in the Mayo Valley until they were rounded up by the Mexican army in 1890 and shipped to Baja California to work in the mines. Santa Teresa's influence reached up into the Sierra Madre Mountains and inspired a revolt among the Tarahumaras, and was also reputed to have inspired a famous raid on the customs house at Nogales, Sonora. Ultimately she was forced to leave Mexico and take up residence in the Santa Cruz Valley in Arizona, and later in Los Angeles and elsewhere in Arizona at Clifton.

The influence of Santa Teresa has still not died out. As we learn in this book, she initiated, or perhaps carried on, a tradition of great importance in Mayo life—a deep interest in mystical experience and prophecy. Although this tradition may spring from a base similar to certain beliefs in old Yaqui and other Sonoran Indian cultures, it is distinctively Mayo in the way in which it has developed. That is one theme of this book; as Crumrine says, he tries to help us understand the nature and causes of prophet production among the Mayos.

There is another aspect of Mayo history which the schoolchildren of Sonora ought to know more about. General Obregón tells in his autobiography how he recruited thousands of Mayos for his revolutionary armies, and shows pictures of Mayos with bows and arrows in 1917 ready to join his troops and fight for the new Mexico which was to follow the destruction of landlord Mexico in the 1910 Revolution. It is true that many Mayos fought in that great effort. Nevertheless when the Revolution was over, Mayos did not find themselves possessed of any new freedom. On the contrary, when the Calles administration in the mid-1920s began its anticlerical campaign throughout Mexico, destructive prejudice was unleashed against the Mayos and their religious ways. Mestizos sacked and burned the churches which had become the strongholds of Mayo tradition and pride in their way of life. The sacred statues in the churches, and the crosses, which were symbols with complex meaning for Mayos, were also broken up or burned.

This attack of the 1920s is far fresher in Mayo memory than their participation in the Revolution, etched more sharply even than the loss of their land and their impressment into the haciendas during the nineteenth century. Mayos retell these events of their recent history in terms that seem consistent with their general approach to religious vision. They speak of the churches as their Holy Mother and the sacred images, that is, the saints of the church altars, as her children. Not merely a building, but the Holy Mother and her children, were destroyed in the outbreak of violence. Moreover the blame is securely fixed on a particular mestizo, who is named and who now, along with others like him, personifies evil for Mayos. Here is another theme of this book—the symbolization of historical events which have played crucial roles in Mayos' understanding of themselves and their relationships with the dominant society which enfolds them.

Thus Ross Crumrine inducts us into a deeper understanding of this people of a region of dynamic new economic and social developments, and advances our knowledge greatly beyond its former base. A study by Ralph Beals conveyed an impression of a very fragmentary culture, perhaps on the verge of disintegration in the 1930s. Erasmus during the 1950s examined some processes by which Mayos were being absorbed into the mestizo Mexican population. The processes of assimilation have indeed gone far among the Mayos, but it now appears that additional circumstances must be taken into account if we are to have a whole view of these people and their place in the burgeoning life of the northwest coast of Mexico. Processes besides those of cultural assimilation are affecting at least 7,000 to 10,000 Mayos among the 30,000 of the Mayo River Valley.

Crumrine knows the Mayos' devotion to their own traditions and rejection of those of the technological society which pervades nearly every aspect of their life. He is quite aware of the power of the technological society and in fact gives us in a few paragraphs one of the most graphic descriptions of its fragmented ugliness, coupled with a peculiar promise, as it manifests itself there in the Mayo River Valley. But he has also become aware, as happens so rarely for those not born Mayo, of the reality of a distinctively Mayo world view based deeply not only in the seventeenth-century re-synthesis but also in the successive Mayo retellings, aided by their prophets, of their historical experience down to the present.

Ross and Lynne Crumrine went to the Mayo country determined to learn the Mayo language and to live and work in it. This they did. At every point they have used the language. They have taken texts in it, short but deeply significant texts often, but also longer and more formal ones. They conversed with Mayos, to the extent that they were able, in the course of their daily activities. An intimate relationship developed over ten years; Crumrine returns regularly to see the world again for a time through the eyes of his friends among the Mayos. His work has continued on the interpretation of the texts in the Mayo language that he has collected over this extended period, and he has kept a focus on "Banari," where he first became acquainted with the Mayos. It is only through the following of the discipline of the fieldworker that the remarkably revealing little parables, phrases, and stories could have been gathered and could have wrought the changes in the Crumrines which were necessary to enable them to enter into the world in which the Mayos live, gaining some understanding of what lies deeply hidden from representatives of the technological society.

Another virtue of this book is that it makes bold use of modern theory in cultural anthropology. The models which Crumrine has constructed of the several modes of integration of the region's divergent societies and cultures are extremely useful and can be built on by future students. The theory derived from the epoch-making "Rites of Passage" by the Frenchman Van Gennep and developed further by the English anthropologist Victor Turner, is challenging as Crumrine employs it to interpret the Mayo position in Mexican society. The liminal condition (transitional state) which Turner posits as being fundamentally like the uncertain state in which an individual is placed as he passes from one recognized social status to another in primitive societies is applied by Crumrine in an effort to understand the direction in which Mayos are changing. It is this transitional state, he asserts, which stimulates the creative activity so striking in their religious life under present circumstances.

Thus Ross Crumrine has not accepted the usual pronouncements about small Indian groups surrounded by an overwhelming invasion of new peoples and their everywhere-dominant institutions. His study has applied the best of current theories to aid in understanding the processes through which the Mayos are maintaining their own identity. And most important, Crumrine has done this only after gaining a deep sense of Mayo ways of thought through intimate contact with Mayos themselves. We are most fortunate to have such a book.

EDWARD H. SPICER

Preface

The field research upon which this study is based was initiated in the fall of 1960 and has continued, on and off, ever since. I lived in the Mayo River valley from November, 1960 to December, 1961. I returned for short visits in the spring and early summer of 1965, and in the springs of 1970, 1971, and 1972. Financial support in 1960-61 was provided by the National Institute of Mental Health of the U.S. Public Health Service and the Social Science Research Council; in 1965, by the National Science Foundation; and in 1970, 1971, and 1972, by research grants from the University of Victoria.

My interest in culture change and in belief, symbolic, and linguistic systems was stimulated by personal communications from Charles Erasmus to several anthropologists at the University of Arizona. Erasmus, who was engaged in field work in southern Sonora, reported that a young Mayo man had seen God and that a cult, centering upon his experience, was emerging. The young prophet as well as the whole Mayo way of life and the interrelationship between it and mestizo culture seemed fascinating. Although the cult was rooted in Mayo culture, it appeared possible that it was generated in part by the effect of the mestizo way of life upon Mayos. Thus the major aims of this work focus upon the understanding of an enclaved group's way of life and the quality of fit between its culture and social structure and those of the dominant society. In understanding the types and intensities of stresses generated by the misfit between the two ways of life, reasons for the continual emergence of prophets and prophetic cults as well as the continued existence of ethnic groups are revealed.

I am especially indebted to Edward H. Spicer for initial and continuing encouragement, to Edward Dozier, Charles Erasmus, Fred Eggan, Manning Nash, and Sol Tax for numerous stimulating discussions and ideas, and to my colleagues at the University of Victoria, especially Donald Ball, Leland Donald, William Alkire, and Rennie Warburton, for sympathetic ears and specific suggestions. I wish to express special thanks to my wife, Louise Crumrine, for numerous proof readings, many valuable suggestions, and constant inspiration. Lynne Durward and Sharon Keen drew the illustrations and James Boudreau took the majority of the photographs during Easter Week, 1971, in Banari. I am especially grateful to these individuals for the illustrative materials. Also I wish to thank Lynne Crumrine, who died before the completion of this study. Her contribution, especially in the collection of the initial 1960-61 data, was significant. The major contribution, however, is that of the Mayos themselves, who extended the hand of friendship, trust, and sympathy. This book is intended as partial repayment for the time and effort they spent teaching me the Mayo language and showing me the Mayo way of life. In order to safeguard their autonomy and privacy, I have changed the names of all individuals and villages, except the major river valley towns—Alamos, Navojoa, Etchojoa, and Huatabampo. One of the major aims of this study involves the presentation and appreciation of the fascinating complexity of their way of life.

Pronunciation of Mayo consonants and vowels is quite similar to pronunciation in Spanish and not terribly different from that in English. č stands for the "ch" sound as in the English "church," and ? (the glottal) represents a sudden break or hesitation in sound production. The accent falls on the first syllable in a Mayo word unless otherwise marked. The plural of many Mayo words is formed by adding m.

Introduction

THE PROPHET AND THE VISITATION OF GOD

Before noon, on Tuesday, October 8, 1957, a Mayo Indian stood near his home, which consisted of two rooms of cane and mud, close to a small village in the Fuerte River valley of northern Sinaloa, Mexico. Damian Bohoroqui had recently turned twenty. His mother lay critically ill within, and he felt helpless in the face of poverty and death. As Damian describes the events of this fateful day, precisely at noon, a gray-bearded old man appeared, standing under a mesquite tree near Damian's house. This old man, dressed in white and wearing a red cross upon his shoulder, greeted Damian, who did not see him until the third time he spoke. Then the old man asked him to approach. Damian felt fear and began to tremble, as he had never before seen the Señor. Requesting permission to talk with Damian and offer him a few words of advice and instruction, He revealed, "The clouds will not lift until a season far distant from the present, and there will be many strange signs and much rain for the next few years." As a climax he claimed to be El Señor (the Lord) from Heaven. In Damian's own words:

> Damian Bohoroqui, in this place, in the pueblo in general, at this point, Our Father Old Man God. Under a mesquite tree, to me came an old man much bearded. He talked several words. "*Paskom* [ceremonies] you shall make, [to be on] eight Mondays, [and to include] three flowers, red, white, blue. [You] shall make that, our pasko, for several [two or three] years. Those who believe in God, on Monday until Tuesday's sunrise [will be] *pasko persona* [ritual hosts] [and] will make [the ceremony]." Thusly it was said by the old man, much will it rain in the pasko year [or season]. In truth it will come to pass as has been said. Nineteen hundred eight, Tuesday, last day of the pasko.
>
> Our Father, Jesus Christ, said thusly: "Go and take [your] inheritance in this weeping earth, all who are *Yoremes* [Mayos], [and] twelve pasko persona." God thusly ordered. For this reason work the *paskolam* [masked dancers], *masom* [deer dancer], *matačinim* [church dancers], *go?im* [coyote dancers], *maestrom* [lay ministers], [they all are searching or seeking out the fulfilment of God's command]. God said that three crosses [would] testify to the work [of] all pueblos who believe in God.

Thus the Old Man told Damian to give religious ceremonies in each pueblo, and explained how the special ceremonies should be given and what individuals and groups should participate. He also showed the young man the locations and distances at which crosses should be placed. These three crosses would signify those pueblos which had kept God's commandments. He warned that the world would end soon if His instructions were not heeded. Next El Señor asked for a drink of water which Damian obtained in a glass. After drinking He returned the glass to the young man and said, ''I have already drunk.'' In taking the glass Damian discovered it was still completely full of water. He informed Damian that when He returned He would like to be offered water from a traditional gourd cup, as He is accustomed. Then He disappeared.

This account is regarded as factual by a great number of Mayos and is not conceived as representing a vision or a dream, but as an actual visitation of a supernatural to an individual chosen to act as the instrument in a divine revelation. Even those Mayos who reject the ceremonies and the cult which arose in connection with the experiences described by Damian do not challenge the validity of the visitation.

Subsequently many changes took place in Damian's life. Several written transcriptions were made by both Mayos and mestizos (non-Indian Mexicans) who had come to hear his story and find something of personal interest in it. Most of them added ideas of their own concerning the significance of God's visit. This news travelled quickly from pueblo to pueblo in Mayo country. But many Mayos, characteristically distrustful of hearsay and gossip, sent reliable representatives from their communities to visit Damian personally in order to get the full story. They were charged to evaluate the quality of his personal character and honesty and thus to determine the truth or lack of it in his version of the story. Of those communities which eventually produced converts, at least thirty Mayo River pueblos or smaller settlements had held ceremonies by 1960 (Erasmus 1967:102). One of these pueblos, which I shall call Banari, was selected as the focus of this study.

Though the number of converts is impossible to estimate with much accuracy, certainly most Mayos have heard some version of God's visit to Damian and have participated, as observers at least, in the ceremonies which God directed through Damian. By participating, they hope to prevent the destruction of the world. Not all Mayos necessarily became believers, but the popularity and general appeal of the cult in 1960 cannot be denied.

THE MEANING OF THE VISITATION: THE ANTHROPOLOGICAL PROBLEM

Damian's experience, as well as the amazing spread of the new religion, generates numerous anthropological questions. What form did the new religion take and why did it spread so quickly? What kinds of social conditions might encourage or block this spread? Is it indicative of a more general process of revitalization or change taking place in Mayo life? Do other studies reveal this process may be more general, existing in other enclaved ethnic or social groups?

In seeking specific answers to these and similar questions I practiced the traditional anthropological role of participant observer and accepted on face value
Mayo statements concerning the prophecy as well as all other phenomena which
are part of the Mayo and mestizo ways of life that coexist in southern Sonora.

God had appeared to Damian and promised to return. His threat of a huge
flood was fear producing; more than once after a heavy or unusually long rain I
drove by the river simply to check its level. When excess water is released from
the earthen dam upriver, the small stream, which is the modern Mayo River,
turns into a raging torrent several hundred feet wide. The floods which occurred
before the construction of the dam devastated the river valley. Today, if the dam
should break, Damian's prophecy would quite literally come true.

In this study the Mayo way of life and its Mayo structure and meaning are
accepted as given. Then these insights are examined in terms of more general
anthropological questions. In order to examine such questions data had to be
collected on both the structure and meaning of the movement and other Mayo
movements as well as on Mayo history, Mayo ethnography, and the structure of
Mayo-mestizo social contacts. Lastly, to be more generally meaningful these
data had to become an integral part of a set of more general and theoretical
hypotheses concerning the structure of social and cultural change.

First, I shall present Damian in somewhat more detail by describing my
initial visit to his home in 1961. A mestizo man, Jose, who speaks rather
acceptable Mayo and knows the location of Damian's home in Sinaloa, accompanied me. The Mayo River and Fuerte River valleys are separated by a strip of
85 miles of giant cacti and desert brush broken by small areas of clearing where
peasant farmers hope to grow crops with the sparse rainfall or future irrigation
water. Soon we dropped into the Fuerte River valley, crossed the river, turned
off the main highway and drove down the river on a dusty road which parallels an
irrigation canal. Although the vegetation of the Mayo River valley is relatively
dense, that of the Fuerte is impressive especially after the long desert drive. The
trees appear gigantic in comparison with those farther north. Suddenly Jose
waved his hand to stop. We saw a rather heavy-set man standing in front of a
small jacal house set somewhat below the road which runs along the edge of the
elevated irrigation canal. Jose called to the man in a joking manner, "Where
does Damian live?" Climbing out of the pickup, we greeted Damian, who
invited us in and sent for chairs. Damian appeared heavier than in his pictures,
which had been taken several years earlier, and Jose even commented that
Damian had gained weight. Damian chatted politely in Spanish and Mayo and
seemed unconcerned about the presence of strangers. Later he proudly pointed to
the wooden cane and foot-shaped piece of wood (see Fig. 7.3) which symbolize
his position as *Pilato*, head of the important Lenten ceremonial society. Finally,
Damian obtained a piece of paper with the Spanish version of the visitation and
gave us orally the Mayo statement which appears in translation at the beginning
of this introduction. Here is a rather different young man from the monolingual
boy who had been visited by God.

On the return drive to the Mayo River valley, Jose mentioned how much

Damian had changed especially after being visited by two women from Mexico City who were making a movie, a Padre from Mexico City, numerous gringos (Americans), the state governor from Sinaloa and Governor Obregon from Sonora. Since the visit of Obregon, who gave Damian 500 pesos for the ceremonies, the ceremonies have been dying out, said Jose. That was to be the first of several visits to the home and sacred ramada of San Damian. Following visits revealed that the ceremonies were under negative governmental pressure. Thus data on the cult were difficult to obtain and were often of a conflicting nature and outsiders were not welcome at cult ceremonies. Even though I observed some of the new rituals and discussed the new ceremonies with numerous Mayos, the data collected on other aspects of Mayo life are more reliable than those specifically on the cult itself.

Although one wishes to understand the new ceremonies in Mayo terms, the examination of the movement within a more general context also proves extremely enlightening and generally productive. What does the movement suggest about the present condition and the future of Mayo Indians? Before going to Sonora I had been told by some Mexican Yaqui Indians, refugees in Arizona, that there were no more real Mayos. "Modern Mayos are no different from Mexicans. They are just poor Catholic peasants and no longer Indians." Is this new ceremonial the last dying gasp of Mayos as a unique group? Or, on the other hand, does it symbolize an active Mayo people still creating new ritual and ceremonialism? Charles Erasmus (1961:289) tends to prefer the former suggestion:

> Although these fiestas for God are burdensome...they do not really reverse or even slow the trend of disintegration of the church fiestas. In the first place, the very mood of the fiestas and the rationale behind them is despair at the lapse of the traditional ceremonial system. The Mayos believe that their fiesta system is disappearing, and those most concerned about it are the ones who put their words of despair into the mouth of God.

He (Erasmus 1961:301) also tends to lump Mayos and mestizos together as "country people" especially when considering economic activities:

> Regional development...is contributing to the further Mexicanization of the Indian, particularly the less ethnically integrated Mayos. The process is slow and makes the country people look retarded by comparison with the people of the faster-changing towns.

If this should be true, I hoped that additional field work would salvage and record what remained or could be remembered of Mayo Indian traditions. On the other hand, it seemed likely that more Mayo traditions remained than had been recognized. Certainly the new religion is a dramatic event, but an event which also might be more productively interpreted as symbolizing adjustment and reintegration rather than disintegration for at least some groups of Mayos. For this reason the field work also focused upon the existence of Mayos as a separate ethnic group and the maintenance or breakdown of ethnic group boundaries.

Although Ralph Beals (1945) studied upper river Mayos in 1931, no intense study of lower river Mayos had been made. Therefore, I researched the lower Mayo River valley with the explicit purpose of gathering information on the relations between Mayos and mestizos, the geographic and economic conditions in the river valley, present Mayo social and ceremonial organization, and the meaning of the new ceremonies in the total Mayo belief system and religious life. As much of this information as possible was collected in the Mayo language. Thus, in part, this book represents a synthesis and description of the modern Mayo way of life in the general area of Banari, a small community of some 250 Mayo and mestizo persons, on the lower Mayo River. Although official census figures are considerably lower, I estimated the Banari Mayo church serviced some 7,500 Mayos in 1965 (Crumrine, 1968:63-65). Therefore, this book not only examines but also challenges the statement, "There are no more real Mayos. They are just poor religious peasants."

The observation of Damian's new religion and the data on its rapid spread suggest a re-examination of Mayo identity and of group identity in general. What does it mean to be a Mayo or to be a member of a bounded group? Of course group membership involves sharing values, beliefs, and rituals or stereotyped behavior with other members of the group. A large part of this work describes a way of life which Mayos share. Full group membership also includes a process of becoming a member, of changing status from non-member to member, of learning the beliefs and rituals of the group. This change of status often involves a complex set of ceremonies or initiation rituals at the time of birth, adolescence, marriage and death. These rituals mark the passage from membership in one group to membership in another. Chapter six examines how Mayos learn to become Mayo. Also, membership in a group may no longer prove satisfying due to change and disintegration of the shared beliefs and rituals of the group itself or due to changes in the environment external to but affecting the organization of the group itself. Prophetic movements appear to be associated with groups whose members feel dissatisfaction. Kenelm Burridge (1969), Guglielmo Guariglia (1959), Vittorio Lanternari (1963), Anthony Wallace (1956, 1966), Peter Worsley (1968) and others have examined and analyzed hundreds of such prophetic or more general revitalization movements, such as the Handsome Lake religion, the Ghost Dance, and the peyote cult among North American Indians: the *terre sans mal* movement and Quechua messiahs among the South American Indians; "Cargo Cults" in the Pacific Island area; the Xosa rebellion and numerous new religions in Africa; the Taiping rebellion and Communist revolution in China; the Protestant Reformation and later John Wesley's Methodism in Europe; and Mohammedanism in the Near East. Anthony Wallace (1956:265) conceives of this type of creativity as a revitalization movement.

A revitalization movement is defined as a deliberate conscious effort by members of a society to construct a more satisfying culture. Revitalization is thus, from a cultural standpoint, a special kind of culture change phenomenon; the persons involved in the process of revitalization must perceive their culture, or some major areas of it, as a system (whether accurately or not); they must feel that this cultural system is unsatisfactory; and they must innovate not merely discrete items, but a new cultural system, specifying new relationships as well as, in some areas, new traits.

A number of anthropologists have suggested that revitalization movements are the results of deprivation felt by members of the group in question, often an enclaved or dominated one. David Aberle (1962, 1965) discusses "relative deprivation" as a factor in the genesis of such "cult movements." When members of a group expect some state of affairs that is not fulfilled, they feel relative deprivation or a "negative discrepancy between legitimate expectation and actuality" (Aberle, 1962: 209–210). He suggests three reference points which persons utilize in judging whether they are deprived or not; "(1) one's past versus one's present circumstances; (2) one's present versus one's future circumstances; (3) one's own versus someone else's present circumstances"; and four types of deprivation: "possessions, status, behavior, and worth." The continued experience of a high level of deprivation triggers certain individuals to attempt to create a more satisfying culture. For example, just preceding and during the period of initial contact between North American Indian societies and Anglo-American societies, the indigenous groups experienced considerable cultural and social distortion due to disease, conquest, and modified subsistence relationships. In the Pacific Northwest missionization, new legislation prohibiting native curing and the changes just mentioned disrupted "traditional" Northwest Indian groups. David Aberle (1959:74-75), in part quoting Leslie Spier's work, argues that the Prophet Dance of the interior Plateau Indians, especially a Christianized form which developed in the 1830's and thereafter, could have been a response to this type of deprivation,

> "...among these people there was an old belief in the impending destruction and renewal of the world, when the dead would return, in conjunction with which there was a dance based on supposed imitation of the dances of the dead, and a conviction that intense preoccupation with the dance would hasten the happy day...." Under this stimulus, from time to time men "died" and returned to confirm the doctrine.

Anthony Wallace (1956, 1966) set up a most elaborate analysis of the five stages of development in a successful revitalization movement:

1. Steady state: a society and its culture are in relative equilibrium;
2. Period of individual stress: individuals are brought under stress by results of contact with another society or by natural catastrophe or hardship;
3. Period of cultural distortion: socially dysfunctional methods, such as alcoholism, scapegoating, and other anti-social behaviors, are used to restore individual equilibrium (while they may help the individual these methods bring about further socio-cultural disorganization);
4. Period of revitalization, including (a) the formulation of a code: an innovator or innovators construct the blueprint of a new socio-cultural organization, (b) communication: the innovators spread their ideas, (c)

organization: the social organization of the movement crystallizes into a church or sect, with established leadership, (d) adaptation: the code hardens, an opposition party forms, and it may then be adapted to win more converts; (e) cultural transformation: the movement captures a large proportion of the members of the society and of the technological apparatus and there appears a resulting decline in cultural distortions and individual stress; (f) routinization: the movement shifts from the role of innovation to one of maintenance;

5. New steady state: a new series of slower changes take place.

Although these stages can be somewhat simplified (Macklin and Crumrine, 1973), for our argument the major process is one of identification with a new social group and the learning of a new set of beliefs and social relations. A revitalization movement then is a type of ritual process in which a new and more satisfying culture is created and in which this new way of life is learned by participating within the process of the movement itself. Thus a revitalization movement is a kind of rite of passage, defined by van Gennep (1909) as the movement from one role to another, from membership in one group to membership in another. Rites of passage such as those at the time of birth, marriage, or death are characterized by three stages: *separation* from profane society (preliminal stage), *transition* or movement into sacred society (liminal stage), and *incorporation* or return to profane society (postliminal stage). Ritual aspects of rites of passage include activities such as passing through doors, portals and barriers, and purifications such as washing and may be dramatized by a ritual enactment of death. The second stage, transition, is a period of restrictions and taboos. The relationship between teacher and neophyte becomes very important and neophytes are brought into close proximity to the deity or supernatural power and the mysteries of their situation. Since they are not in society, but removed from it, they may be hidden from view, concealed or disguised in masks or bizarre costumes, or with body paints (Turner, 1964). Frequently this liminal period involves reversal of normal procedures. Often it is marked by the presentation of deeply sacred esoteric articles which may be grotesque or bizarre in form and which impress the neophytes with the important factors of their culture's symbolism (Turner, 1964; Crumrine, 1969). Most insightful for our argument, Victor Turner (1968), elaborating upon this period, suggests that whole societies may pass through liminal periods. In these liminal periods the traditional social structures break down or are suspended and they are in part replaced by intense ritual and mythological creativity. I hypothesize that the new Mayo religious cult, as well as revitalization movements in general, are associated with societies moving through this liminal period as they adjust to the change from tribal and relatively autonomous societies to enclaved or ethnic groups. Thus a structure, that of the rite of passage, (1) may communicate a new set of ritual symbols, or restructure, or revitalize an old set, and in doing so may aid the individual moving from one role to another as well as (2) represent a crucial stage in the dramatic adaptation of an enclaved group to the dominant society.

Another new religion in the Pacific Coast area exemplifies this passage pattern. Erna Gunther (1949) and Homer Barnett (1957) provide full descriptions of the original experience of John Slocum in 1881 or 1882 and of the cure attributed to the shaking behavior of his wife from which came the name the Shaker Religion. The religion diffused both north and south of the Puget Sound area and still remains a recognized chartered church today.

The pattern is quite typical of both societies and individuals passing into the liminal or in-between status. John Slocum "died" and was wrapped for burial. He returned from the dead, however, with specific insight. This innovation involved a fusion or combination of certain traditional and Christian patterns into a new religious system, as well as a rejection of other traditional patterns, such as the shamanistic curing ritual. A church was constructed and Slocum began to preach the new religion. He fell ill a second time and again rejected the native curer. His wife experienced supernatural power, began to shake over her husband and cured him. The shaking behavior was interpreted as medicine, a curing method, sent by God to all the people not just to a specific shaman. In this case the shaman vs. non-shaman hierarchy had been re-interpreted in terms of an equality of believers vs. outsiders. This equality of members (neophytes) is clearly characteristic of a society in a liminal stage.

The Shaker Religion involves symbols and rituals transmitted to Slocum and others both through the traditional culture and by Christian missionaries. For example, the proportions of the churches are similar to those of the traditional houses. The rubbing of faces and brushing off of evil, part of the church service, is also characteristic of persons about to be possessed by a guardian spirit at the traditional winter guardian spirit dances. The use of a white wooden cross, two brass bells, Catholic holy pictures, and certain Shaker songs can be traced back to the Christian missionaries. Thus the Shaker religion represents a unique response of one Indian group, yet a response which is hypothesized as typical for social groups undergoing rapid change and moving through a liminal period in their re-adjustment both to themselves and to broader social and environmental changes. As if emphasizing the liminal stage of Northwest Coast groups, one Shaker minister says, "Remember we are just camping here."

At the most general level I wish to test this hypothesis, the model of the liminal process, against the field data collected on the new Mayo cult, on Mayo-mestizo relations, and on traditional and modern Mayo culture and society.

The chapters of this work focus around the presentation of data that are generally descriptive, comparative with other studies or revitalization movements and also meaningful in terms of the more specific hypothesis outlined above. Chapter 1 provides a general introduction to the history and geography of the Mayo River valley and more concrete examples of revival in Mayo mythology, beliefs, and social and ceremonial organization. A kind of Mayo folk model, the "Holy Family (Sagrada Familia, *Utes Yoʔoriwa*)," which aids Mayos in understanding and re-integrating their changing way of life, is introduced. The "Holy Family" model manifests a deeper more general structure, thus providing a descriptive and analytical tool and additional evidence of Mayo liminal status. Chapter 2 presents materials that document the social structure of contact between Mayos and mestizos and concludes that Mayo individuals may assimilate by giving up all Mayo identity and becoming low-class mestizos or those individuals who wish to continue being Mayo must maintain their own way of life in opposition to that of the mestizos. This contact structure contributes to the reduction of autonomous Mayo socio-political organization and to the resulting liminal stage in which those individuals who continue to identify as Mayo intensify their mythico-ritual activity, creativity, and productivity. Chapter 3 presents means of subsistence and patterns of economic interaction showing that Mayos participate both in the mestizo markets and national exchange system and also in a unique Mayo system of exchanges and ceremonial participation. This Mayo exchange pattern integrates the Mayo section of the dual economic realm with Mayo ceremonialism, which in turn is modeled upon the "Holy Family" structure. The Mayo family functions as one of the major production units, the consumption unit and the basis of ceremonial exchange. In addition to these functions it also represents the basic manifestation of the "Holy Family" model. Chapter 4 elaborates upon the patterns of social interaction within the family, the ceremonial kinship unit, the church, and church sodalities, (1) developing the concept of the "Holy Family," (2) showing the interrelationship between this concept and changes taking place within the kinship system, and (3) explaining the Mayo emphasis placed upon ceremonial kinship and the church itself as a social group. Chapter 5 describes the ceremonial organization and its symbolism tracing in more detail the full elaboration of the model, the "Holy Family." Chapter 6 discusses the values and beliefs which a Mayo learns, showing the importance of the family and church sodalities in this learning process. The final chapter returns to the general hypothesis, explaining Mayo prophet production in terms of societal liminality and cultural revival. A more abstract model of a permutational structure incorporates the "Holy Family" metaphorical model and provides additional understanding of Mayo revitalization and the entire process of societal liminality.

Although Damian's new ceremonialism produces a dramatic and exciting introduction to modern Mayo life, in the following analysis his experience becomes an indicator of more general processes. Could such events be symbolic of a disintegrating culture and a dying society? Or more likely, do they represent the creative product of a dynamic way of life still capable of adjustment to changing socio-political and technological situations? This book develops a kind of dialectic between these two horns of our dilemma and suggests a complex answer which lies between death and complete freedom to recreate a Mayo culture and society independent of the modern Mexican nation.

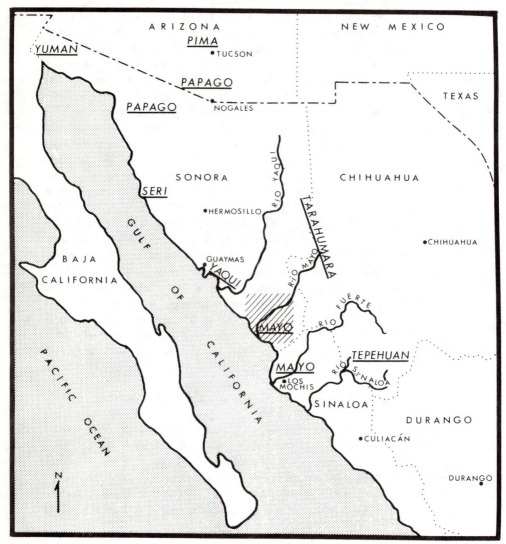

1.1   Northwest Mexico, 1971

1. Mayo Historical and Cultural Ecology

Northwest Mexico, the area in which Mayos live, consists of three major geographical zones: temperate highlands, hot lowlands, and a desert peninsula. At the time of contact with Europeans it included two different types of Indian societies—hunting and gathering bands and agricultural villages. These Indian groups were speakers of two great families of languages: (1) the Hocan family, whose present day speakers are the Seri living along the west central coast of Sonora and the Yuman speakers living along the lower Colorado River valley and on the peninsula of Baja California; and (2) the Uto-Aztecan family, whose remaining speakers include the Hopi of northern Arizona, the Pima and the Papago of southern Arizona and northern Sonora, the Tarahumara of the southwestern mountains of Chihuahua, the Yaqui and the Mayo of southern coastal Sonora and northern coastal Sinaloa, the Tepehuan and Tepecano of southwestern Chihuahua and southern Durango, and the Cora and Huichol of Nayarit and Jalisco (Fig. 1.1). Interesting descriptions of these groups by various authors, as well as a useful introduction to northwest Mexico by Edward Spicer, appear in volume 8 of the *Handbook of Middle American Indians, Ethnology Part II*, edited by Evon Vogt (1969).

Today people who call themselves Mayo (Yoreme, The People) are found along the Mayo River valley in southern Sonora and the Fuerte (*Močikahui*) River valley in northern Sinaloa (Fig. 1.2). Yoremem live either in several hundred scattered rancherías, in more than forty small pueblos of one to several hundred people, or in urban barrios. With the possible exception of rancherías, Mayos reside interspersed with non-Mayos, although some communities have larger percentages of Mayos than do others. Almost all communities include at least 10% to 20% mestizos and a large number consist of more than half mestizos. In many Mayo households and churches the Mayo language is still spoken, and Mayos maintain at least the ideal if not the reality of a separate way of life.

GEOGRAPHY AND ECONOMICS

The upper reaches of the Mayo River extend into the eastern part of northwest Mexico, the highland temperate mountainous region of the rugged Sierra Madre Occidental. Cutting into the western flank of the Sierra Madre Occidental

[11]

1.2   Mayo River Valley pueblos, 1971

are great canyons whose violent rivers drain westward onto the narrow coastal plain of the Gulf of California. This hot lowland coastal area, the Sonoran Desert, consists of a subtropical section south of the Mayo River and a hot dry section with highly distinctive desert vegetation north of the Mayo River. The peninsula desert of Baja California lies to the west across the waters of the Gulf of California. Baja California shows major similarities to the mainland's coastal desert strip but the peninsula lacks the large rivers with their dependable although often violent water supply.

In spite of the rivers, many of the desert lowlands are uninhabitable due to inadequate water supply. The major rainfall occurs in July and August, although there are also slow winter rains in December and January. In general the region averages between 40 and 80 cm. (15.5 and 31 inches) of rainfall per year, but many areas receive less than the minimum average. Desert strips exist between the nine major river valleys—moving from south to north, the Santiago, Piaxtla, San Lorenzo, Culiacan, Sinaloa, Fuerte, Mayo, Yaqui, and Sonora. Before the arrival of the Spanish, tribal groups that relied mainly on the annual floods of these rivers to water their crops of corn, beans, and squash built numerous settlements up and down the river valleys. Abundant wild food resources, such as venison, small game, fish and shellfish, fruits of numerous cacti, mesquite pods, agave plants, and many other types of seeds and fruits, provided a variation in diet in addition to the cultivated foods. Even without complex irrigation sizable population densities existed in the river valleys at the time of contact with Europeans.

From the gulf up the Mayo valley there are three ecological zones besides the area of intense vegetation along the river itself, which consists of huge cottonwood, oak, and mesquite trees and *carizo (Arundo donax,* cane). The first zone includes the wide sand beach and dune coastline backed directly by an area of brackish, muddy, smelly mangrove swamp which produces abundant supplies of fish, shellfish, and salt. The second zone is the coastal plain proper, with pitahaya cactus, numerous other cacti, and thick growth of a whole range of scrub desert plants, which provide building materials, medicines, and natural fruits and seeds. Third, above Navojoa, the foothills zone consists of thorn forest with a great range of vegetation, such as giant pitahaya (*Pachycereus pringlei*) and other cacti, agaves, and larger hardwood trees including mesquite, palo blanco (*Acacia willardiana*), palo santo (*Ipomea arbeorescens*), and oak. These trees provide woods for tool handles, construction, and cooking fire fuel. This zone also has abundant animal life: mice, wood rats, rock squirrels, foxes, cholugos (*Nasua narica),* raccoons, bobcats, pumas, jaguars, javelinas (peccaries), some fish, and a bird population which includes doves, quails, sparrows, towhees, flycatchers, eagles, kingfishers and herons (Gentry 1942, 1963). Rainfall and temperature also vary with the three zones: a typical winter minimum of around 10°c. (52°F.) in all zones, typical summer maximum of 36°c. (97°F.) in Huatabampo, 39°c. (102°F.) in Navojoa, and 42°c. (107.5°F.) in Alamos. The average rainfall is 30.9 cm. (12 inches) in Huatabampo 40.5 cm. (16 inches) in

1.3   Mayo house, near Banari, Easter 1971

Navojoa, and 66.1 cm. (26 inches) in Alamos (Proyecto, 1957). Much of the soil is rich and of a chestnut type with adequate humus but inadequate moisture.

With irrigation and modern farming technology, many of the traditional corn, bean, and squash crops have been replaced with those of cotton, wheat, sesame, other oil grains, and barley, which are used for commercial beer production. Many families either own small plots or are members in ejidos. Peasant plots are generally inadequate, often no more than 4 hectares (10 acres), and such operating costs as seed, irrigation water, and land taxes are heavy so the actual margin of profit is quite small. Besides the semi-commercial farming of the above-named crops, Mayos work as wage laborers in the harvesting of cotton, oranges, mangos, papayas, and truck-farm produce, such as tomatoes, peas, chiles, and watermelon. While some Mayos catch fish which they sell, farm-wage labor provides the greatest single source of cash income for a large majority of Mayo families. For farming loans they turn to the government-operated ejido bank and for food which they do not grow, clothing, tools and manufactured items Mayos go to the town market, and to mestizo-operated grocery, clothing and furniture stores. Although many families have a bicycle for transportation, a radio, a single electric light bulb, and some form of running water, often at a neighborhood tap, most still cook on a wood fire and build their own jacal or adobe brick homes, wooden chairs or benches, tables, and beds (Fig. 1.3). In summary, modern Mayo residence and most of the material culture and economic activities are an integral part of the modern state of Sonora and of the Mexican nation.

MAYO CULTURAL RELATIONS

As mentioned earlier, at the time of contact with Europeans most of the people in northwest Mexico spoke a language of the Uto-Aztecan stock. In addition to membership in this Uto-Aztecan stock, Mayo belongs to the Taracahitan family, Cahitan subfamily, and Cahita language group. Today Yaqui and Mayo, which are mutually intelligible, represent the Cahita group. In the past, however, there were at least five dialects. "Cahita" means "nothing" or "there is none." When the early Jesuit missionaries asked the Indians what language they spoke the answer was "cahita" (it has no name, or nothing). Mistaking the response, the Jesuits named these dialects "Cahita."

The present Indian population estimates for northwest Mexico relate directly to language spoken because recent censuses no longer utilize the Indian-mestizo distinction but instead note numbers of Indian language speakers. The 1950 census (Flores, 1967:22) lists 31,053 Mayo speakers of which 2,509 or 8.1% are monolingual in Mayo. Nolasco Armas (1969) counted 15,000 Mayos in the Mayo River area in 1963. My estimates indicate that by 1965, due to population growth and difficulties in counting Mayos, the figure in Flores could be doubled and by including 15,000 Yaquis (Spicer, 1969:830) it seems possible that Cahitan peoples in the 1960s included perhaps 75,000 individuals. Many Mayo friends indicated, "When the census taker discovered we could speak any Spanish, even if it was only 'si', he neglected to ask if we also spoke Mayo." This would result in inaccurate recording of the population. Even taking the 1950 census as accurate, Mayo population shows a growth beyond the 25,000 figure for the early 1600s (Perez de Ribas, 1645), the time of first major contacts with Europeans.

Very little is known about the cultural relations of the Indians in northwest Mexico in pre-Conquest times. What is known comes from two major time levels: early explorers' and Jesuit missionaries' accounts of the seventeenth century which appear reasonably accurate and give a kind of baseline Indian culture, and more recent accounts of late nineteenth century travellers and twentieth century ethnographers. Although there are no archaeological reports from the Mayo River valley, the linguistic distributions in northwest Mexico prove useful in thinking about pre-contact cultural relations of the Indians. The Uto-Aztecan languages of northwest Mexico are closely related and show a relative lack of dialectical variation. This uniformity suggests the Uto-Aztecans were recent inhabitants of the area, indicating population movement and migrating shifting tribal groups in the 1400s and 1500s (Spicer, 1969:782). The arrival of the Spanish, in the early 1600s, stabilized the tribal groups around missions up and down the Mayo River valley, around mines in the Alamos area, and in haciendas gradually spreading down the Mayo River valley from the Alamos area.

Without extensive artificial irrigation but relying upon river flooding, the pre-Conquest Mayos raised two crops a year. Wild foods also were abundant and constituted perhaps up to 40% of the diet (Spicer, 1961:12). The Jesuit missionaries introduced new livestock, such as sheep, goats, and cattle, and new crops, including wheat, as well as irrigation agriculture, but the Mayo economy was not basically changed although it increased in efficiency. Mayos lived in loose clusters of houses, rancherías, generally consisting of under 300 persons. An occasional ranchería, however, might have reached 1,000 persons. New churches provided a focus for the mission communities which the Jesuits had consolidated into seven towns of 2,000 to 3,000 persons. Although some Mayo households are contiguous, especially in new ejido villages and urban sections, many Mayo families still construct their homes at some distance from their neighbors.

In pre-contact times Mayos built flat, earthen-roofed rectangular houses covered with heavy, twilled cane mats. They made coiled basketry and pottery and they wove cotton cloth. Men wore breechclouts and cloaks for special occasions and women wore knee-length skirts. Spanish contact encouraged native crafts, especially weaving, which is still practiced by some Mayo families today. Men did most of the farming and the hunting while women assisted in farming and were the main wild-food collectors. Even though land rights generally were based upon family use, the Mayo community also had some power in assigning lands. Mayos traded for luxury items, such as shells, parrot feathers, and colored stones, but neither money nor markets existed. Nor does wealth seem to have functioned as the basis for the development of an established wealthy class or a system of social stratification.

Following Spicer's (1969:839) suggestions for Yaquis, Mayo descent and kinship organization was probably traced bilaterally through both the mother's and the father's line, with perhaps some bias toward the male line. The kinship terminology, which Mayos most likely used to refer to and address their relatives, was bifurcate collateral with a separate term for each of the following: father, mother, father's brother, father's sister, mother's brother, mother's sister. Probably it was also "Hawaiian" with the same terms used for cousins and siblings. The general rule of ranchería exogamy suggests that the members of the ranchería conceived of themselves as related in one way or another. Formal supra-ranchería political organization did not exist except during times of warfare when a set of hierarchically organized war leaders took control of warrior groups both within and among sets of rancherías. After peace was re-established, the rancherías became autonomous units led by a group of elders who met and discussed community policy with all the adult males. In this way leadership in times of war drew out the aggressive authoritarian individuals and relied upon a more highly explicit ranking of positions for military action. In peace times leadership was based upon age and achievement in the supernatural realm and was coupled with a more egalitarian social structure. Underlying this elaboration in social space, and existing as a geographically bounded area of lands, the ranchería, with its diffuse organization, usually was capable of solving the crucial problem of allocation of the rather limited river bottom lands among the members of a rather dense population. Probably there was warfare between the differing river valleys, but this informal ranchería kind of political organization appears to have been successful in maintaining a delicate short-term peace between neighboring rancherías and in permitting them to organize against outside enemies. After contact, the Jesuit missionaries placed emphasis on ceremonial kinship and godparenthood, upon certain ceremonial sodalities, and upon the newly introduced village government which actually had much in common with the ranchería political organization. Both political systems valued equality and individuality of adults, but they consisted of ceremonial sodalities whose leadership depended in some degree upon authority and hierarchy of positions or roles within the sodality. When confronted by difficult problems, heads of these sodalities would meet in open town councils at which each household had some representation and say in the final decision. Mayos have lost much of their secular political control and the secular village governors have become part of the church organization, yet this type of village government still exists in a modified form in Banari.

Many Mayo pre-contact beliefs were shared by the Uto-Aztecans of northwest Mexico in general.

> The cosmology included conceptions of stages in creation and a universal flood, a view of life as involved in an opposition between supernaturals controlling wet and dry seasons, a belief in serpents associated with springs and other sources of water which were the source of supernatural power, a dominant male and a dominant female supernatural probably connected with heavenly bodies, and the attachment of high ritual value to the deer and to flowers (Spicer, 1969:789).

The shaman, one of the important ritual leaders who obtained power through dreams, had the ability to control the weather, to foresee future events, to diagnose diseases and cure them by sucking out the evil or constructing a painting made of colored sand. Many ceremonies involved drinks fermented from corn or cactus fruit while the cult of war included ceremonial cannibalism, a scalp-pole dance, and other victory dances. Both men and women participated in other ceremonial sodalities characterized by formal initiation with a ritual sponsor, a hierarchy of officers, and utilization of masks. Tending to enrich rather than break down the native Mayo belief system, Jesuits introduced new supernaturals—the Virgin of Guadalupe, Jesus and a number of other saints, the Christian flood myth, the Catholic system of godparents, and Catholic brother and sisterhoods. The unique Mayo fusion of indigenous beliefs and organizations with those introduced by the Jesuits and the linking of this sacred system to the village-government has produced a type of highly integrated Catholic folk culture, which with some modification still survives in the Mayo River valley.

MAYO HISTORY

An extremely brief summary of Mayo history places this Mayo Catholic folk culture in a broader perspective (Spicer, 1961; 1962). In the early 1500s the Spanish were expanding up the western coast of Mexico. By 1533, in the first record of Yaqui-Mayo contact with the Spanish, Diego de Guzman, on a slave raid, met and dispersed a force of Yaquis along the banks of the Yaqui River. In 1564 a Spanish prospecting expedition camped with the Yaquis and aided them in a battle against the Mayos. By early 1600, a Captain Hurdaide had conquered the Indians south of the Mayos and Jesuit missionaries were at work among them. In 1609 he made a treaty with the Mayos and in that same year he and his Mayo supporters were defeated by a force of some 7,000 Yaquis. Then the Yaquis proposed peace and both Mayos and Yaquis requested missionaries who were supplied in 1614 to the Mayos and in 1617 to the Yaquis. Although there were never more than several missionaries in the area, their techniques of learning the language, working through the native leaders, living with the Indians and utilizing the army no more than was absolutely necessary produced broad changes in the Mayo belief and technological systems. The mission villages became economic as well as religious centers. Except for the epidemics, which killed half the Mayo population in the first fifty years, the Mayo River valley was stable until 1684 when one of the richest silver mines of northwest Mexico was discovered at Alamos just above the river valley. Gradually, as Spanish settlers flocked to Alamos and slowly moved down the valley, and as more and more Mayos were taken to work in the mines, resentment grew until 1740, which marks a general Indian revolt. After this revolt the Jesuits returned, only to be expelled from the New World in 1767. By this time Mayo population was recorded as under 6,000. Many Mayos may have been missed, however because they were away working in the mines or on the haciendas. In 1768 several Franciscan missionaries arrived but were replaced by the secular clergy in 1771. Thus a widespread kind of colonial conflict between missionaries, seeking souls and the establishment of mission communities, and secular authorities, pursuing cheap lands and labor for the mines and haciendas, became important for the Mayos during the 1700s.

Toward the end of the 1700s Spanish authority began to fail and by the 1820s Mexico had become a free and independent nation. The new Occidente State government (Sonora and Sinaloa combined) attempted to integrate the Indians but lacked the power to successfully carry out plans of land distribution, taxation, and localization of political power away from Indian villages in the mestizo community of Buenavista. After a number of highly destructive revolts, caused in part by mestizo land encroachment, the Mayos were essentially pacified by the 1880s. In the years just preceding 1890 a number of Mayo prophets appeared predicting floods and in September, 1890 they were deported to the mines in Baja California. Through these bitter experiences, The Land and Personal Freedom became crucial political issues and intensely sacred symbols for Mayos. Dissatisfaction increased during the period of the Mexican dictator Porfirio Diaz, from 1876 to the 1910 Revolution, as many Mayos virtually became slaves on the haciendas in the Mayo River valley. Both the visit of radical Francisco Madero to the area and mestizo revolutionary promises of freedom from the haciendas and the return of alienated lands crystallized Mayo opinion. So it was that many Mayos joined the young local mestizo leader, Alvaro Obregon, who was anti-Porfirio Diaz and was destined to become a president of Mexico. In 1912 they gathered in Huatabampo and under his leadership marched off to join the revolution. After a very confused period of intensely bitter, bloody civil war, they began to return to the Mayo River valley in 1915 only to discover that their families, lands, and homes had been destroyed and that mestizos had taken the lands which the revolution had promised to them. Even though in this same year the law establishing the reconstruction of ejidos and small properties was enacted, it was to have little effect in the Mayo area until the late 1920s and the early 1930s when the Banari ejido was set up and the Banari church was reconstructed.

This brief historical sketch delineates the importance of the periods of initial contact and missionization, of slowly eroding socio-political autonomy and land loss, of prophetic movements, of revolution and finally of reconstruction and revival of a way of life. This revival will concern us for the remainder of the book.

BANARI MAYO SACRED HISTORY: THE POWER OF BELIEF

Since the 1870s and 1880s, and especially up to the 1920s, the general historical processes increasingly involve conflict, loss of Mayo lands, removal of Mayo leaders, and breakdown in the structure of social relations between individuals representing mestizo and Mayo societies and even between Mayo secular leadership and Mayos in general. If Mayo society is not completely disintegrated but rather is passing through a liminal stage in its adjustments to these processes, my hypothesis would predict co-existent intensification in ritual, mythology, and ceremonialism. While Mayo prophetic movements probably existed earlier, they are reported for the late 1880s up to the present time. Thus the hypothesis is, in part, verified. In order to proceed in this examination of the interrelationship between liminality, reduction or breakdown in the complexity of the structure of social relations, and intensification and revitalization of ritual, I shall briefly discuss recent Mayo history and the conversion of past events into a sacred myth. This mythico-history provides a partial basis for Mayo re-integration of the ceremonials whose production requires the re-establishment of a complex set of Mayo social relations. In other words, recent history provides the basis for a sacred Mayo interpretation, a myth. The actualization or realization of the myth requires a ceremony and making the ceremony necessitates the utilization and, therefore, revival of numerous Mayo cooperative relationships.

To show the power of a set of integrated beliefs and introduce Mayo culture I shall outline several of the more exciting contemporary historical and mythical occurrences. These kinds of beliefs are responsible for the return of many Mayo men to southern Sonora and northern Sinaloa and for the re-establishment of numerous traditional rituals and the social organization required to make the ceremonials. In a fascinating manner, the rituals re-enact the events described in the sacred history and in so doing recreate the sacred mythical past as present experience. Mayo belief is reinforced through this experience of and participation in the events of their sacred history.

1.4 Banari church and bells, Easter Sunday, 1971

1.5 Banari cemetery and typical Mayo-mestizo cart

Banari represents a Mayo ceremonial center consisting of two most important Mayo landmarks, a church and a cemetery (Figs. 1.4, 1.5). Travelling into
Banari, one notes that the sides of the old dirt road, the site of innumerable
processions, are littered with wooden crosses which are decorated with flowers
of different colors throughout the year. At first the stranger meets only with
silence when asking about these crosses. One can only observe that in almost
every Mayo ceremony held at the church of Banari there are salutes and ritual
decorations and prayers to these crosses. When one has become a friend, Mayos
will often point them out, identifying and distinguishing the crosses by name and
classification. Eventually, the full story is told. "That is the Pueblo Cross. It
marks the boundary of the pueblo of Banari. During Lent the Way of the Cross
goes down this path, toward the place where the Little Children were martyred,
at *Crucecitas,* The Little Crosses. This cross separates us from 'the others,'
those of Huatabampo. That is the *Tiopo Kurus Yo?owe* (the great church
cross)"—and so on. The sacred paths marked by crosses (*konti bo?om*) provide
rich and moving symbols of Mayo history. Present rituals taking place on each
sacred path link the past with the present and sacred history (myth) with social
interaction and intensify the sacred quality and power of both Mayo lands and
Mayo social unity.

Dates are not usually mentioned when the following account is told, but
Mayos note that the event took place on a Tuesday. In 1926 Plutarco Elías
Calles, the President of Mexico, ordered a local mestizo to burn the churches and
the santos in the Mayo River valley. The central aim was enforcement of
Mexico's anti-church legislation. Similar church burnings took place at that time
all over Mexico, although the people of Banari frequently add that in their area
the churches of the rich and powerful were not burned. They feel that the local
powers saw in this occasion an opportunity to take revenge upon Mayos by
destroying their humble church buildings. As expressed by one Mayo:

> Rodriguez did it. He just walked into the church. At that time the
> church doors were never locked as they are now. He set fire to the church. It
> was just a little mud and cane building with one bell. It burned and fell. And
> he gathered up all the Little Children (images) and carried them away. As
> they came to the river and started to cross San Juan jumped away from
> Rodriguez and hopped into the river where the little bridge is now. Rod-
> riguez pulled out his gun to shoot San Juan, but the little santo ducked under
> the water and Rodriguez could not harm him. That is why the cross stands
> under the big oak at the place where it happened. Rodriguez went on to the
> place in the bush where Crucecitas now stand, and there he burned up the
> Little Children. That is why Crucecitas are in that place now. The charred
> bodies of the Little Children lie there. *Itom Ačai O?ola* (Our Father, Old
> Man) will burn him down for that pain. Those little bodies suffered agony.
> Rodriguez and his issue will be destroyed by Father Sun (Itom Ačai)
> (Figs. 1.6–1.8).

Some Mayos report that one of Rodriguez's children drowned and this was
part of his punishment. There exist numerous other versions and commentaries

1.6 Tree and cross above the Mayo River where
Rodriguez carried the saints' images across the river

1.7 Looking down from the bank and tree toward the
river, the point where San Juan jumped into the river

1.8   The cross where the saints were burned, decorated with flowers
and several coins as a wish for health and good luck

especially on this last part of the story. Some mestizos and more assimilated
Mayos argue that the failure of God to kill Rodriguez proves that Mayo religion
is useless (Erasmus, 1961:276-7). But when told by those who clearly identify
themselves as Mayos there is no expression of doubt that Itom Ačai and the
saints are still very powerful and that they are thoroughly identified with Mayo
causes and Mayo concept of justice. ''Itom Ačai knows that man, he knows
Rodriguez. San Juan knows him, too. They know who he is, and what he has
done. '' No person in Banari who told us this sacred history was in doubt about
the truth of the story and of its significance with regard to the martyrdom of the

santos. It strikes a deep chord in their sense of Mayo history. But more crucial
for my hypothesis, they also relate it to present ritual and custom. The Burning of
the Little Children was linked by one Mayo to the locking of the church doors, a
guard against the repetition of such a betrayal. After relating the myth another
man explained that this was why Roman Catholic priests are not welcomed in
some of the conservative Mayo churches. The greed of the priests is blamed for
the anger of the government which started the holocaust. Almost all accounts
present the event as the reason for the positions and ritual treatment of these two
groups of crosses, Crucecitas and the large cross below the oak tree at the river.
Even though one man argued that the image was away at a house ceremony at the
time and thus escaped being burned, the miraculous survival of San Juan is
clearly an important Mayo symbol. Still another account dwells upon the
treachery of Rodriguez and his imminent downfall, as a very personification of
mestizo ruthlessness. The burning provides the rationale for the direction of the
first Lenten Way of the Cross at Banari, whose crosses are planted in the path of
the martyred santos, toward the Mayo River, instead of around the church or in a
circle as in so many other Mayo and Yaqui village churches. It even accounts for
one of the reasons for the sayings, "Bad things happen on Tuesdays," and
"Those who love God should not go out on Tuesdays." More generally the
sacred history provides the reason for the San Juan procession to the Mayo River
described in the next section.

Mayo religious life was suppressed for years during and following the era of
the church burning. But in the long run the religious suppression seemed to have
intensified a kind of resynthesis which resulted in the eventual revival of
village-wide ceremonies. Mayo men began to filter home from all parts of
Mexico where they had been fighting during and after the Mexican Revolution.
Boys who had left Banari with bows and arrows returned as men who had given
their service to their country. They had left their fathers and brothers in un-
marked graves, sometimes not knowing when or how they had died, a sad thing
for a Mayo. Now they came home to a situation of religious suppression and land
encroachment as bad as or worse than ever, and without political machinery for
so much as a hearing of Mayo petitions. Some even found their women married
to mestizos, who had taken their land and cattle, or their families all dead due to
the long period of hunger, sickness and the state of chaos and lawlessness that
had prevailed in the last years of the war in the northwest. One of these veterans
whom we shall call Juan, told this story with a deeply moving quietness (See
Fig. 2.2).

> I was a federal in Colima. We fought this battle there. Men were shot
> to pieces all over the place. All you could hear was their moans of pain, like
> one voice. It was terrible. Terrible! There was a man beside me who was
> dead but had not been buried. Men were just left for the coyotes to eat. My
> leg was badly wounded and I couldn't move.
> I made a *manda* (religious promise) that if I lived and could return to
> my home I would pay my promise in the *Hurasim* (men's masked Lenten
> ceremonial society).

Then when I got here I had to pay my manda. I went to my old grandmother, who was the only relative I had left. I told her I had this promise. She didn't say anything. She just took me to the church. There were only a few charred pieces of cane and one cross standing. I just stood there and looked at it. "What will I do?" I asked. "I must keep my promise." I talked to the old people and they told me what had happened. "The government isn't mad at us," I told them. "It's the priests who have sent all the money to Rome whom they are mad at." So they took up a collection to start building a church.

We didn't have the bells then. When the church was burned some schoolteachers had taken the bells to Huícori. A young virgin girl from Huatabampo went to the governor and got a paper that said Banari could have the bells back. She is now called a saint in Banari.

Thus the Mayo way of life survived a series of crises in the recent historical period, and out of the struggles and tragedies of constant war and suppression came some of the most important segments of Mayo sacred history. Accounts such as The Burning of the Little Children are vividly and intensely related to present issues and are constantly being incorporated into the rituals of Mayo religious life. These narratives provide ample proof that Mayo sacred history and belief is a dynamic cultural system which relates to the recent past as well as to the sacred time of the origin of Mayo culture and society. Innovation, reorganization, and the striving for consistency are constant ongoing processes in Mayo mythology and culture in general. Seen in this light, Damian's visitation represents one of many attempts to achieve consistency and organization in the ideological system called Mayo culture, yet remaining within the bounds of Mayo social organization. This suggests that anthropologists have been mistaken in tending to assume that culture and especially mythology are rather conservative and unchanging in relation to social organization. Also, on a deeper level perhaps these innovations and reorganizations provide embellishments and consistency corrections on a basic underlying Mayo mythic and cultural structure. To investigate the degree of stability or change within Mayo cultural and social structure is one of the main purposes of this case study.

A BANARI MAYO CEREMONIAL:
THE SOCIAL ORGANIZATION OF BELIEVERS

What types of social organizations or systems of cooperation do Mayos find necessary to produce or act out their sacred history, and more generally, their mythological and belief systems? Even though these patterns of elaborate social interaction, ceremonials, may be ancient or recent innovations, they correspond as closely as possible to the Mayo idea of what their religious life was always like. Most of the images that Banari people feel the church should have were replaced after the church was burned and many of the calendrical ceremonials which Mayos remembered were reinstated, as well as some which were new for

Banari. A short description of a specific ceremonial will exemplify one of these patterns of elaborate social interaction.

In the new Banari church Mayos have revived the ceremonial for San Juan Bautista (Saint John the Baptist), the little santo which is called "the companion of Christ. The comparatively simple ceremony takes place on San Juan's Day, June 24. On the preceding Sunday a large number of crosses in Banari appear with new red flowers, the specific flower associated with San Juan. "San Juan *sikili sewaka*," it is said (San Juan always has, inalienable possession, red flowers). House yard crosses (*tebatpo kurusim*) are covered in red laurel in homes where some household member has promised to serve San Juan in the coming nativity day ceremonies. And a great deal of activity takes place around the church. Most deeply concerned with the preparations are the paskome, the ceremonial hosts dedicated to the cults of the *Santisima Tiniran* (The Holy Trinity) of Banari and the *Santa Kurus* (The Holy Cross) of Homecarit, a neighboring community. These two sets of Paskome are responsible for reciting the proper prayers, preparing the food, obtaining deer and paskola dancers and musicians who provide the entertainment for the guests on the feast day climaxing the ceremonial.

In the ramada several hundred yards away from the front door of the church, their music and dancing at first seems very wild and "primitive." The long-bearded black masks of the paskolam, and the deer headdress of the Maso are quite foreign and exciting to non-Mayos. Only after a longer acquaintance with the ramada dancers and their literature does it become obvious that their symbolic and social meanings are subtle, complex, and far more mysterious than first meets the eye. The animal impersonations, burlesques of life situations, and allegorically obscene speech of the paskolam are authorized by special permission of the saints only for the limited period of the pasko, which the head paskola explains in a ritual sermon. Paskola dancers are treated with considerable respect in Banari, and many rituals require their presence. The deer dance and the songs of the deer singers describe, in highly allegorical and poetic Mayo language, activities and attributes of a mysterious sacred "Little Brother" Deer, usually associated with flowers and the dawn. One of the musicians plays a water drum, a half of a large gourd turned opening down in a pan of water buried in the ground. Its resonant thump seems to jar the earth and can be heard for great distances, especially in the early morning hours when the fog hangs low over the villages. Three others, who also sing, play rasps of a hard brazil wood, which are graduated as to the size of the notches so that each rasp has a higher tone than the preceding one. This group (*maso bwikame*, deer-singers) sings the traditional songs in harmony with one another on an interval of consecutive fifths with strong steady voices and vigorous rhythm accented by the drum. Starting at a slow regular pace and gradually building in speed, the drum and rasps accompany the dancer in helping create the vivid sound illusion of the pursued animal or the subject of the song. These dancers always play a significant role in processions and are felt to be an integral part of almost every religious ceremony in the Mayo valley.

To San Juan in particular the paskolam and masom have a special ritual relationship dramatized on San Juan's Day. This ceremony took place as follows on June 24, 1961 in Banari. Upon approaching the empty church in the cool of early dawn, I was startled by the eerie reverberating sound of crowing roosters which were tied to the pillars in the church. About mid-morning a procession formed headed by the paskome carrying two of the birds and followed first by the ceremonial dancers and musicians from the ramada, then by San Juan's image, the church group, and the women and men of the pueblo. The matačin dance society, a group of ceremonial dancers closely connected with the church organization, should have been leading the procession but many members, including the dance leader, were ill. As the procession left the church and moved down the konti boʔo it made thirteen stops. Each pause involved the reading of a section of sacred Christian scripture by the maestro, and the singing of traditional hymns by his women assistants. This ritual was complete by the time the procession reached the pueblo boundary, marked by the pueblo cross. Then the group marched quickly to the river's edge where San Juan originally jumped into the river and near the hill where the San Juan kurus yoʔowe stands under the oak tree (Fig. 1.9). On a low spot at the river's edge the paskola and maso dancers and their musicians began singing and dancing. The image of San Juan was placed upon a large square cloth facing the river. The *moʔoro* (ceremonial advisor of the hosts) of the Santa Kurus paskome partially undressed the little santo, taking from him the characteristic water gourds and the little straw hat with a red feather in it that the santo customarily wears. The santo retained his red robe and still clung to the tall round metal cross that is his other insignia. In front of San Juan the sacristan placed a plate for small contributions. Also on the cloth were placed a large cup-shaped irridescent shell, the two drums of the moʔorom, one for each of the two sets of paskome, and the insignia of the paskome, their fox tails and rosaries and ribbons. Before the paskome put their insignia on the cloth they knelt on the downriver side of San Juan, to his left, and addressed prayers eastward toward the river.

One Paskola who does the speaking for the ramada group in rituals, the paskola Yoʔowe (head paskola) made a short speech (*hinabaka*) in Mayo addressing himself not to the congregation, not to the paskome, but to the river. Then he and another paskola took San Juan, carried him to the river, and waded into the water. They lowered the image three times to each of the four directions, laid him face down and lowered him three more times, each time nearer the water, and the last time put his face in the water. They made this ritual also toward each of the four directions. Finally they put San Juan back on the cloth. The Santa Kurus moʔoro adjusted San Juan's neck scarf, rose and took the head paskola with his own left hand, led the paskola into the water, and with his right hand made the sign of the cross with his first finger in the river water. He made a sign of the cross upriver, acrossriver and downriver, and with each sign said "In the name of the Father " [cross], "...the Son" [cross], "the Holy Spirit" [cross]. Then the moʔoro baptized the paskola by taking water three different times and patting him on the head with it. Then the other paskolam baptized the paskome and vice versa. The maso also took part in this baptizing. The men baptized in the manner described above, but the women members of the paskome cupped both hands and dropped water on the heads of the paskolam. Then the sacristan was baptized and baptized the paskolam in return. The head maestro and others in the procession also joined the baptizing by patting water on their own heads, and children who were in the procession now jumped into the river in their clothes and swam and played in the water. This ritual is performed in remembrance of the baptism of Itom Ačai Usi, and the paskolam are said to be like San Juan Bautista, companions of Cristo.

The paskome put on the insignia, sandals and other items of clothing which they had shed for the rituals. The sacristan filled the shell near San Juan with river water and the paskome dipped their fingers in it and crossed themselves. Then the paskola and maso began to dance again, in their positions upriver from San Juan and to his left. After a short dance the procession reformed and started back toward the Banari church. A large firecracker (*kamara*) signaled the end of this segment of the ceremonial, as fireworks had signaled its beginning when we had first reached the river. The dancers danced up to the kurus yo?owe under the tree on the high bank of the river. The procession then fell into a march, the dancers walking briskly with the other participants, until we reached the Banari pueblo cross marking the boundary of the village. At the cross the dancers resumed the procession style of dancing and continued in this way to the door of the church. The roosters, which had gone to the river, were again tied to pillars in the church. The matačin sodality would have baptized them at the river had the sodality been present. The paskola and maso and their musicians returned to the ramada escorted by the Banari paskome, who ended this segment of the ceremonial with a long flag-waving exercise at the cross which stands in front of the dance ramada. Leaving their flag at the kurus yo?owe of the dance ramada, the paskome returned to the food ramada, where they served ritual foods as a feast to the people who had come to the ceremonies. There was eating and visiting until the second main event of the day, the rooster fight.

The *totorenasoa*, a ritual fight between Mayos using roosters, took place around mid-afternoon in the paskola ramada. The paskome knelt on all fours facing the paskolam and musicians. Making the sign of the cross three times with their right hands in the fine alluvial dust of the ramada floor, the paskome said, "In the name of the Father" [cross], "in the name of the Son" [cross], "in the name of the Holy Spirit" [cross]. Then they hit the paskolam over their backs three times with a rooster. And the paskolam repeated the same ritual, doing as the paskome had done, and striking the paskome three times with a rooster.

About four o'clock the paskola and maso groups and the paskome faced each other in a characteristic formation in the dance ramada while the head paskola, with his long-bearded mask on, gave the traditional farewell speech in Mayo. A generous supply of blood of the fowls on the shirts of the deer musicians and others was pointed to with pride as evidence of the success of the rooster fight. After the farewell speech the paskome gave the paskolam fireworks which were set off outside near the paskola ramada cross. The maso and paskolam danced once, the paskolam grabbed the deer musician's gourd resonators, filled them with water from the water drum and ran after people in the crowd, who scattered, laughing and squealing. The paskolam were trying to hit the spectators with the water which is said to bestow fertility. Someone picked up the drum and threw out what water remained in a curved throw. The paskome pulled up the kurus yoʔowe of the paskola ramada and some of the Santa Kurus paskome went to get their remaining roosters and belongings. Following a short church service, all the paskome marched out several hundred feet from the church bells and said goodbye in a characteristic ritual salute to the Santa Kurus paskome of Homecarit. They returned home, while the Santisima Tiniran paskome of Banari returned to the church to repeat before the altar the flag-waving exercise which they had performed earlier before the kurus yoʔowe of the dance ramada. This ended the church segment of the ceremonies, as the ramada speech had ended the pasko part of the ritual.

In general, these kinds of events and types of social groups characterize Mayo ceremonialism. The preceding description reveals a well organized system of ceremonial roles and a general structure of activities including: flower offerings to crosses confirming mandas to be discharged, the *velación* or novena (nine days of prayers), the opening and continuation of paskola ramada activity (opening of the pasko), *vísperas* (evening prayers), often matačin activity, prayers and and hymns (*alabanzas*), and readings frequently including the Mass of the Dead, rituals concerned with welcoming visiting saints and cortege, special rituals connected with the occasion and the particular santo, feasting and other special symbolic unity rituals, a series of farewell rituals ending the ceremony.

The environment, pre-contact culture, and the history of the Mayo area were discussed briefly above. The last two sections show the complex interrelationships between a dynamic sacred Mayo history and belief system and an intricate set of social and ritual activities carried on by interacting Mayo social groups. The sacred history provides an explanatory blueprint for and a logically prior system to the pattern of social interaction activities. If, as the evidence presented in this chapter shows, Mayo sacred history and mythology provide a model upon which Mayos have reconstructed their society, can we suggest a more general Mayo model which aids them both in understanding changes taking place in their environment and society, and in reconstructing a workable Mayo society in the modern river valley? We do not wish to suggest that Mayos necessarily can analytically explain or control certain changes which have and are taking place but rather that some of these changes can be made meaningful and useful as a basis for integration. If Mayos have created or borrowed an explanatory model which transforms change and disorganization into the charter for a dynamic Mayo enclaved society, then the discovery of the Mayo model proves to be the missing link in our explanation of Mayo revitalization.

Societies undergoing the liminal or transitional stage, in passing from one state to another, may be characterized as experimenting with revitalization movements within which are embedded newly created or borrowed explanatory models. In May 1970, I returned to Sonora to attend the yearly ceremony given by San Damian for his Santa Cruz. But no ceremony materialized. In order not to have travelled so far in vain, I suggested to several Mayo friends that it would be just as good to go by a small church near Banari and pay our respects to the Santa Cruz there. Sensing my disappointment and their own inability to provide the ceremony, they were pleased to find a solution and happily agreed to take me to the church. After paying our respects to the saints, the Paskome, who were decorating the altar and the Santa Cruz image (a wooden cross wrapped in blue ribbon), brought us chairs and coffee. Growing out of some words of explanation, one of my friends drifted into a long Mayo hinabaka including a discussion of some of the images in the church. He talked at length of the Holy Family while pointing to a picture of God, Mary, and the Christ Child (Itom Ačai, *Itom Aye*, Itom Ačai Usi). Since the Holy Family was functioning as an integrating symbol in his hinabaka, I made a mental note to think somewhat more about the concept in a freer moment. After contemplation, I concluded that the Holy Family provides a general Mayo model and the hinabaka represents a discussion of the structure of Mayo ceremonialism and the reintegration of Mayo life. Holy Family elements parallel the types of major actors both in Damian's visitation by God and in the church burning myth. Deeply concerned about the health of his *mother*, Damian, the *son* who becomes a powerful curer and a living saint, is visited by an old man, who in fact is God, the *Father (* Itom Ačai). The church, sometimes symbolized as Itom Aye (Our *Mother*), and the saints' images, called *Ili Usim* (little *children*), are burned. But through a trick, jumping into the river, San Juan escapes. Itom Ačai, The Sun, will burn up those who destroyed the church and his Ili Usim. Mayos directly link members of the Holy Family to phenomena of nature: The Sun is Itom Ačai, The Moon is Itom Aye and The Stars are the Ili Usim; the *Bawe Hamyoʔola* (the old woman of the sea) and her husband protect their little children, the fish of the sea; the *Huya Oʔola* (old man of the forest) and his wife protect their children, the animals of the forest; Señor Santiago (a manifestation of Itom Ačai) protects the domesticated animals; and the productive earth (sometimes linked with Itom Aye) has a contract with man, who is nourished by the earth and in turn is eaten by the earth after death and burial.

In future chapters, I shall develop the role of Holy Family imagery in Mayo-mestizo relations, in Mayo social organization, and in Mayo ceremonialism. For example, Mayo ritual is usually coded in terms of the meeting and "embrace" of a male image (Itom Ačai) and a female image (Itom Aye) occurring in front of the Ili Usim, the human members of the church community. Certainly this folk model, the Holy Family, cannot be considered as a major independent variable in Mayo socio-economic changes because, as I shall discuss in the following chapter, Mayo society represents an enclaved system. Today, Mayos must confront external forces for change as well as recent modifications within their way of life. Through the symbolic power of the folk model these changes are understood, accepted, and creatively utilized by Mayos in the revitalization and adaptation of their mythico-ritual and social systems. Thus the folk model provides a symbolic manifestation of an underlying Mayo structure which is sufficiently elastic and dynamic to integrate recent contingent Mayo history and to provide a structure for complex ritual organization without relying upon the local mestizo political organization. In summary, my friend's discussion of the Holy Family suggests the last variable in our hypothesis. In final form this hypothesis may be stated as follows: societies undergoing change, whose social organization has collapsed, or at least has been radically modified, move into a liminal or transitional period in which myth and ritual are intensified. Numbers of models providing explanations of the changes and bases for reintegration will be generated. These innovative, often prophetic models, are tested through embodiment in sporadic ritual cults. The Mayo data, specifically the concept of the Holy Family, provide an opportunity to examine and test this hypothesis.

2. Where Mayos And Mestizos Meet

To understand whether being Mayo involves a distinct way of life and if so, why Mayo culture is being revived, one must consider the types of social groups and social events in which mestizos and Mayos participate. The model developed here is a refinement of an earlier discussion (Crumrine and Crumrine, 1969).

SOCIETIES IN CONTRAST: A MESTIZO FIESTA, A MAYO PASKO

An old mining town, Las Sierritas, celebrates a patron saint's fiesta on November 20. A great crowd of people and hundreds of cars, busses, trucks and pickups are parked along the dry river in this little village. People of all customs and classes mill along the narrow paths forming a crowd so thick that one needs to push one's way through. Colored rockets shoot high into the air from the church, which is a few hundred yards from the ferris wheel, merry-go-round and a large billboard of a snake with the head of a man. Nearby, a ferocious voice growls out of the loudspeaker, evidently the animal pictured, competing with the mariachis playing for the social dancing on the hill above, while a number of beer stands cater to many customers. One is shoved and pushed toward the church, as there is scarcely room for the people to walk through the square in front of the church. The sound of the music and the shouts of the adults riding the merry-go-round resound everywhere. Seemingly everyone anywhere near this place who has something to sell has come. Various foods and herbs, elaborately painted guitars, rubber masks, plastic ducks, brass saints and rosaries and many more such items are displayed on small wooden tables. Some eighty stands line one of the paths to the church. These vendors' booths extend right up to the doors of the church itself. From the church radiate the songs of mariachis and the prayers of the worshippers. Leaving, one may take a side path where small groups of people lie wrapped in blankets, heating coffee and ears of corn on their respective fires. They have come for the duration of the fiesta and will not go home for several nights. Rural schools are empty in adjacent pueblos and even a few gringos (Americans) from Alamos have dropped by. Although some of these people

[32]

include ceremonial leaders in nearby Mayo pueblos, they attend and participate like the mestizo crowds and not as leaders or representatives of Mayo communities or traditions. This fiesta at Las Sierritas provides a graphic example of a type of social group and activity in which Mexicans participate without special reference to their identity as Mayos or mestizos.

As a contrasting example, elsewhere and at another time one may attend a Mayo house fiesta. Pasko is a better word for it is not the same sort of social event as the Las Sierritas festival. No more people attend than can sit and stand around a pascola half of the ramada, perhaps two hundred, including all participants. Almost all should be from relatively close to the house and many are kin. The procession bringing the visiting santos, the routines of the paskome, the maestro and the *cantoras* (church singers) praying on the altar side of the house ramada—all are performed much the same as everyone knows it should be done. When the paskolas begin to dance, the order of dancing and the kind of dancing are prescribed. The women sit on one side of the ramada, the men on the other. A hat is passed to pay for gifts for the paskola and maso dancers and musicians. Everyone has *wakabaki* (beef stew), eating together to symbolize Mayo unity. The central theme of the gathering is sacred in character rather than secular. This social gathering, the Yoreme home pasko, is a homogeneous activity or "the same kind of people doing the same kind of thing" (Redfield, 1941:347). In contrast to the Las Sierritas fiesta, Mayos are participating, not as mestizos, but as Mayos in a distinctly Mayo social activity.

This social contrast of a village full of milling strangers with a house full of lifelong associates, involves conscious selection of polar situations. But members of the polar societies meet and behave in terms of polar value systems. Even in strongholds of Yoreme culture like Banari, where all the Friday processions of Lent (*Warehma*) are still practiced with great care to every detail and great sincerity on the part of the Mayos, their neighbors, who are not Mayo, mistake the activities of the Čapayeka for pure horseplay. Mestizos drive over sacred areas, though probably not intentionally, pull into processions, honk their horns loudly and capitalize commercially on the large Yoreme ceremonials. All these activities are in harmony with their own idea of a fiesta which is basically fun-loving and secular. Here tension is caused by people living in the same cities and pueblos, sharing the same roads, schools, markets and even in some cases the same churches and working in the same ejidos, but having very different and incompatible concepts of the proper units of society and the central meanings of the occasions for the formation of those units. Also Mayos, who are trying to participate simultaneously in two differing social systems based on two varying systems of meaning, feel confused when these systems do not match. In order to understand these stresses I shall examine the opportunities for Mayos and mestizos to meet and communicate.

These two examples of social activities in the river valley prove instructive in the construction of a more general framework useful in the description of Mayo-mestizo interaction. They reveal the existence of two classes of societal structures and activities, one Mayo and the other mestizo, the former a societal organization as manifest in the pasko and the latter an organization exemplified in the Las Sierritas fiesta or in Mexican social institutions such as the school or federal government systems. In these types of polar situations, it is perhaps too easy to contrast Mayos against mestizos. Yet the level of reality of Mayo culture and society is indeed illusive and difficult to pin down. Certainly today a Mayo "nation" does not exist and Mayos are very much an enclaved people, proud of as well as frustrated by living within the modern Mexican nation. Without even assuming a Mayo society, in a group of persons there are groups of individuals who first of all speak adequate-to-excellent Mayo; secondly, support special ceremonies in which the Mayo language is often used; and, thirdly, identify themselves not only as Mexican but also as Yoreme or Mayo. This chapter concerns itself with how often and in which social situations these "Mayos" interact with non-Mayos, what meanings and emotional tones Mayo-mestizo interaction carries, and how this structure of contact affects the lives of these persons who call themselves Yoreme.

In order to productively analyze "where Mayos meet mestizos" one requires a system or means of organizing and classifying numerous observations of Mayo-mestizo interaction into a social structure of contact. Yet this classificatory scheme must manifest the power of a model which permits one to classify and organize the data in terms of a specific purpose. The model not only describes the present contact structure but also predicts logical outcomes of Mayo-mestizo social interaction. In terms of the quantification of the data the model will predict a certain type of socio-cultural change as the logical product of the present configuration of Mayo-mestizo interaction. The initial contrast between a Mayo pasko and the mestizo fiesta at Las Sierritas suggests the existence of two societal structures as well as two types of participation. A person may participate in a societal institution either as a Mexican individual disregarding his Mayo identity or as a representative either of a Mayo social group and Mayo traditions or of a mestizo group and mestizo traditions. That is to say, social structures are characterized by at least two sets of rules and resulting relationships. One focuses upon the individual and who he or she is in relation to others and is relative to the individual while the other set finds its reference points in named positions, statuses and roles, parts of the societal structure. In this way Mayo-mestizo "individual integration" means persons interacting as unique individuals (as compared with Mayo-mestizo "societal integration" which refers to interaction between individuals who represent Mayo and mestizo societal statuses or sodalities. By combining the two classes of societal groups (Mayo vs. mestizo) with the two types of participation, individual (or family) vs. representative, the following possible social contexts are derived for "where Mayos meet mestizos": (1) Mayo individuals integrated with mestizo individuals, (2) mestizo individuals integrated with Mayos representing Mayo societal groups, (3) Mayo individuals integrated with mestizos representing Mexican societal groups, and (4) Mayos representing Mayo societal groups integrated with mestizos representing mestizo societal groups. This may be diagrammed as:

Individual (Mayo) ← (3) → mestizo societal group

↑   ↑

(1)   (4)

↓   ↓

Individual (mestizo) ← (2) → Mayo societal group

For example, at the time of the Mexican Revolution, many Mayo battalions, structured along traditional Mayo lines, including Mayo war symbols and leadership, fought in the Mexican army under mestizo generals. This is type 4, societal integration, because Mayo individuals participating in the Mexican army also held or represented statuses (positions) in a uniquely Mayo war organization, a societal unit. In the sixties, the situation, an example of type 3 (Mayo individual-mestizo societal integration), is quite different. Mayo young men often still join the Mexican Army, however, as type-3 individuals and not as members representing Mayo societal groups, type 4. This framework, which aids in organizing a great deal of data on Mayo-mestizo relations, provides crucial insight into the degree of level of isolation of present Mayo culture and society. With a predominance of individual integration, types 1 and 3, I would predict some Mayo individuals will accept mestizo culture, lose their Mayo identity and assimilate (become mestizo). Others will become more conservative, reject mestization, and retain as much of the traditional Mayo culture and society as possible within the context of the present conditions in the valley. These results are predicted because under these circumstances communication and adjustment would be taking place at the level of the individual. Thus acculturation would be manifest as an individual process (assimilation) and not as group evolution and adaptation. On the other hand, a high level of societal integration, type 4, would suggest that information exchange is taking place at the level of societal units. If this type of integration could be shown to exist for Mayos, then the subordinate Mayo society would still retain the potentiality of group adjustment to the structure of the dominant mestizo society and Mayo society would not be isolated but rather would be linked to mestizo society. In order to discover whether the Mayo are characterized by a dominant process of either individual (types 1, 2, 3) or societal integration (type 4), I shall classify the full range of social contexts which are potential contributors to Mayo-mestizo social interaction or meeting. If the process of individual integration (types 1, 3) proves to be dominant, the necessary social conditions as suggested by the logical model exist for the formation and continuation of a separate unique Mayo way of life.

INDIVIDUAL INTEGRATION, TYPE 1

Residence

Mayos live in both rural villages and semi-urban mestizo centers. The three larger towns of the area, Huatabampo, Etchojoa, and Navojoa were, but no longer are, Mayo church centers and predominantly Mayo pueblos. Many of the residents of these towns consider that the *solares* (house plots) belong to Mayos

2.1   Manuel, 1971

and have been Mayo from ancient times. Therefore, they will not move even though the growth of the mestizo commercial centers crowds them greatly, continues to pressure them more and more toward marginal areas, and changes their accustomed way of life. In rural and especially urban living, Mayo areas are recognized by all as the "old" parts of town. Exemplifying this type of inhabitant, Manuel (Fig. 2.1), an older and extremely poor Mayo, fought as a warrior, was deported to Yucatan, and walked back to Sonora. Manuel considers Huatabampo, where he was born and raised, "My pueblo." His home is in an impoverished and low, easily flooded area. Still he insists upon living near similar Mayo families beside the cemetery and railroad. Poor mestizos live in many of these mixed sections of town, but there is a statistical tendency for Mayos to cluster in Mayo areas of a larger settlement. Typifying a second class, Juan, (Fig. 2.2) the man instrumental in the reconstruction of the Banari church, lives on ejido lands in a mixed settlement of some ten families. He frequently stops by and eats with the family of his sister's son who lives next to the Banari church and identifies as Mayo. Somewhat more traditional than Juan and an example of a third class, Loreto lives close by on ejido lands but in a ranchería consisting of several houses occupied by relatives: the families of his son, his sister's daughter, and his wife's younger brother, all of whom identify as Mayo

2.2   Juan, 1971

(Figs. 2.3-2.6). Thus, there are limitations on the amount of neighboring of mestizos and Mayos in the towns, as well as on the ejidos and in the rural areas. But, on the other hand, where people live next door, use the same roads and streets, and go to the same schools, stores and markets, eventually a certain number of Mayos and mestizos become friendly, visit, and choose each other as compadres and as marriage partners.

Land disputes, even between Mayos, and certainly between mestizos and Mayos, are increasingly being turned over to Mexican agrarian authorities or handled by local lawyers in municipal courts. This constitutes an important common participation of Mayos and mestizos. Mayos formerly took such disputes to the head of the *wawari* in the case of relatives or to a court of elders representing the council of wawarim of an area. This still happens occasionally. In one case a Mayo family went to both courts. The wawarim's decision to divide the plot equally was also the decision of the Mexican court.

Briefly, Mayo residence and neighboring with mestizos, as well as *solar* inheritance and disputes have become individual and nuclear family concerns, rather than those of a Mayo societal corporate unit like a clan, sodality, or village. The modern Mayo residence reflects a pattern of individual integration, type 1.

2.3   Loreto, 1971

2.4   Loreto's wife, 1971

2.5   Loreto's ancient mother, 1971

2.6   Children of Loreto's household, 1971

[39]

Intermarriage

Mayos are probably as much or more prejudiced against intermarriage in principle than are mestizos. They know that a mestizo spouse may not wish to sponsor the ceremonies a Mayo is likely to need to give in the course of the growth of a family, and that the generalized hostility of the Mayo community toward *yoris* (derogatory Mayo term for mestizos) should be avoided. Manuel, who at present is married to a mestizo, is criticized by her and her grown daughter (by her former mestizo husband) for spending his time and what little money they can scrape up in Mayo ceremonialism. However, mestizos marrying into Mayo families are tolerated with kindness, for Mayos tend in fact to accept mestizo individuals as individuals on their own merits though they are prejudiced against non-Mayos on principle. The ancestor cult of the Mayos makes one who has no dead buried in the land an outsider forever, or until such time as the person produces graves filled with his or her own kin. Most Mayos recognize in principle the equal rights of persons to live in Mayo country if they have ancestors buried there, as long as they do not occupy lands out of proportion to their immediate needs, restrict the rights of others, or refuse to share their good fortune in ceremonial participation.

Mestizo prejudice against Mayos focuses upon the Mayos' insufficient motivation to enrich their positions of wealth and status, as mestizos conceive it. "Mayos spend all their money for ceremonies." Such group attitudes would not seem to aid in successful marriages of Mayo and mestizo. Nevertheless, of the ceremonially participating Banari males of marriageable age, not fewer than one-fifth have married mestizo women. Loreto has a Mayo wife. Juan, whose wife is now dead, married a mestizo whom he met while in the army. For Mayo males in general the percentage of mixed marriages might be higher than one-fifth while a comparable fraction of women have been married to mestizo men. In examining some 170 marriages of Mayo River and Fuerte River villagers, Erasmus (1967:8) found that about an eighth were mixed marriages. In addition, estimates of intermarriage would be higher in the more urban towns of Huatabampo and Navojoa. It was not possible to ascertain whether intermarriages were more brittle than intramarriages. All marriages tend to be brittle, and probably, in the 50-or-older age group, one person out of fifteen or twenty had had only one spouse. This pattern was intensified by war and migrations. A man leaving Banari in the second decade of the 1900s would sometimes take a mestizo wife, and his first wife, if she stayed home, might also remarry. Then upon returning he might take a third wife. This was not always true, however, for some Mayo women accompanied or followed their husbands to battle areas.

In cases of successful intermarriages that had lasted many years, Mayos like Jose, who lives near Navojoa, had become almost totally mestizoized. In other cases, like that of Manuel, Mayos have maintained long and important participation in Mayo society while living with mestizo spouses. That intermarriage has had an important effect on both the spouses and children involved in such unions as well as on Mayo leadership is undeniable. A mestizo parent or stepparent often gives a Mayo a relative mastery of the Spanish language. ''My stepmother, a mestizo, taught me Spanish and beat me when I spoke Mayo,'' explained Juan, who speaks both Spanish and Mayo well. Bilingualism is generally valued in Mayo leadership in order that the leader has the power and ease of interaction with the mestizo power structure.

Intermarriage is a second indicator of the first type of social contact, individual integration. In individual cases, mestizo spouses and neighbors are often accepted by Mayos with love, affection and trust, but, nevertheless, most of the marriages, neighbor, and even visiting relations of Mayos are with other Mayos. In general, more Mayos participating in the Banari church have mestizo neighbors and compadres than have mestizo marriage ties.

Compadre ties

Compadre ties with mestizos are not as easily measured in overall frequency as are mixed marriages, but they seem to pattern closely with the values and aspirations of particular family heads. Those who hold the dominant values of Mayo society and participate frequently in the ceremonial life seem to seek Mayo compadres, whereas those who fail to agree with all major aims and values of Mayo society, even though they might participate in the ceremonial activities, frequently seek mestizo compadres. Generally a Mayo selects as a compadre a person he loves and admires and a person whose resources he can use but never only with an economic motive in mind. The Mayo institution of ceremonial kinship is much too permeated with respect for this aspect to be shed lightly.

Employer-employee ties

One of the roles in which Mayos habitually participate with mestizos ties together the employer and employee. Both Mayo men and women work as low-paid unskilled farm wage labor and are employed by mestizos. A majority of mestizos share this poverty with Mayos and play similar roles, although other mestizos are self-employed as vendors or as merchants in small businesses. Few Mayos enter such trades and if they do, they usually cease to identify themselves as Mayos and cease to participate in Mayo ceremonial life.

Social dances

Social dances of the lower class are open to both Mayos and mestizos, but there is a polarization of participation and attendance. Mayo social dancing is generally an adjunct to a religious ceremony dedicated to a santo as a result of a promise. The tendency of some people to look upon the dancing connected with such events as more important than the religious aspects is disparaged by older Mayos and likened to yori behavior or a yoripasko (mestizo fiesta) because most mestizo dances are expressly secular.

In conclusion, social dances as well as residence patterns and neighboring, intermarriage, compadre, and employer-employee relations provide social contexts for integration between Mayos and mestizos. In these contexts the structure of contact is predominantly of the first type, individual integration, in which the general pattern of interaction is between persons acting as individuals rather than as representatives of either institutionalized Mayo or mestizo societal statuses or roles.

INDIVIDUAL INTEGRATION, TYPE 2

A second way to look at the meeting of Mayos and mestizos involves mestizo participation in Mayo societal units. Although there are rare exceptions, the mestizo participants in Mayo religious life are few and their participation is sporadic and generally incomplete. In all the Banari church sodalities, I met only one person who claimed not to know a word of Mayo nor to have Mayo parentage. Nevertheless, this girl was working off a three-year promise which was Mayo in cultural structure, not mestizo. Her manda to the Virgin Maria Santisima originated in her miraculous survival of a serious accident in her childhood. At the time of the promise her mestizo parents lived in a small pueblo which was almost entirely Mayo. But this case is highly atypical. Participation in Mayo ceremonies has little or no status appeal in the mestizo communities, for many consider the Mayos to be fanatic in their religion. Although mestizos may make promises to santos in illnesses, their contracts seldom stipulate the form, length and intensity of ceremonial service that Mayo manda contracts require, even though they are sometimes consummated in Mayo churches. Furthermore, mestizos are explicitly unwelcome in some Mayo churches unless they conduct themselves as Mayos.

Far more often mestizos show commercial rather than religious interest in Mayo ceremmonial events. Again and again, Mayos give this conflict as a major reason for the removal of the saints' images from Huatabampo, the commercial center, and for their establishment in Banari. The community of Banari does not even receive the taxes placed on the mestizo carnival concessions which fill the church plaza for the feast of the Santisima Tiniran, a fact much resented by Mayos. The selling of sideshows, rides, and trinkets on the sacred way from the church to the dance ramada, and between Banari's church and *campo santo* (cemetery), is regarded as a violation of sacred ground. Dire supernatural sanctions are promised by the old men and women of Banari against the mestizos who sell things there, though it is doubtful that the mestizos feel they are doing anything wrong or irreligious in these activities. ''Much money fell within the four corners of that holy church ground. It will not come out right for those who sold there. That is the place to give,'' explained an elderly woman. Mestizo merchants and vendors pursue Mayos relentlessly. Much cash is spent at these times and new clothes, trinkets, and so forth are bought with little consideration of their cost. Mestizos also use the Mayo language in radio commercials and on large advertising posters with deer dancers painted on them publicizing the so-and-so ''Sale.'' But the use of Mayo symbols by mestizos in this way represents only a manipulation of these symbols to uniquely mestizo ends and does not mean that any real understanding between Mayos and mestizos is produced in this particular social conjunction.

A few individual mestizos do participate in Mayo societal contexts. However, their participation generally is structured in terms of mestizo values and
models for proper behavior. Therefore, this participation does not represent a
real basis for either communication to mestizos or mestizo learning of any part of
Mayo culture. As a result, very little mestizo individual integration with Mayo
societal units (type 2) exists. Mayo societal units and associated values are either
rejected or never understood by individual mestizos.

INDIVIDUAL INTEGRATION, TYPE 3

The situation is quite different, however, in Mayo individual integration
with mestizo societal units, type 3.

Schools

Education has a high rating in Mayo estimation, at least ideally. They talk
to their children very positively on the subject of getting a good education in the
mestizo world and going to school. But the average formal education of most of
the Mayo adults of Banari certainly does not exceed two years, and many have
none at all. Mayo children cannot be kept in school during the major ceremonies
which involve a great many days of the year. Sheer hardship and necessity also
play a great part in the picture, together with the low quality of physical equipment and personnel in poorer school areas. Nevertheless, some poorer mestizo
children and Mayo children meet in the schoolroom during a short period of their
lives, although in this meeting the children who have already learned Spanish at
home are at an advantage.

The Ejido

The ejido may be either collective (plots farmed by the group as a whole) or
parcelled (plots farmed individually), for example, into four hectare units, as in
Banari ejido. The contiguity of mestizo and Mayo plots, even on parcelled
ejidos, brings about the necessity of cooperation at times above and beyond
questions of ethnic identity. For example, a mestizo farmer sprays his cotton,
then loans the equipment to a Mayo, for, "If I do not do so, the insects will
simply go over to the other field and will soon return and destroy my own crop."

Mayos and mestizos sit together in the ejido organizations as members
although there is a tendency for ejidos to become dominantly either Mayo or
mestizo in actual composition. Erasmus (1962:216) reports that membership in
22 of 35 Mayo ejidos is more than 90% Mayo speaking. Many people, both
Mayos and mestizos, who do not have farming parcels in the ejido, live on the
common lands of the ejido. Mestizos are the doctors in the ejido infirmaries and
the teachers in the local schools. At present, mestizo medicine is in rather low
repute with Banari Mayos, though Mayos do go to the ejido infirmary where they
join mestizo patients, are cared for by mestizo doctors, and are treated like
mestizos. Both Mayos and mestizos participate as officers and vigilantes in the
ejido organization, but this organization is separate and distinct from the Mayo

social organization. Although Mayos constitute a considerable majority in the Banari Ejido, they find the ejido organization exasperating, in some respects, and complain that they do not control its affairs to the extent they feel they should.

Military Service

In the army Mayos participate with poorer mestizos on more or less equal terms. According to Mayos, "This is one of the few ways open to a Mayo who wants to improve his lot and remain a Mayo." Even though he may remain a Mayo, it cannot be denied, however, that in army service he will experience a new life, mestizo in structure, aim and quality. On the other hand, a record of service in the Mexican army produces advantages in the mestizo-dominated sphere of life, such as the receipt of an ejido parcel or a passport.

Protestant Church

Even though several Banari Mayo have converted to Protestantism, the movement does not represent as much of a threat in this area as it may farther north in the valley. Mayo individuals who become *evangelistas* (Protestants) puzzle ordinary Mayos, who consider them defectors from the Mayo way of life every bit as much as those who simply turn away from all religion when they become yoris. One turns one's face away when one passes. Therefore, the present evangelista movement cannot promote societal integration of Mayos with mestizos, when former Mayos presently identifying as Protestant no longer interact with other Mayos and withdraw from Mayo society.

Political Organization

One of the most compelling forms of symbolism connecting Mayos with poorer mestizos focuses upon the Mexican Revolution. All radiate pride in being Mexicans and share a prejudice against some of the wealthy landowners, lawyers and politicians. Mayos and poor mestizos vote in the state, municipal and national elections, and almost unanimously support the PRI (Partido Revolucionario Institucional) because it is the party of the Revolution and they fought to put it in power. The *comisario* (manager) of Banari pueblo happens to speak Mayo, but is appointed to the office by the municipal president of Huatabampo who is placed on the PRI ticket by higher PRI officials. Thus Mayos realize that the nomination of candidates for the PRI in the state is controlled by the rich (ricos), and they are provoked by having only one candidate for which to vote, if they continue to support their party.

The authority and power wielded by mestizos is not uniformly distrusted by any means. Mestizo municipal authorities have strong Mayo support when Mayos believe that these men understand Mayo problems. However, unreasonable and unwise use of power and authority by mestizo officials, priests, and wealthy landowners is regarded with much resentment. Mayos list alleged wrongs, such as the persistent use of peasant labor for community works and the lack of certain physical improvements in their villages, of an audience for poor people's problems in important offices and courts, and of enforcement of the collection of delinquent wages. These types of difficulties between Mayos and the exploitation of power by mestizos harden Mayo resistance to establishing complete peace and becoming completely assimilated.

Catholic Church

Often priests of the Mexican Catholic church inspire similar, or even more deeply felt, reactions, especially when they express disapproval of uniquely native Catholic rituals and paraphernalia in the Mayo churches. The several resident priests in the Mayo valley administer mainly to the large urban mestizo churches though they also occasionally say mass in the Mayo churches and have some influence over a very small number of Mayo maestrom affiliated with those churches. In terms of the numbers of Indian churches, the rural locations of most of those churches, and the tactics and attitudes of the priests, the degree of Banari Mayo resistance to the organized modern church is not surprising. Because they so often fail to act with a full understanding of Mayo religious symbolism or economic point of view, the activities of priests, well intentioned though they may tend to widen rather than narrow the gap between modern and native Catholicisms.

In conclusion, Mayos and mestizos are bound together through marriage and compadre ties, as well as through residence, use of common legal sanctions, common municipal, state and national government agencies (medical, educational, agrarian and other), the land-holding ejido system, the total symbolic aims of the Mexican Revolution and service to the country in the armed services. Within all these social contexts, the dominant kind of integration is that of the first or third type—individual integration in which either Mayo individuals are integrated with mestizo individuals or individual Mayos are integrated within mestizo societal units. In other words, Mayos participate with other Mexicans in all these kinds of institutions without reference to their identity as members of Mayo societal units or as carriers of Mayo traditions. Therefore, with the exception of ceremonial exchange, which I shall now discuss, Mayos have no encouragement or opportunity to participate as "Mayos" with mestizos or in mestizo societal groups.

SOCIETAL INTEGRATION, TYPE 4

Ceremonial exchange provides the only remaining potential point of societal integration between Mayo and mestizo societies, type 4. The relationship of the Mayo churches to other Mayo churches as against the mestizo church of Huatabampo provides the crucial data. Some essential elements of Mayo church-to-church exchange which involves the patron saints of two autonomous Mayo churches, have already been introduced in the description of the San Juan ceremony in Chapter 2. A fuller discussion of these elements appears in Chapter 5 on Mayo ceremonial exchange. Regular exchanges take place throughout the year between numerous Mayo pueblos in which all essential elements are met.

But the relationship of Mayo to mestizo churches proves to be very different from that which prevails between Mayo churches since it lacks the basic social elements of exchange characteristic of Mayo pueblo relationships. Also, its forms and meanings have different symbolic values for the mestizos of the Huatabampo church than for the Mayos of the village churches.

In the yearly round, perhaps the most impressive visit of the Banari church to Huatabampo takes place during the exchange with the Mayo church of Etchojoa. On the way to Etchojoa, the group stops at the mestizo Huatabampo church. Here a short service takes place. Many elements, such as reciprocity are missing, however, for no saint's sodality or even individuals identified with the Huatabampo church return the visit to Banari. Mayos who live in Huatabampo go to one of the outlying Mayo churches if they wish to maintain their Mayo identity. On reaching the town of Huatabampo, paskola and maso ceremonial dance groups and their musicians, essential in all processions involving traditional Mayo patron saint exchanges, are replaced by mariachis. Fireworks are not supposed to be used. Rest stops of the Santisima Tiniran in Huatabampo are abbreviated to a shadow of the traditional ceremony. Also there is no ceremonial feasting between Huatabampo, as a church, and any other Mayo church, nor any salute of images, face to face, since no images from Huatabampo go out in these processions.

In summary, a very different kind of basic relationship exists between the Huatabampo mestizo church and the Mayo churches than among the Mayo churches themselves. Mayos are highly aware of the integrative aspects of Mayo ceremonial exchange and also of which churches are included in or excluded from the exchange pattern. Therefore, very little, if any, integration of the societal type exists between Mayo and mestizo societies. Representatives of mestizo societal statuses do not interact with nor understand Mayos who are acting as Mayo status holders and in terms of Mayo societal roles and their associated norms and values.

The great majority of mestizos popularly rank Mayo culture much lower than their own. Refusing to credit Mayo language with the capacity for transmitting complex thoughts, they call it *la lengua,* or tongue, whereas Spanish is commonly referred to as *la idioma*, the language. Mayos often are regarded as rather stupid because they are Indians and have a comparatively low standard of living. Occasionally one hears mestizos refer to Mayos as *indios* (Indians) or as animals. Of course, by far the majority of mestizos have better taste and do not often apply such epithets to any human being. Similarly Mayos politely refrain from using the rather bitter term "yori" unless sorely pressed. Generally, it may be said that mestizo awareness of Mayos becomes increasingly vague as one rises on the social ladder. An exception may exist in the general fear of Indian religious fanaticism and the violence which, through a persistent myth, mestizos believe can arise from Mayo religion. They feel that everything particularly and uniquely Indian in form is somehow symbolic of plans for military uprising, even if it is in fact only a ritual connected with a family funeral. Most Mayos actually show a deep interest in keeping the peace, as they know far better than most people the ravages which violence can have upon a people already at the margin of subsistence. With such a set of negative mestizo attitudes, Mayo identity and traditions prove disadvantageous as a basis for Mayo-mestizo integration. In terms of the mestizo prestige and stratification system and attitudes associated with this system, a Mayo becoming mestizo would be well advised to dissociate with his Mayo background.

In summary, mestizo attitudes provide no basis for societal integration, type 4, between mestizo and Mayo societies, but encourage individual Mayo assimilation to mestizo society, type 3.

On the other hand, if Mayos wish to participate chiefly in mestizo society they are severely limited to essentially several positions, all of which they share with poor mestizos: unskilled farm laborers and fishermen, small farmers (both independent and ejidatarios), and soldiers. The economic rewards of these positions are also relatively scant, and the relative statuses are very low in the total Mexican society. Mayos do not obtain any practical skills because the schools do not offer them and because Mayos are not likely to attend school enough to reach any level of attainment. Apprenticeship possibilities are limited, and what few exist tend to be passed on to relatives by the mestizo possessors. Also, Mayos reject types of skills not connected with primary resources and hesitate to stay with jobs which do not give them the opportunity to arrange their work time in order to be free to participate in ceremonial activities. The times of day on which events are held in Banari are governed by supernatural sanctions, e.g., Friday processions during Lent must end at the pueblo cross at the moment of sunset, as the image of Itom Ačai is turned toward the west. *Tiniran komčepte* (the appearance of the Saint's image in the church nine days before the major ritual) must take place at straight up noon. The feasts of the saints take place almost always precisely on the date specified in the Catholic ceremonial calendar. These factors add additional restrictions to the positive adaptation of Mayo culture and society, as such, and force individual assimilating Mayos to enter mestizo society at the very bottom.

In conclusion, the Mayo data definitely indicate a contact social structure, characterized by the dominance of individual integration (types 1, 2, 3) with little, if any, societal integration (type 4). With this kind of contact, the model predicts that some Mayo individuals will assimilate, becoming mestizos, while others will revive and maintain traditional Mayo culture and society. These conditions of change are dominant within the river valley and are intensified by the limitations of positions which Mayos themselves can fill in mestizo society and still maintain their ethnic identity as Mayos. In other words, in order to participate chiefly in mestizo society, a Mayo must reject his Mayo culture and enter mestizo society at the bottom level, that of peasant farmer with very few real alternatives open to him. Thus it is not surprising that numbers of Mayos prefer to seek prestige within Mayo culture and society and that traditional Mayo culture has become a value in itself. As long as the traditional Mayo group, which presently is not decreasing and may be increasing in number, retains a certain minimal size, Mayo culture will continue to exist.

The process of individual assimilation is recognized implicitly by the Mayos themselves. Mestizos with Mayo ancestry who have turned away from Mayo traditions, specifically the religious traditions, are held in the lowest possible esteem by Mayos. The special name applied to such people in general is *yoris revueltos* (turned yori). By far the greatest amount of Mayo verbal hostility toward mestizos is directed toward their own defectors, those people who had an opportunity to choose the Mayo way and rejected it in favor of a mestizo pattern of life. The enclaved Mayo group's way of life has become a symbol which Mayos utilize to distinguish themselves from the members of the dominant mestizo society. In other words, the group as a unit is rationally attempting to stop its evolution toward the dominant society and is synthesizing an "opposition" way of life from traditional and new elements.

In terms of the interrelationships between Mayos and mestizos, the necessary social variables for the production and revival of the Mayo way of life definitely exist. Since a potentiality is not an actuality I now must turn to a description of this "opposition" way of life, of present Mayo society and culture. Mayos, neither able to adapt to mestizo culture and remain Mayo nor able to assimilate except into the lowest stratum of mestizo society, have recreated a way of life. Reinforcing Mayo identity, this "opposition" way of life symbolically establishes a clear boundary between Mayos and non-Mayos and in doing so has become a kind of sacred drama integrated around the symbol of the Holy Family. This folk model brings additional insight to Mayo-mestizo interrelationships. Assimilation into mestizo society is taking place at the level of the individual and the family. Therefore, the folk model focuses our attention at the crucial point in either the maintenance or the ultimate loss of the Mayo way of life. Whether Mayo culture disappears or continues to flourish would seem to depend upon processes taking place within the Mayo family, one kind of Holy Family. The Holy Family imagery provides a powerful logical link between individual family members and the entire superstructure of Mayo belief, ritual, worldview, and ceremonialism. By metaphorically tying individuals and families to general Mayo ritual symbolism, the Holy Family model symbolically reinforces Mayo identity. In light of the fact that individual assimilation provides a critical threat to the continuity of the Mayo way of life, the creative application and elaboration of the Holy Family metaphor represents a major Mayo symbolic attempt to block assimilation by providing a logico-symbolic means of integrating the individual and his or her family within more general Mayo belief and ceremonialism.

3. The Mayo River Valley: Mayo Subsistence and Economic Patterns

THE ENVIRONMENT, SETTLEMENTS AND POPULATION

The face of the land is changing as the native forest gives way to vast modern farming lands in the rich Mayo River valley. Bright new cities expand into the traditional barrios, gobbling up the thinly scattered earth houses, and digesting them into crowded rows of small shacks or sweeping them away entirely for the use of markets or some other urban need. Complex features of (1) the spatial distribution of population into groups which identify predominantly as Mayos vs. others who do not so identify; (2) the visible contrast between the city and the village, and (3) the vast modern farm fields vs. the small plots and thorn forest at its edge reveal patterns which show the points of articulation as well as the deep cleavage in differing human world views. These patterns of articulation and cleavage concerning the physical environment and economic production and exchange in the area provide the central theme of this chapter. Although production often depnds upon both individual and family effort, consumption and distribution are family matters. Therefore, the Mayo family provides the basic unit in the structure of Mayo economic production, consumption, and exchange.

The land itself mirrors recent and continuing social and economic changes. The central flood plain of the Mayo River bears a vast band of irrigated gold, green and brown fields. This rich sandy loam soil produces cotton, corn, field grains, vegetables and melons, oil grains, wheat, and other crops for enormous markets, some of which are international. Modern irrigation has transformed the river valley into a high-yield agricultural area. This transformation results from economic activities of mestizos whose self-image reflects that of a frontier people. They believe they have the right to dominate and exploit the land and native population. The state or federal government has not set aside any reservation lands for Mayos, which symbolizes a lack of governmental recognition of Mayos as a separate ''Indian'' group. At the edges of the commercial fields and in scattered spots along the river small stands of virgin growth help recreate an impression of the earlier appearance of the land, an image so alive in the minds of Mayos today. Near the upper reaches of the plain and at its edges, which are watered by runoff from the Alamos mountains, and its foothills, stands of mesquite, acacia, cactus, pitahaya, and agave provide fruits, seeds, woods and liquids still used by Mayos for a range of practical items from cooking dishes to combs and medicines. This and the much heavier thorn forest still extending in patches to the northwest of Etchojoa also shelter animals like the rabbit, deer and peccary, which are still used by Mayos in certain ceremonies. Along the coast mangrove swamps compete with fields of salt where the sea water has been trapped after high tide while the water itself teems with edible fish. In contrast to the widespread commercialization, scattered crosses mark mountain tops of Mayo mythical significance and near the mouth of the Mayo River crosses stand at the division of the fresh and salt water.

Rain and river flooding is adequate for a lush desert growth and two uncertain crops a year, without modern irrigation. In spite of potential year-round modern agriculture, Mayos traditionally plant only two crops a year for the heavy summer showers and the gentle winter rains. The Mayo River, originating in the western Sierra Madre above and beyond traditional Mayo Indian country, once carried a relatively narrow ribbon of fresh water onto the desert plain. A dense strip of cottonwood and oak trees shaded the actual river. At flood times in the late fall and winter, it spread its reviving load widely over the plain in its rush to the sea, whipping out new channels. Today the river, too, like the land, has been greatly, though not entirely, subdued through the dam constructed by means of the technological knowledge of the dominant society. And the giant trees are being cut so that the shiny new fleet of little red spray planes resting on the outskirts of Huatabampo can drop down to the fields with their cargos of insecticide. Canals carry the water southward and westward, far from the original banks of the Mayo, into neatly plowed and ditched fields stretching far out of sight on the coastal plain. Still, at the end of the rains in some years an enormous weight of water presses against the edge of the earth dam. When a great volume of it is released, at least once or twice during the year, the canals are full and the river itself overflows, submerging small bridges leading to the villages at its mouth. The water level rises and shallow drinking wells in the villages near the ocean become salty. Thus the reverence of Mayos for the power of the river is periodically renewed.

The population and settlement patterns of the area have been discussed, although I must re-emphasize the changes in composition and quantity which are as startling as the changes on the face of the land. Since the first appearance of the Jesuit Fathers among an estimated 30,000 Mayos the total population of the towns of Huatabampo, Etchojoa, and Navojoa has increased to 120,000 in 1960 with somewhat more than one-third of this number consisting of people who identify themselves as Mayo and participate regularly in Mayo Indian culture. This population is distributed into at least four types of settlement, each with distinctive social and cultural implications: the scattered rural household clusters, or rancherías, apparently a pre-contact pattern; a modified Spanish village and ceremonial center, or basically Spanish mission pattern; a modern northwest Mexican urban market center pattern; and a more recent ejido community pattern. In the ranchería type, houses are scattered throughout the fields of bush country and are hard to see from any distance. Socially the pattern means distance from neighbors of whatever ethnic affiliation and privacy relative to city or even village standards. A drum in an all-night practice session of ceremonial dancers is not likely to arouse the police so that the pattern not only removes necessity for frequent contact with strangers but also contributes to the maintenance of ritual which may come into conflict with the dominant society. The modified ceremonial center—for example, Banari—whose entrance is usually marked by a cross or group of crosses, has two foci. The Mayo segment of town reveals adobe and jacal houses scattered around the church in a seemingly unpatterned way, and includes, in most cases, the cemetery area. The second focus of the community consists of the plaza, around which are found the mestizo homes, the rural school, the grocery store or stores, the *comisaría* (police station and town hall), and other such buildings representing Mexican institutions.

The typical modern northwest Mexican urban center appears once to have been a variety of church-centered Mayo settlement in which the mestizo segment has crowded and finally pushed the Mayo segment to the outermost edges of the community. In Huatabampo, for example, even the old Mayo church was finally abandoned by Mayos and became a market, while the mestizo community constructed a new church. The Mayo saints were moved to Banari, about six or seven miles away, and a Mayo ceremonial-center type pueblo grew up around the Banari church with mestizo merchants ultimately following and establishing themselves around the plaza. Today, the land of Huatabampo which was once Mayo *solar*, is covered with new patterns of buildings and people with new kinds of beliefs. This pattern includes a plaza with a municipal palace, banks, a Mexican church, a bandstand, a centralized enclosed market, usually a central park, a large number of stores, saloons, a police station, some schools, a new group of social security buildings, and an infirmary or small hospital. Wealthy and imposing houses of the large landowners dominate the high-class residential areas.

Though many ejido communities on dominantly Mayo ejido lands are of the ceremonial type, another pattern, typified by San Juan founded in the 1930's about two miles southeast of Huatabampo, is different because it is laid out entirely in blockgrid. Although the school, stores, church, and such buildings tend to cluster around a central plaza, one characteristic seems to justify a separate classification of this pattern. Mayo compounds tend to be found interspersed with mestizo ones, apparently with no forced and little spontaneous zoning. Mayo extended families do control groups of houses close to one another, but larger Mayo groupings seem to have little clustering. Mayo institutional structures, such as church and dance ramada or cemetery, which form the focus of large clusters in Mayo ceremonial centers, are missing. There seems to be, therefore, relatively more neighborly contact between Mayos and mestizos, contact perhaps on a much more equal basis than in any of the other community types. Fishing communities seem to fall into a combined grid and random settlement pattern, with houses constructed of tin or sheetrock scraps or planks due to the lack of vegetation and soil yielding the adobe and mud-and-cane materials traditional elsewhere. Cutting across these varying types of settlement patterns, the Mayo family functions as the basic, most elemental, and minimal meaningful settlement unit. The ranchería pattern in which relatives live in neighboring houses suggests an earlier pattern of kin rather than nuclear family settlement. Therefore, the change in land ownership and settlement pattern is from a kin or extended family unit toward a nuclear or Holy Family type.

The urban center provides the spatial heart of the mestizo population of the municipality, around which all commerce and important social life pulsates. Village and ejido mestizos go to the urban market centers to attend church and visit, to buy clothes and food items, and to seek employment. The Mayo village ceremonial center, on the other hand, is the heart of Mayo society. This center is characterized by a different sort of rhythm in the flow of its people, and is regulated by a ceremonial cycle which colors even its economic character, in spite of the fact that Mayos often go to urban centers to purchase goods and seek work. Although a few are ceremonial center residents, most Mayos live elsewhere and gather in several major Mayo centers at certain times of the year. Much of the descriptive material used in this book concerns ritual activities centering around two of these Mayo ceremonial centers, Banari and Homecarit, both located several miles west of Huatabampo, and commercial transactions occurring often in Huatabampo. The major interest guiding the organization of these data involves the question of Mayo revitalization and the explanatory utility of the Holy Family model.

MAYO ECONOMIC PRODUCTION AND ROLES

How do the Mayo people of Banari, and those who conceive of themselves as belonging to the Banari church, fit into a pattern of activities or roles in economic production? What does this participation mean to them both as Mayos and also as participants in the economy of the larger area? In the municipio of Huatabampo many Mayo household heads have rights to some land, either privately owned or in ejidos, which they farm as a family unit. Nearly all of these family members, men and women alike, work part of the year as laborers on larger Mexican farms to supplement their own small-scale farming activities. Generally men do the majority of the heavy work, although husbands and wives will go together to pick cotton, chile, or tomatoes. A few males either belong to fishing co-operatives or occasionally participate in part-time fishing, selling some of their catches for a small cash income. A few families own some cattle, often no more than a milk cow and the occasional offspring, or a few pigs, chickens, sheep, plow horses and goats. Some households also have members who know and practice the native crafts, such as weaving wool blankets and carrizo mats, which often are sold for cash. Fireworks-making, and some dancing and curing specialties also provide a cash income for a limited number of persons. Hunting and gathering of wild products are now diminished in economic importance although the techniques are well remembered by many Mayos, and are practiced by those who have access to stands of native forest. While visiting in Mayo homes one often sees women preparing cactus fruits, ground seed pods to be cooked in tortillas, ground cactus seeds, and other wild seeds and fruits.

A common economic role is exemplified by Juan, who considers himself primarily a farmer. Juan holds an ejido parcel consisting of eight hectares but actually farms only some four hectares, or about ten acres of his land. The other part of his holding lies miles away in heavy pitahaya cactus forest. He is not working very hard to clear that portion of his holdings, because he is not able to financially, and also because in November he goes to that land to hunt deer, and in June to pick pitahaya fruit. On his four hectares of cleared land he would like to plant corn, and does so if he can finance himself. But generally he must plant cotton because this crop is required by the ejido bank which supplies his capital for seeds. Whether or not his cotton is good he must pay annual costs of 175 pesos ($14) per hectare for water and 100 pesos ($8) per hectare road tax. In Juan's case, from a total cash income of 1,100 pesos ($88) from all sources some 20 per cent goes into these two taxes alone. Needless to say Juan cannot live on the income from ten acres of cropland alone and must raise a small subsistence garden near his house, in which he grows squash, onions, and beans and is experimenting with fruit trees. In one of his larger trees he keeps a beehive for honey, and he grew his own coffee until a government official came through and chopped down all the coffee trees in Mayo country. Juan also keeps a few chickens and a dog although, by our standards, they are not well cared for.

His two-room house constructed of adobe is warmer and sturdier, but was more difficult to build, than the jacal houses common in the area (Fig.3.1) Juan

3.1   Juan, standing in the doorway of his house near Banari

and a group of relatives and compadres built it over a period of months. His house is on Mayo village land, Juan says, though the deed to the plots is actually owned by some of the Mayos who live near by. The fact that his house is made of earth and covered with an earth roof has great significance to him because he sees this earthen roof as part of his identity as Yoreme or Mayo. Like almost all Mayo houses, his has a large shade ramada across the entire front where the women cook. In contrast to many other Mayo houses, Juan has no cane and mud kitchen separate from the bedroom section of the house. In the patio of his house stands a tebatpo kurus which he made himself.

In Juan's household live six persons: himself, his mother, his son, his daughter-in-law and two small grandchildren. He and his son cooperate in certain productive activities, such as fishing when the moon is new or full. At the time of high tides they take their circular nets (*temestim*), which they have either woven themselves or bought for about 50 pesos (U.S. $4), to the sea. At night so the fish cannot see them, they fish with temestim and set up another kind of net trap across the mouth of an estuary. The fish swim into these traps, the tide goes out, and the catch is picked up. Good food fish available in these waters include types of mackerel, white bass, red snapper, mullet, and halibut, as well as shrimp, which are caught in small circular casting nets in August and September. Fiddler crabs and ocean catfish are not considered fit to eat. Some people eat the flesh from the stomach of the manta ray. Ordinary crabs are quite good to eat on the spot while one waits all night for the tide to go out (Crumrine and Crumrine, 1967:25-33). The sea and shore also supply a large variety of medicinal plants and animals, and the very valuable commodity of salt (*óna*) used for the preservation of the fish. Natural salt deposits are traditionally free to Mayos of the areas near the ocean, although in some places they have been claimed by mestizos and the salt from the deposits is now sold. Juan does not belong to a fishing cooperative and in contrast to the Mayo coastal villagers he would not go out in a boat to fish. People in the coastal villages are fishing specialists or fishermen (*biróme*) and use hollowed log or plank canoes or modern commercial boats in regular fishing. Fishing is simply an important adjunct to his farming, as far as Juan is concerned. Corn farming is the proper base economic activity for a Banari man, as fishing is for the coast dwellers.

One or two older girls or women stay home to tend the children, to shell and grind the corn, coffee, cactus seeds, tree pods, and other vegetable products, to cook, air the bedding, and iron the clothes. The other adults in the household usually are employed in some kind of part-time work during the times of the year when fields need little care. Juan knows how to pick cotton and tomatoes, how to plant with horse and plow, and even how to build adobe houses, all of which he does for cash income at the appropriate seasons. The majority of other Mayos of Banari living in rancherías and in the nearby modern ejido villages have basically the same economic roles.

Another type of Banari farmer, almost identical with Juan in the significant aspects of economic role, is Loreto, who lives more remotely located from the roads and villages, out on his ejido parcel of four hectares (ten acres) (see Fig.

3.2   A Mayo bread oven

2.3). Perhaps related to the fact that he speaks Spanish only with a most broken Mayo accent, Loreto will neither grow strange kinds of fruit or vegetable crops, nor engage in certain types of labor. He does not work with a large number of impersonal *patrons* (farm employers) as does Juan, nor would he remotely consider leaving the municipio to take a job in some city. He considers himself an *etléro* (farmer) by speciality, and also plants crops for one or two regular patrons whom he has known for years. This personal relationship with his patrons involves an element of pride for Loreto. He believes they value his service as a peon above the work of all other farm laborers and expects the help and protection of these patrons when he is in legal or financial difficulties. Loreto also has an extensive knowledge of a native specialty, that of harpist for the paskola dancers, which he uses for both a hobby and a small source of income. Loreto's mother-in-law, a conservative old Mayo, has special skills also of blanket weaving and bread baking (Fig. 3.2). She makes her blankets on a crude semi-vertical loom, from the wool of the white, brown and black sheep in her flock. Sometimes she adds a dark blue to the diamond and stripe designs, which she calls "flower" *(sewa)*. A few of her blankets are sold to a Mexican shopkeeper at one hundred pesos for resale at two hundred to five hundred pesos. Almost every Mayo house in the area of Banari has one or two of these Mayo blankets, bought or bartered directly from her or other Mayo weavers.

In summary, both Juan's and Loreto's economic roles are overwhelmingly characterized by a close relation to primary resources, a value for a fervent intimacy with the land and water and their products, particularly corn, and preference for a type of wage labor which is related only to the land.

Other skills bring income to the specialist, including curing and manufacturing of alcohol, pottery, mats, musical instruments and ceremonial masks especially those of the paskola and Capayeka (Fig. 3.3). Of the clearly remunerative skills and crafts, the one most likely to become full-time is that of *Hitolío,*

3.3 A range of Capayeka (Parisero) masks, Easter week, Banari

general diagnostician and curer of diseases believed to be caused directly or indirectly by witches (*moriaram*). This dangerous though highly profitable specialty involves a doctor-clientele role relationship, in which the services of curing are rendered by the hitolío in exchange for goods and sometimes cash. In addition to their expressive roles as pasko entertainers, the deer singers also act as curers in a similar relationship with a clientele. Nevertheless, all persons who perform ceremonial specialties also see themselves as farmers or farmers' wives.

Many households have no members with land rights, and these people are drawn much closer to the Mexican economy than are those who can maintain some independent economic means. A description of Manuel's role personality will illuminate the landless laborer's economic life (see Fig. 2.1). Manuel neither received an ejido parcel as a veteran of the 1910 Revolution, nor obtained a deed to his early land rights. His single economically productive asset, above and beyond helpful relatives, is unskilled farm labor on a more or less open market. He picks cotton, and some kinds of vegetables and fruits, on various large Mexican farms and orchards in the area. Even the kinds of labor he can do are limited by his health and age of some sixty years. Manuel does not fish, just as he refuses to pick some types of vegetables, because he believes it would make him sick. There is no doubt his hungry and ill-clothed conditions do dispose him to sickness. He or his wife walk several miles to gather firewood for cooking and for heating in the cold winter months, or pick up wood scraps around the railroad tracks running near his house. If spoiled fruits or vegetables are discarded around the railroad yards nearby they may gather them and sell them for a little cash. Manuel's very existence and, needless to say, the expenses of his heavy ceremonial participation, must be in large part supported by his more able relatives and compadres. Through membership in two important Banari ceremonial societies Manuel has acquired a large group of compadres who are loyal and helpful to him. The aid from his compadres and his Mayo sons provides the means for his intensive participation in Mayo ceremonial life. For reasons of sheer economic necessity this role of independent sedentary full-time laborer is at any time transmutable into resident full-time hacienda laborer. The individual who must remain on the hacienda sacrifices his freedom of movement in exchange for job security.

In many of these economic roles, the individual functions as the major producer. Nevertheless, running across them all are the importance of the family unit and the individual's labor as affected by and as a major contributor to the family. A large amount of the money earned is contributed to the family, to be spent as a family unit or given to kin or ritual kin in support of their ceremonial participation. Often husbands and wives, brothers, fathers and sons, or other relatives will pick cotton or other crops, working together as wage labor. Members of the families who hold lands will at times cooperate in the clearing, planting, or harvesting of the fields. Also male relatives may cooperate in placing a fishing net across an estuary. And lastly, some of the monies from home craft manufacture or other specializations return to the families of their producers.

In conclusion, individuals often act as producers although their work is an integral part of the family unit in which they are members. The Mayo family is a crucial unit in production if in fact it is not also the primary production unit.

MAYO ECONOMIC VALUES, DISTRIBUTION AND CONSUMPTION SYSTEMS

Distribution patterns have two major foci because two distinct yet meshed systems exist in which Mayos spend goods and money, a Mayo system and a mestizo one. The Mayo system includes exchange between hunters, farmers, fishermen and native craft and ritual specialists in which barter of foods, fish, and salt play an important part. The mestizo system involves the exchange of money for labor services, taxes, utilities, and a limited number of durable goods such as pottery, enameled spoons, pots and pans, iron tools, meat-grinders, clothes, cooking shortening, and even radios and bicycles in the cases of more affluent Mayos. But all of this commerce is patterned quite separately from the Mayo distribution system, which uses food rather than money to secure obligations, respect, and health. In striking contrast to the mestizo system, the Mayo one is overwhelmingly concerned with ceremonialism and dependent upon family and ceremonial kin group cooperation rather than upon an open market economy. The common pattern of goods exchange between families as well as between compadres so characteristic of Mayo distribution also serves as a sort of social security insurance to Mayo families. When one family visits another, small food gifts are taken, several ears of corn, a couple of eggs, a pitcher of fresh, warm milk, or a few onions. Theoretically, the receiving family should bring a gift of equal value on its return visit. Ideally these gifts should be home-produced items. In actuality, the goods gradually tend to increase in value as the visiting cycle continues, increasing the ties of obligation between the visiting families and establishing the generosity of the giver. Since, when they visit, Mayos chat all day and since one offers food to any person present in the home at a mealtime, meals also are exchanged between families and friends. Accommodations, such as sleepiing mats, beds, and blankets, are given generously if an individual stays overnight.

Some community services, such as painting the church, are taken on as a part of the official work roles of the matačin or some other ceremonial sodality. But church repair is paid for by the church treasury in cash from a common fund, employing villagers who are jobless and who possess the required skills. Mayo services to other non-related Mayos—housebuilding and the curing of illness,for example—as well as such manufactured goods as mats, fireworks and homemade liquor are generally paid for in cash. Yet the social patterns associated with the exchange or the cash payment are uniquely Mayo. The value of services is fairly standard and payment of specialists, such as fireworks makers, paskolam and masom, is ritualized, with food offerings supplementing the cash. To illustrate, to be paid, the paskolam gather in a row of chairs facing the paskome. The paskola yoʔowe speaks for the paskolam and the parina yoʔowe (head ceremonial host) speaks for his group, the paskome. They offer some institutionalized greetings, restate formally and at length the terms of the exchange, and relate the exchange and work to be done to the general purpose of the ceremonial and the supernaturals. Therefore, the payment itself becomes a social occasion for a ritual which states and re-establishes Mayo values and traditional symbols.

Money-lending takes place from time to time between families and compadres, but Mayos generally prefer to give food rather than money, for money owed too long tends to put strains on a relationship. Ideally, Mayos say that 20 pesos (U.S. $1.60) is a comparatively large amount to borrow from any one person. More common and comfortable than the lending of money with expectation of an exact return is the *limosna* (very small cash gift or contribution) pattern. Typically a paskome group, the *Pariserom*, or a household about to give a pasko, gathers limosnas from the pueblo at large, and often from the nearby urban center, usually carrying a saint in a procession. Only a few centavos are expected at each house, as well as gifts of food or coffee. Since the limosna rationale involves spreading the load very thinly and very widely, quite large limosnas may be regarded as rather bad taste.

Another complete subsystem of distribution within the Mayo economic system deserves special attention. It functions, like the limosna distribution system, as a supplier of needed capital for the religious system rather than for individuals. To illustrate this system, which may be called the pasko exchange pattern, let us take the Banari Tiniran paskome as a representative host group and describe the operation of its economic payments and services. The paskome group at Banari consists of three head paskome, parina yoʔowe, *alperes* yoʔowe (second host), and *alawasin* yoʔowe (helper host) and three assistants for each yoʔowe. Within the sphere of the paskome authority, the parina ''commands much.'' The four alparesim are charged with errands, such as providing and supervising transportation of fireworks and paskolam to the pasko village. Alawasim are responsible for such heavy physical tasks of the pasko as wood-chopping. Food is provided by all paskome and is served in a long temporary ramada erected through the cooperative labor of the paskome group. Usually about twelve tables provide food for the milling crowd at a pasko, each with its own fire on which a pot of food simmers. Homemade bread, coffee, sugar, a sweet cornmeal drink (*bannari;* Spanish, *atole*) are usually served together with wakabaki or *kobabaki* (head stew). Food should not be paid for by those who come to eat at the ramada but is given. Any offer to buy food is a grave insult. Mayos on the lower Mayo River do not like people selling at paskos because the whole principle of such a ceremonial is based on giving —giving great amounts of food, fireworks, entertainment, and one's labor to the saints by way of the pasko crowd. The ceremony is an occasion to give not to sell. The concessions invariably attracted to patron saint paskos are run by mestizos and have no connection with the Mayo part of the ceremonies. But, of course, in purely economic terms someone has to pay for what is given in the Mayo food ramadas, and these are the paskome and their families and ritual kin. In 1961, the cost of a single major pasko and associated ceremonies ran as high as 3,000 or 4,000 pesos (U.S. $240 to $320) for each of the paskome. Considering the actual daily wage in 1961, which was about 10 to 15 pesos (U.S. $.80 to $1.20), this is without much doubt the greatest sum of money ever handled by a typical Mayo in a comparatively short time. It constitutes his most impressive spending experience.

People flock from far and near to become members of the paskome groups in the lower Mayo River ceremonial centers. They finance at least eight area-wide ceremonials a year and a number of home rituals and attend religious ceremonies in other neighboring ceremonial centers. Their economic capacity to perform these rituals derives from a cooperative distribution pattern which is family and compadre based. Perhaps the most impressive economic exchange which is purely Mayo in character involves ceremonial exchanges between entire villages, in which the people of one or more village churches gather for the patron saint ceremonies of a host village. The host village feasts the guests and thus obliges the guests to reciprocate, either as a village or as individuals. The food exchanges here concern thousands of pesos worth of goods, but when discussing it Mayos are more likely to emphasize the ceremonial significance of the exchange. Viewed as an economic system, the inter-village exchange chiefly broadens the distribution base for luxury foods, wakabaki, bannari and the sugar supplied for coffee. The people of Banari, who would like but certainly cannot afford to eat meat daily, consider the pasko stews a treat. Nor can they regularly afford large amounts of sugar and honey to sweeten bannari and even the cornmeal which goes into bannari often has to be bought with cash. Daily, Mayos of Banari eat a lot of fish and eggs, and on special occasions, such as San Juan's Day or for home paskos, the better situated families have chicken. Pork is generally eaten in October or early November if possible, in the form of tamales (*kowi nohim*) or pork stew (*kowibaki*), which is connected with the festivals of the dead. But many a poor family eats beans (*munnim*) even for special occasions, though they consider this a deprivation.

A range of native specialties, like Loreto's harp playing skill or the other paskola and maso musicians' and dancers' skills, receive some cash or goods, though the pivotal role determinant is ceremonial rather than economic. Sometimes individuals serve in these roles as a "gift" without being paid by the ceremonial hosts. The people of Banari consider some of these especially talented individuals as beyond salvation. They have sold themselves to an old man living in a cave in the mountains, and will go there to live with him when they die. This old man, who is identified by some as *El Diablo* (the devil), gives these extraordinary individuals great power and skill and so little fear of an excess of money. In contrast with these persons the average man's value for at least an appearance of uniform poverty becomes clear. Even most of the paskola and maso specialists themselves will deny that they have very great skill or wealth in order to avoid classification too much apart from other Mayos. An occasional deer dancer may admit that he has supernatural skill acquired in a contract with the little old man in the mountains. He will live gloriously and die young, with the definite and irrevocable expectation of being distinguished also in the afterlife from those who have not chosen such a way.

A Mayo myth illuminates the value for certain goods, such as traditional foods, over money and for these kinds of goods over skills other than farming. The *tomi ania* (money world) also provides a focus for Mayo gossip. Concealed near the ocean in the sand hills not far from Banari, a place of buried treasure glows at night. If one digs up this treasure without the proper ceremonial precautions, a swarm of *čičialim*, terrible black bat-like creatures causing sickness, is released. The čičialim will follow each piece of money wherever it goes, from person to person even to the innocents, the little children. A person may safely take the money from the tomi ania only if he first has a dream wherein the soul of the person who buried the money appears. The deceased must ask him to dig up the treasure, telling him where and how to get it. If one uses it to give a pasko, in fulfilment of a manda made by the deceased, the danger is lessened. But it is always a dangerous business, and generally only those with evil motives are said to attempt it. To visit the ocean at night or on certain days is to invite criticism—"He has been to the tomi ania."—so it takes courage to be a fisherman and remain at the ocean all night. Clearly for Mayos, this rather common Mexican myth links money and wealth with evil, sickness, and death.

The relative value of each of the productive roles is clear in Mayo thinking. The etléro, or farmer, is the best and in a sense the only proper economic role for a Mayo of Banari. He considers himself a farmer above all, even if he farms only a few acres. Being a fisherman, biróme, is also a traditional and accepted economic activity though Mayos consider eating much fish as characteristic of abject poverty. Almost everyone works as a peon, or wage-laborer, at some time during the year, and all Mayo people over fifty years of age remember the savagely oppressive pre-1910 debt peonage. In the 1960s Mayos, still distrusting anyone who offered a loan, resisted entering into any kind of full-time permanent labor contract wherein they felt they might become trapped. Symbolizing autonomy, the little piece of Mayo land, cultivated or not, and the grazing and hunting territory, along with the coastal land, are intensely sacred anchor points in the Banari Mayo's self concept of his economic life. This deep attachment to the land contrasts strikingly with dependence upon cash derived from seasonal wage labor on large mestizo farms and formerly from labor as braceros in the U.S.A. The land produces the primary resources of corn and other vegetables which are deeply sacred and symbolically much more valuable than money. From the hunting and grazing territory come animal products and wild fruits, woods, and medicines, and from the coast, salt and fish. All of these products once provided the basis for a self-sufficient Mayo exchange system. Still recognized as such by Mayos of the sixties, they have been transformed into symbols of Mayo autonomy. The real system has been basically modified by the increasing integration of Mayos into a cash economy, yet in striking contrast the symbolic value of the traditional system is still formidable. Briefly, production activities in the Mayo system are characterized by (1) preference for raising corn and food crops, fishing and hunting; (2) demand for personal working relations with patrons, and (3) the perpetuation of traditional Mayo crafts and expressive skills. Mayo distribution activities involve barter and a small amount of cash exchange for some specialty services, and, chiefly, exchange of foods—mostly meat, corn, fish, and salt—among families, ritual kin groups, sodalities, and villages. Mayos have learned to operate with more or less finesse in the mestizo market. Yet, most monolinguals and real ranchería Mayos minimize their economic dealings with mestizos as much as possible.

The most important conflicts between the two economic systems involve the Mayo value for the production of food crops as against pressure from the other system to grow cash crops or sell their lands. A Mayo reasons he cannot lose his land or control of his parcel if he raises food crops and does not borrow money, thus incurring debt. Furthermore, he needs food to distribute in the religious pasko system. On the other hand, if he borrows money, even from the Ejido Bank, and is slow in paying, as is often the case, the control of the bank over him increases. Mestizo individuals and money lending institutions reason that if they do not require the borrower to plant a cash crop, he will eat it and they will lose their entire investment. Many a Mayo farmer considers it easier to split the crop with a private money lender than deal with the bank. Of course, the loss of an ejido parcel or deeded land is an irrevocable loss for any poor Mexican, be he Mayo or mestizo.

The Mayo world view attaches a negative mental set to money, the accumulation of riches in general, and almost all non-agricultural occupations outside Mayo traditional culture, and positively values the appearance of relative poverty. These represent views antithetical to highly successful participation in the local mestizo and general Mexican economy, although Mayos do in fact participate in and contribute considerably to the economy. At the level of participation in the Mexican economic system, Mayos are indistinguishable from poor rural mestizos. Yet in intense contrast, the economic values and symbolism as well as the whole complex of ceremonial exchange is very much a part of a unique Mayo way of life which is not shared with mestizos in the Mayo River valley. The symbolism of the Holy Family provides a means of understanding the structure and changes taking place in Mayo economics. Both the modern settlement patterns and landholding system reveal a shift away from an extended family unit to a nuclear family of father, mother, and children, a type of Holy Family. The system of production while mostly rooted in the individual also is very much a family organized and regulated affair, often involving specific patterns of cooperation among family members. Lastly the Mayo family functions as the basic concrete unit in the Mayo system of consumption, distribution, and exchange of economic commodities. Mayo families build up reciprocal patterns of visiting at which time small gifts of food are exchanged and small loans may be requested. Much broader in scope and more expensive in terms of family contribution are the ceremonial exchanges or paskom, in which the paskome families, aided by their real and ritual kin, prepare and give food to the crowd attending the ceremonial. For a successful ceremonial the paskome must have the largest possible show of food, decorations, fireworks, and the greatest imaginable number of persons attending. Symbolically these ceremonials are built upon the code and structure of the Holy Family metaphor and specifically represent the meeting and embrace of Itom Ačai and Itom Aye. Practically they involve Mayo families, the minimal Holy Family, as the concrete basic social units, which produce the ceremonial. Clearly the symbol of the Holy Family provides a kind of thread which not only runs through the Mayo economic system and ties it together in a conceptual whole, but also symbolically opposes Mayo versus mestizo economic systems. Mayo-Mayo exchange patterns which cut across and integrate all the levels of Mayo social organization, from the family to the village levels, are symbolized in terms of the Holy Family metaphor. On the other hand, Mayo participation within the mestizo economic system takes place chiefly at the level of the Mayo individual and in terms of mestizo values and norms.

In summary, present data indicate the simultaneous existence of two differently structured and at some points opposed economic exchange systems. The presence of elements of the Holy Family metaphor also suggest the presence of Mayo exchange and of the Mayo economic system while the absence of these Holy Family symbols indicates the functioning of individual Mayos within the mestizo economic system.

4. The Sacred Mayo Political Organization: Where Mayos Meet Mayos

Is there a distinguishable and distinctively Mayo field of social relations or social organization? The preceding chapter indicates some exclusively Mayo networks of exchange which characterize Mayo economic organization. Certainly other types of economic behavior integrate the Mayo economic system with a general state and national system. Perhaps too, the subsystems of Mayo social organization such as family, church and community, may be dual in nature relating Mayos to each other and linking them to the wider mestizo society. In light of earlier discussions, especially in Chapter 2, one would expect societal relations linking Mayo society to mestizo society to be considerably less significant than the economic ties. I will be tracing the Holy Family model like a kind of red thread which symbolically unifies the constantly adapting systems of the Mayo family, community, and church.

FAMILY AND HOUSEHOLD

For Mayos, kin represent a broad bilateral group, wawari, with relationships traced through both mother's and father's sides of the family. Whether members actually reside there or not, the wawari is inseparably connected with the land, *solar,* where the dead are located. This concept of the wawari as including the dead is confirmed in all saint's ceremonies, house ceremonies, and unelicited but explicit statements by many informants. Families also keep the *balem,* books of the dead, in which the names of one's *animam* (dead) kin are listed.

In the 1960s most families used the Mexican kinship system characterized by a lineal, Eskimo terminology with separate terms for parents versus aunts and uncles, and brothers and sisters versus cousins (Fig. 4.1). For parents, siblings, children, and sometimes grandparents, Mayo terms are almost invariably retained (in Fig. 4.1, the area marked by larger dots). Conservative families also use Mayo terminology for more distant relatives and may punish children who use Spanish terms within the immediate family, while in other less conservative families children use Spanish kinship terms exclusively.

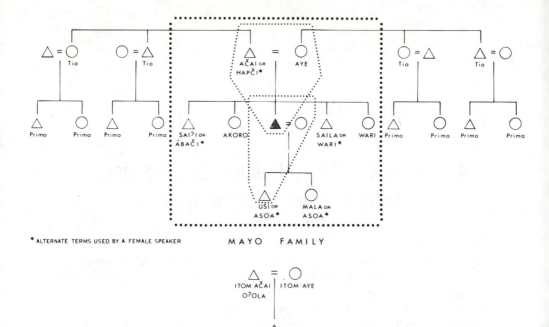

MAYO   FAMILY

HOLY   FAMILY

4.1   The Mayo Family and the Holy Family

It is additionally true that some Mayos remain unaware even of those kinds of distinctions made in the old system, while others realize there were distinct terms for maternal versus paternal uncles and aunts and also older-younger term distinctions. The Spanish terms *tia* (aunt) and *tio* (uncle) have replaced the more complex second ascending generational terminology. *Primo* (male cousin) and *prima* (female cousin) replace the old cousin terminology and even lineal relatives may be referred to or called by Spanish rather than Mayo terms. Or a male speaker may confuse terms used by women with those used by men if he has been taught by a female relative, or vice versa. The Mayo kinship terms also distinguish between siblings (*sai?i* versus *saila* and *akoro* versus *wari*) and parents' siblings in regard to relative age. A person may know all the Mayo terms for these relatives, but he may not know which term applies to which relative. Nevertheless, some informants who claimed not to know the Mayo terminology were heard using Mayo terms for more distant relatives on occasions when they needed to specify the exact relationship, as in litigation concerning lands. It would seem that this breakdown of Mayo kinship terminology is relatively recent.

The degree to which Spanish kinship terminology had replaced Mayo in most households reflects the amount of intermarriage with non-Mayos. A mestizo as a wife, husband, mother, father, or in-law, certainly influences the children's learning. The opposite process also takes place and there exists ample evidence of "Mayoization" of a few intermarried individuals. Although still recognizably different from Mayos, such persons who did not speak Mayo and were neither born in Mayo country nor of Mayo parents have become Mayo speakers, practice Mayo crafts, and participate in Mayo ceremonies. On the other hand, the Mayo use of Mexican Spanish kinship terminology is not always particularly accurate. For example, a woman may call a father's sister (tia) of approximately the same age as herself, *prima hermana* (first female cousin). Mayo terminology provides for this kind of categorizing. A man can call any younger man *insaila,* my little brother, or take him into a little brother relationship (*sailariapo*) or take a younger woman into the relationship of little sister (*waririapo*). Relative age plays a part in actual Mayo social relationships and their inaccurate use of Spanish kinship terms sometimes reflects this fact.

Mayo terms have been retained for relationships within the nuclear family, those denoting parents, children, and siblings, which reveal extremely interesting parallels to the Holy Family model (Fig. 4.1). Recent periods of extremely disruptive warfare coupled with patterns of wage labor and small plot farming, have forced large kin groups to split into small nuclear families or informal groupings of several relatives—for example, a mother, her son and his family, two brothers and their families, or an older man and his nephew and nephew's family. Therefore, this disruption of traditional Mayo kinship terminology and the increasing importance of the Holy Family model seems relatively recent. Still reinforced through the use of Mayo kinship terminology, the two major cooperative relations link parents with children and siblings with each other. The strong Mayo value and respect for age provides a means of structuring these relations, parents and older siblings having power and control over children and younger siblings. Although the sibling relationship is not emphasized, the Holy Family provides the model and the ultimate basis and sanction for the age-respect principle and for these changes in kinship and family structure. Within the Holy Family, Itom Ačai Oʔola, the oldest, holds the most power, followed by Itom Aye and by Itom Ačai Usi, the youngest.

In order to examine this Holy Family metaphor and the age-respect principle in somewhat greater detail, a brief description of the types of relationships which existed within the Mayo family in the 1960s will be useful. Mother-child relationships are permissive and close in the early years and children respond becoming generally affectionate and respectful in the mature years. A girl entering adolescence is gradually encouraged and if necessary pressured into helping around the house (Fig. 4.2). Her mother or elder sister will praise her efficiency or scold her laziness. The boy as he matures spends an increasing amount of time with his father, learning men's work. His discipline then becomes of less concern to his mother than does that of an older girl. Fathers, although they are less responsible for younger children, generally also treat children permissively and

4.2 Girls drawing water at household tap, Banari

affectionately, participating in their ceremonial training, giving ceremonies for them, and helping them make matačin costumes. On the other hand, mothers accompany both boys and girls on Lenten processions and pick or buy flowers for their crowns. This split in the roles of father and mother is symbolized in the positioning of the Christ Child and the mature Christ. The Christ Child is often placed on Mary's side of the church altar and the grown Christ on the male side. Even after their children marry, parents continue to be directly concerned with their health and welfare and help them in every way possible. Yet at the same time the parents represent authority figures, an attitude which is extended to all older members of the household. As long as the parents live the children maintain this type of emotional dependence on them. Grandchildren in general are treated like children, and grandparents like parents, although more teasing exists in the grandparent grandchild relationship than in the parent-child relationship. Beyond this level a Mayo myth symbolically ties children to old people through a primordial rejuvenation process in which children came from flesh and bones of old people.

As if mirroring the relationship between the sun and the moon or between male and female saints, a cooperative and respectful relationship prevails between husband and wife. Complete loyalty and patience as well as the ideal of family solidarity, especially before children and strangers, are major values which characterize this relationship. The division of labor assigns the large part of the household tasks to women and the bulk of food obtaining activities to men. Yet this is not invariable, for men help in caring for and disciplining even small children. And women work in the fields from time to time, especially during harvest, although no woman was seen planting crops or fishing. Either spouse may assume authority in the household. Mayos believe a church wedding is important and elopement is discouraged but is nonetheless common, especially when parents do not approve the choice. "Those which the parents decided were always the best marriages," one old man observed, emphasizing the power of parents even in the choice of a spouse. In this context the Holy Family symbolizes the crucial importance of the marriage bond, discouraging elopement and divorce or separation. Thus modern Mayo mythology emphasizes and ritualizes this crucial bond and critical weak point in the maintenance of an "opposition" Mayo culture.

Sibling relationships are characterized by cooperation first in play groups and later in work groups. Brothers and sisters are increasingly separated in activities after they grow older, but they maintain close emotional ties and turn to one another for help in ceremonial obligations and family crises. Older siblings, particularly sisters, have more authority and responsibility, and are like "little mothers." Siblings and siblings-in-law very often live in a close cluster of several houses within a village or ranchería. The women work together and help to maintain the clothes, prepare food and watch all the children. They take turns doing these tasks freeing some adult women to participate in ceremonies, go to market or work as wage labor. Often male siblings and siblings in-law cooperate in farm labor, fishing and food gathering.

The behavior characterizing this system of family roles demonstrates that the basic principles inherent in the traditional kinship system, especially that of age-respect, still carried meaning in Mayo life of the sixties. Nevertheless, they have been transformed and integrated into a nuclear family system and a Holy Family sacred model. Symbolic of this transformation, Spanish kinship terms have replaced the Mayo terms for persons outside of the family, a replacement which contrasts with the firm use of Mayo terms for members of one's family. The marriage bond, too, crucial for the modern continuity of Mayo culture, is creatively elaborated as one of the key relationships in the Holy Family.

Often larger than the family, the household (*hoakame*) is ideally lineal and consists of a couple and their children, grandchildren and the couple's living parents. Both married daughters and married sons may live with the parents or parents' siblings. Families that are able to do so build separate rooms or houses for each nuclear family, but all continue to eat, work and make decisions together. A brother's widow and her children or a wife's widowed sister or cousin and her children exemplify other common additions in household organization. The hoakame tends to change in composition frequently as individuals join the army, go away to work, or move from one parent, who has remarried, to the home of the other parent. Although extremely diffuse and hard to pinpoint in terms of specific membership, the household includes a number of ritual activities which act to unite it as a unit. Hoakame members pray together and hold common ceremonies at the house patio cross and the household altar. The altar includes the ceremonial paraphernalia of household members, flowers and burning candles offered to the santos. Even the santos themselves form part of the household pantheon and are believed to look after the interests of its members. Resting on a table or shelf on the wall of a bedroom, the altar generally faces the patio house cross, which forms a symbolic tomb during the funeral of a household member (Crumrine, 1964). The taboo extending over the household after a member's funeral prohibits, among other things, the sweeping of the patio for nine days, so that the dead soul may return and "gather up its steps." No member of the household is supposed to attend a ceremonial for ninety days after the death of a household member, nor is he or she supposed to be a ceremonial host for a period of one year. The depth of a person's attachment to a particular house and the land on which the house stands involves the number of ancestors and relatives who have died there, and for a woman, particularly her dead babies.

In the month of October a *tapanko*, which is a table made of four Y-shaped posts, is erected, usually to the east of the household cross. On the tapanko are placed a large red water jar, food including bananas, oranges, pork tamales (*nóhim*), homemade bread, wreaths of red and white flowers, and a basket with some of the same foods, together with water from the jar. This food and water is taken to the cemetery on All Saints' Eve and offered on the graves of each of the household's dead while large candles are burned. At the gravesides a maestro and a cantora pray for each of the dead by name and are paid in cash and food from the grave. During October, the dead hover about the house and see and hear what household members are doing, so Mayos are circumspect in word and deed, for should the dead become angry, they can bring sickness upon the household. The dead are also said to bring the fall rains in the form of low-flying clouds which roll in off the sea producing the first really cold rains of the year along with actual human colds and sickness. The authority of the oldest household member or the oldest male and oldest female members is justified in Mayo thinking because the old ones are "close to the dead." They know the traditions which must be kept to please the dead. Along with this group of rituals and beliefs, the everyday activities which household members perform together link them into a unit, the hoakame, against nonresident kin and all others. Ideally each hoakame should include a set of old people (*In Ačai*, My Father and *In Aye*, My Mother) along with the children of the household. The hoakame is, therefore, an expanded transformed version of the Holy Family.

CEREMONIAL KINSHIP: THE KOMPAÑÍA

The Mayo ritual kin group is an exogamous system of persons related by sets of ties closely resembling real kinship relationships (Fig. 4.3). These ritual ties are consummated through religious ceremonies and, theoretically, last for the lifetime of the persons involved. Compadres are acquired in such ceremonies as the original baptism of one's children, the formal induction of one's children into ceremonial societies—for example, the matačini society for both boys and girls, and, every three years for a Parisero member. Notice that the Mayo officials and leaders always have tremendously wide compadre connections often both inside and outside Mayo society. Distant kin ties may be reaffirmed through compadre ties, or real kin ties may be ignored. Much is left up to the family in choosing those individuals and families with whom it can cooperate most successfully and ignoring those with whom it cannot.

The pseudo-lineal relationships first, of *batoačai* (godfather) and *batousi* (godson) or *batomala* (goddaughter), and second, of *batoaye* (godmother) and *batoasoa* (godchild) are respect relationships. The godchildren take part in a series of rituals in which they are accompanied and guided by their godparents. Part of the ritual always takes place before a cross and an altar and involves

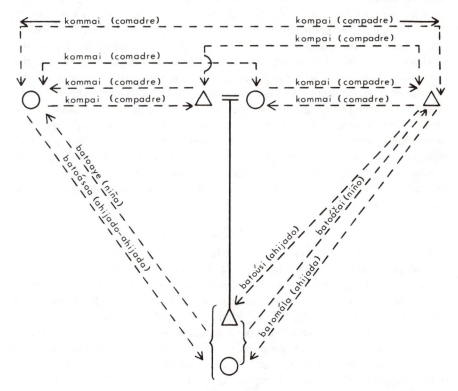

4.3   Mayo ritual kinship terms of reference (adapted from L. Crumrine, 1969, Fig. 1)

making the sign of the cross. In cases of baptism, a family feast for the god-parents follows. When they meet, the godchild must always greet the godparent formally and with the full set of polite Mayo forms. Mayo children are more often scolded and chided in public to obey this custom than perhaps any other single one. The godparents of baptism have a particularly strong obligation to the godchild, as does the child to them. They are expected to take over the responsibility of the child's training if anything happens to the parents and to prepare his or her body for the funeral should the godchild die. In contrast to the godparent-godchild relationship, the most impressive social and economic cooperative group (the *kompañía*), arising from the ritual kinship system, forms between those individuals who are related as compadres (*kompai, compadre and kommai, commadre*). Coparent ties also tend to be extended to include anyone whom the godchild calls "godparent." Within this group of compadres a Mayo forms the associations of deepest trust outside his own wawari. Therefore, within his kompañía he seeks cooperation in ceremonial and economic ventures. For many individuals, whose families died in warfare and social upheaval, compadre ties are fa nore dominant in their lives than wawari ties.

 ι hus the ritual kinship system shows more adaptability than the real kinship system. Its ritual and symbolism provide a wide spectrum of available individuals from which a few are chosen for the most intimate social ties. Symbolically, lineality or fictional lineality, the godparent-godchild relationship is very important in the system. In contrast, for the actual work of social life and for cooperative enterprises the collateral, horizontal group of compadres must bear the burden of social interaction and social labor. Second in importance only to the immediate family, the household and selected members of one's wawari, the ritual kinship group (kompañía) is vital to many of the activities and ceremonies where large cooperative groups are needed, such as funerals and post-funeral rites, the curing of sickness both by native curers and by manda and the resulting production of ceremonials in honor of the santos. In such activities the kompañía is related specifically and centrally to the maintenance of Mayo social life. Finally the kompañía and the ritual kinship system is based upon a transformation and symbolic extension of the structure of the Mayo family and of the Holy Family model.

Pueblo

The concept of pueblo symbolizes for Mayos a very real entity, a united group with religious and civil leadership directly responsible to every single household in the pueblo. Ideally the pueblo is an absolute democracy; yet in actuality each household has a vote for Mayos could hardly conceive of household opinion as not unanimous within itself. On the other hand, a Mayo pueblo is not exactly coterminous with a community. People consider themselves members of a Mayo pueblo even though they live in a broad range of communities. Many of the most influential members of Banari pueblo live in rancherías and other ejido villages miles away from the actual geographic locus of the "pueblo." Some evidence points to lineal descent as an important factor in pueblo allegiance, but modern

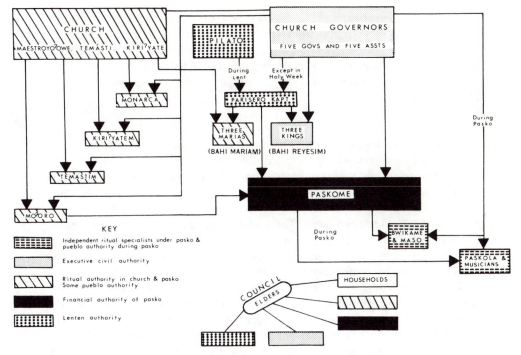

4.4 Mayo pueblo societal units (adapted from L. Crumrine, 1969, Fig. 2)

data do not show any very rigidly patterned system. Most likely the concept of pueblo became increasingly indefinite as Mayo residences shifted so drastically in the 1910-1936 war period. Also in the sixties no Mayo secular government existed as such, although Mayos claim that formerly there was a set of five pueblo governors whose chief function was the settlement of land disputes between family groups. The governors were assisted in this by the *susuakame*, or elders, who were the heads of wawari groups. Today most disputes which are kept within the Mayo pueblo are handled in the extended family, or taken to the church governors or to the heads of other special ceremonial societies. Some of the organization and functions of the secular governors have been incorporated into the church governor's domain, and some have been given over to mestizo authorities in Mexican municipal and ejido organizations. Little is known of the rituals and formal knowledge which once characterized the Mayo military organization (goʔim). The few remaining members help as a police force to control occasional unruly drunks at paskos and cooperate closely with the church governors in maintaining the relationships of the pueblo to other Mayo pueblos. The military organization is recruited by manda and by a ''volunteer'' system and is dedicated to the saints. It has a patron, as do the other sodalities of the church, and formerly had insignia, though the use of these is disappearing since they increase the visibility of the wearer.

The Mayo pueblo, still a very real Mayo symbol, includes a church-cemetery area, a set of church officials and church sodalities, and Mayo membership drawn from a dispersed set of communities (Fig. 4.4). The Mayo members of the pueblo are called the little children (Ili Usim) of the major male and female saints (Itom Ačai and Itom Aye). In this way the pueblo is spoken of as a huge Holy Family.

SAINTS' CULTS

Associated with each pueblo are one or more saints' cults, because a given santo attracts devotees who believe this santo is responsible for curing illness among themselves, their kin, and compadres. Cult devotees are characterized by having taken part in the payment of a manda which may have been made for the paskome participant or for a family member on whose behalf he or she is performing the ceremonial labor. The social component of a santo's cult at any given time does not necessarily correspond to the church area in which it is centered, for devotees flock in from a far wider area crosscutting pueblos and church centers. The experience of having been a pasko persona functions as an initiation to the cult core, whereas the members of the kompañía of the pasko persona are on the fringe of the cult. If the santos grant the cures supplicated, many families eventually belong to at least three different cults situated in three different churches and three different pueblos, the Santisima Tiniran of Banari, the Santa Kurus of Homecarit, and San Juan (Saint John) of Navojoa. Similar allegiances of cult devotees weave together Mayos from the ocean pueblos to Cucusebora, high on the Mayo River and from the Guasave River in the south to Magdalena and the Arizona Yaqui-Mayo village churches in the north.

Although cult members are not restricted to area residents, the patron saint of one's own church-pueblo center does tend to be a very popular curer in the area. In Banari, for example, Mayos agree that their Santisima Tiniran image is more powerful than any other Holy Trinity. Even after a family has dispersed to other areas, individuals tend to return to the patron saint ceremonies, to the Lenten ceremonies, and to discharge other mandas. The most geographically restricted ceremonial group is the cult of the dead, whose members have dead kin, especially parents, buried in the cemetery area associated with a given church. Yet even this extremely exclusive cult integrates individuals of "foreign" origins, because anyone who has dead in this cemetery, particularly a parent, spouse or children, has the right to be present and take part in these ceremonies. These cults, whose members are called the Ili Usim of their saint or in the case of the cult of the dead are the actual relatives of deceased persons, provide the structure for the cooperative organizations which make much of Mayo ceremonialism. Often a ceremonial involves the presence of a visiting saint of the opposite sex to that of the host saint. Therefore, this ritual integration of saints' cults is coded in terms of the Holy Family with the Saints being named Itom Ačai and Itom Aye and the members of the cults and other participants, the Ili Usim of the saints.

CURER AND CLIENTELE

The saint's cults are also maintained in a fascinating fashion through recommendations by native curers (hitolíom). The diagnostic relationship of the hitolío to his patients is best described as that of shaman to clientele, since he deals with each of them as individuals. The relatives and compadres of the curer and the Mayo patient are also usually involved.

In another quite different type of curing ceremony for rabies, a group of men in the role of curer sing deer songs on horseback at a sacred spot near the ocean. They sing all night until the morning star rises, when they sing the deer song which is always sung to that star (*Santa Mačiria*). At that moment they gallop into the brush near the spot, catch a rabbit by the ears, split it open with a wound in the shape of the cross on its chest, and smear the blood upon the patient. After this they all return to the patient's house and the patient's family feasts them with a fixed series of ceremonial foods beginning with sweetened bannari, wakabaki, coffee, and bread.

Before any cure proper begins, the hitolío diagnoses the cause of illness in the patient. This power (*gracia*) to divine the cause of the sickness and to recommend the proper treatment is given by God. According to his diagnosis, based on revelation and symptoms, the curer recommends his own treatment involving herbs and massage, in the case of witch(sibome or *moriaram*) caused illness, *malpuesto*. In the case of those illnesses which are God-sent (*liohman-dapo kokore*), he normally recommends making a manda to serve in a saint's cult, and may even specify which santo is good for the illness. Therefore, a manda-making link exists between the hitolío and the saints' cults, in which the curer essentially supplies the cult with paskome participants. A santo's popularity waxes and wanes as the powers of the curers who send patients to the santo rise and fall. Any given hitolío tends to act as a mechanism in the maintenance of the cults of specific santos.

THE CHURCH

The church building itself (*tiópo*) is referred to as Itom Aye and the members are conceived of as her children (*asoaka*). The people of Banari are proud of their church, for they say she has many children and in this way her greatness is measured. "Within the four corners" (*naiki eskinapo*) of the holy churchyard lie the cemetery areas of Banari, as well as the church which houses Itom Ačai O?ola and the images of the santos, the Little Children. The social church consists of specific sodalities, cults of the saints, and a general congregation. The sodalities and cults of the saints generally recruit members by means of a ritual contract or manda made with a santo in return for a cure from an illness. If one is cured one must pay the manda. In general terms, leadership in the sodalities is chosen by pueblo consent. However, the head maestro in Banari is extremely instrumental in the nomination of a candidate. The head of each sodality is likely to remain the leader of the group as long as he or she is physically and mentally able to satisfy the pueblo.

The Church Governors

These men (*tiópo kobanarom*) work closely with the Maestro, are chosen at a meeting where the entire pueblo is present and in which everyone can speak out for or against them, remain in office for three years and may be reelected for a term of three more years. The five church governors, *Tiópo Kobanaro* (president), *Hiotelío* (secretary), *Tomita Suayaleo* (business manager), *Bihilante* (watchman) and *Kapitan* (captain), along with five *Bikales* (helpers), are called the "sacred ten." They meet weekly to confer on matters of importance to the church, and are especially important in coordinating ceremonial activities, such as processions and intercommunity ceremonial exchanges.

Being a church officer constitutes a community distinction and carries with it a kind of obligation which is similar to a manda, but is called *tekia*. It is a sacred duty to complete one's tekia. In the major part of the year the church governors work together with the head maestro, *temasti* (sacristan), *Kiri?yate* (cantora), and the matačin monarca (head of the church dancers' sodality). The Pariserom take over nominal command during the Lenten season when special authority is vested in their head Pilato.

Maestrom

Perhaps a dozen maestrom are affiliated with Banari church, all of whom are characterized by a knowledge of the Catholic prayers, rituals, and *alabanzas*, which are sacred songs. They read the balem, pray for the dead by their personal names over each grave on All Saints' night, and give the Mass of the Dead at funerals, during Lent, and on various other occasions. The services of the maestro are also essential at all house and church paskos and especially crucial just before burial of the dead. From the group of maestrom one is elected by popular consent to the position of maestro yo?owe, or head maestro. This official exerts a great influence over the pueblo and is frequently consulted because of his enormous knowledge of church rituals.

Temastim

The sacristans have two chief duties: the care of sacred paraphernalia, and the singing of the hymns and responses in some ceremonial services. Members of this sodality are recruited by manda, and rise in prestige within the organization by popular support both among other temastim and with the pueblo in general. The maestro often has much to do with the nomination of a temasti to the most important position, the temasti yo?owe, or oldest sacristan. At Banari the temasti yo?owe takes care of the sacred images, keeps the key to the church, and is its guardian. He was the only person ever seen touching the sacred bells in front of the church, which are rung for funerals, paskos, Sunday konti and Friday konti during the Lenten season. The temasti also rattles the wooden *matraka*, or substitute for the bells used on Good Friday in the symbolic funeral of Itom Ačai. He sweeps the junta building, where the officials of the church and sodalities gather to discuss plans for paskos. The temasti yo?owe takes care of the procuring and use of holy water, of perfume for baptisms, of incense used in processions on Holy Friday, and of canes which are put in the corners of a grave during a burial ceremony. He acts as the custodian of the additional sacred paraphernalia belonging to the pueblo in general and interpreter of the symbolism connected with that paraphernalia. Aiding him in this work are the junior sacristans. In Banari the position of temasti yo?owe carries considerable authority, often equal to that of the maestro.

Kiri?yatem

The cantoras are a women's sodality which accompanies the maestro and sings various Mayo, Spanish and Latin hymns (*alabanzam)* in response to the maestro's reading in home and church ceremonies. The kiri?yatem kneel with the maestro before the altar, march with him in processions, and accompany him at funerals. After years of participation, some have acquired essentially the same fund of knowledge.

Kopariam

This group looks after the female saints' clothes and helps direct activities and train the young women who bear the female saints in some processions, especially during the Easter ceremony. These girl bearers are supposed to be virgins and speak Mayo flawlessly, though it is said, not without humor, the latter requirement is not always met. The older kopariam are mature married women. Within this sodality a head is chosen who may contribute directly in church decision making and planning meetings. Kopariam serve by manda.

The Matačin Society

This dance sodality is composed of male members for most of the year, but is joined by young female members during a period extending from nine days before the feast of Espiritu Santu on Epiphany Sunday to the feast of Santisima Tiniran on Trinity Sunday (Fig. 4.5). The role is entered either by manda or as a gift to the Santisima Tiniran. Young members are confirmed into the society in a formal church ritual with godparents on Trinity Sunday. A hierarchy of offices exists within the organization. At the top the *monaha yo?owe,* or head of the society, often leads the dances and gives the instruction hinabakam to the matačinim. The second in command, the monaha segunda, takes over if the monaha yo?owe is unable to attend a ceremony. A group of men, called *alwasils,* directs the young women dancers who are always accompanied by their godmothers. All matačinim carry a rattle, a feather wand, and on some occasions wear a crown-like ribboned headdress.

The matačin dances are historically European in the structure of steps and major formation and are performed to violin and guitar music. Yet, the mature men, who are the leading Banari matačinim, dance close to the earth in a crouched position, with a spring-like quality in their legs, which curiously resembles some of the styles seen in the dance ramada where animal dances are done. At least one animal dance is performed by the matačin society, the *moel* (sparrow). The women have a slightly different dancing technique. They do not

4.5   A young Matačin dancer with a Matačin crown, wand, and rattle, Banari, Easter Sunday

lift their feet as high, nor crouch, and, in fact, girls are scolded for imitating the men's style. When dancing in processions, girls precede the men and when dancing in front of a house or church they stand parallel to the front wall before the entry of the building in a formation at right angles to two lines of boy matačinim who dance alternately toward and away from the line of girls.

The matačin society dances for most important paskom during the year except during the Lenten season up to Holy Saturday, at funerals of important persons, and for many home paskos and other rites of passage. The core of the matačin organization at Banari is formed of perhaps a hundred very experienced dancers while as few as seven may dance at once. Yet perhaps four hundred or more boys and girls danced matačin simultaneously for the several miles of procession from Banari to Arocósi for the ceremonies of Espiritu Santu and the Santisima Tiniran in the spring of 1961.

Congregation

The general congregation of any given church involves persons not specifically participating at the time in any of the given sodalities. Most congregations tend to be formed of individuals who have made promises to attend a given pasko either in payment for a cure from sickness or as a gift to the saints of that church. People also come as individuals and households seeking pleasure, fellowship and the more general blessings of the saints. More often persons who do not have promises of their own in regard to a particular ceremony come to help other individuals who are formal participants and who are related to them through kin or compadre ties. Usually, patron saint ceremonies attract enormous and relatively impersonal congregations for the culminating paskos, whereas ceremonies involving the cult of the dead ancestors tend to be very limited and the group is more or less unreceptive if not actually hostile to outsiders. Definite geographical and socio-historical bounds exist within which a person can attend house and church ceremonies. One is not safe going to a ceremony in another pueblo unless his or her home pueblo has "permission" *(licensia)* from the church governors there. An individual attending without permission could be threatened with verbal and/or physical violence. Also, certain times of day are safe to go to major ceremonies in another pueblo. After these hours one should not be in that pueblo, unless staying at the home of a relative or compadre. The congregation of a pueblo shows its most homogeneous aspect during the Lenten season when traditionally one should go only to one's own home pueblo for services.

The members of the congregation play specific roles and functions in the ceremonies. One of the most important duties of all participants involves prayer. People generally *mukti* (pray) as the family arrives at the church ground, before turning to any visiting or work. Mukti patterns differ with churches. At Banari before entering the church one crosses oneself to the kurus yoʔowe of the church and then turns in place and crosses in the direction of the church. On entering the church, the worshipper begins at the center altar greeting the Santisima Tiniran. Then he or she turns to the three-dimensional images of the three Marias, the Christ Child, the Sacred Heart (in the Christmas season), and San Miguel. One returns to the center altar to a small crucifix and a large picture of the Santisima Tiniran of Banari. The Santisima Tiniran, a large picture, includes three figures, which appear to be dressed as males, each holding an object—from left to right, a lamb, a triangle with an eye in it, and a dove. The three stand on a globe surrounded by seraphim and clouds with sunlight streaming downward. San Juan, a three-dimensional image, occasionally stands on this center altar. Sometimes a bronze patriarchal cross sits to the worshipper's left of the large central image of the Santisima Tiniran. The large crucifix with a removable lifesize body of Christ generally stands to the worshipper's left (Fig. 4.6) and farther to the left are placed San Ignacio, Rosario, and occasionally a visiting santo from another pueblo. A small three-dimensional wooden dove sometimes rests here,

4.6   The large crucifix, Itom Ačai, directly in front of the altar, Easter Sunday, Banari

too. The worshippers in Banari cross themselves to each of these supernaturals in the order described and generally proceed to the vestry, where they mukti to Guadalupe (the patron Saint of Mexico), the Banari Santa Kurus (a large wooden cross with a coronet of white flowers), a small group of images often behind a white curtain including an anima in a casket-like box with glass over it, San Isidro, usually another small image of the crucifix, a small Santisima Tiniran, and a Christ in Gethsemane. The wooden open slat wicker-work casket of Christ hangs on the outer wall of the vestry and Mayos, especially Pariseros, cross themselves at this casket as if it were an image. At the end of the line stand the maestro, temasti, and other officials with whom the worshipper shakes hands.

The Mayo sign of the cross is normally made with the right hand. The thumb which makes a small cross when held in front of the forefinger, at right angles to it, is touched to the forehead with the words *"Santa kuruhta"* (Holy Cross), sometimes also inscribing a small cross on the forehead. Then it is placed on the lips with the words, *"Itom beherim betana, aman itom yoretua itom yaučiwa Dios,"* to the left shoulder with "Itom Ačai O?ola," to the right shoulder with "Espiritu Santo," back to the lips and to the lower breast with "Itom Aye." Instead of Itom Aye on the last touch, some say, "Amén Jesús." Very few people do the sign of the cross properly, Mayos claim. Often the ritual is abbreviated into a mere triangle, touching the forehead, the left shoulder, and the right shoulder. But people who do this know how it should be done, and children are taught by their godparents how to do it properly. The meaning of the words. *"Itom beherim betana, aman itom yoretua itom yaučiwa Dios,"* literally, "Liberate us from our enemies, Leader God," was interpreted as signifying that our enemies are evil words, our own and those of others, which will do us harm. Therefore, one touches one's lips with a crossed thumb while saying this part of the sign of the holy cross. The sign of the holy cross, when made before the images, especially those of Itom Ačai, confers the forgiveness of the santos. When doing mukti, worshippers often cross the images, touching them and praying to them in Spanish or Mayo. The prayer, "Our Father," is said to most of the male images. San Isidro, who kneels on one knee and whose other is thrust up as his foot braces him, is often patted on the knee by worshippers who stop to cross him and ask him to send rain for the crops. Individuals with different role or sodality affiliations linger at certain specific images as they mukti. Pariseros invariably spend time with the images of Itom Ačai Usi or Christ Crucified. The small crucifix is frequently offered cotton during harvest seasons. A Parisero explained, "He understands men's prayers better." Women linger longer over the little image of the anima and pick it up and fondle it as they mukti. Women and children also pay more attention to the images of Mary and the Christ Child, especially during the Lenten season. San Juan is offered watermelon in June during the beginning of the melon season. Clearly the members of the congregation are united with each other by sharing this common Holy Family relationship established in prayers and offerings to Itom Aye, Itom Ačai and all the santos. As "Ili Usim" of the Holy Family, all the members of the ceremonial center are children of the church (Itom Aye) and of God (Itom Ačai).

Another ritual kind of behavior, ceremonial feasting, especially characterizes the congregation at any Mayo ceremony and draws it together. Throughout any long ceremony pauses occur between the main events during which all the people gather at the food ramada. This fellowship of eating together is explained as one of the most important aspects of a pasko. The final division of leftover foods invariably demonstrate a surplus, for it is part of the sacred charge of the paskome to feed the congregation well and to give food abundantly.

Paskoria, the term usually used, means to give a feast on someone's behalf, for example, the santo's. Without a congregation to consume the sacred goods, the paskome could not complete his or her manda to the santo (*mandata čupa*). Also, the designation Ili Usim unifies the congregation, called the Ili Usim of the church center, with the santos conceived of as the Ili Usim of God. Obviously symbolically linked in their identification as Ili Usim in the Holy Family, the congregation acts as a replacement or stand-in for the santo.

Lastly the enculturation function of participation as congregation is stressed by Mayos. They argue that one must repeatedly see what is done in a given ceremony "with his or her own eyes," before he or she understands it, or before the meaning can really be explained. To be ignorant of the ceremonial life is not to be truly Mayo.

PASKOME

Paskome simply means "those of the feast (pasko)" and may apply to any of several kinds of groups which are bound by manda and formally dedicated to give feasts and perform services of prayer for a santo. Ranging from informal to quite formal in organization, Banari paskome organizations are dedicated to household, pueblo, or church santos. Although twelve individuals are promised to the Santisima Tiniran, the patron saint of Banari church, essentially twelve households and kompañías participate in the discharge of the duties of the paskome, rather than twelve individuals. Including spouses, the twenty-four paskome are divided into three groups of eight each, the parina or paresin (the captain), the alperesin or flag-bearer, and the alawasin or helper. Both a division of practical labor concerned with the preparation of the feast and a division of ritual labor characterize this organizational division into three ranked groups. Also within each group a secondary ranking is found.

The practical labor—building of structures, wood-splitting, heavy labor of all sorts—is assigned to the alawasim. The alperesim take care of commercial transactions, both with the non-Mayo community, for transportation, machinery and some foods, and with craftsmen native to the Mayo community, such as *kahueterom* (native fireworks' makers) and paskolam. The paresim, highest ranking of the three groups, supervise all the activities of the other paskome and manage the feasting of the highest officials of the church, of the paskolam, and of any honored guests at the ceremony. All the paskome and their families, households, and kompañías are responsible for procuring and dispensing food to the guests. The men butcher and the women cook, wash dishes, and serve the food on the tables. In their ritual activities the Santisima Tiniran paskome are instructed and directed by the moʔoro, an official and ritual expert whom they choose and clothe during the period of his service. He leads them through the rituals, often while drumming on a thin skin-covered drum. The main functions of the Santisima Tiniran paskome are: to pray in the velaciones and feasts of the Santisima Tiniran and of San Juan, and throughout the year; to perform an important part of the weekly Sunday konti ceremony involving the blessing of cottonwood leaves *(abaso sewam)* to the four directions and the decorating of all the crosses, bells and images of the church with leaves; to sweep the church and the konti boʔo; to perform a protective series of duties during Lent, when they accompany and guard images and crosses against the Čapayekam (masked Lenten sodality members) and to take part in certain funerals. In any given pasko the paskome, who have hired and transported the paskolam and deer dancers and their singers, are responsible for the ritual introduction of these performers to the dance ramada in the beginning of the ceremony and the periodic escort of the performers to the church to pray and to take part in the processions. The paskolam thank them for this, among other things, at the end of the pasko.

Still other fascinating differences cut across the paskome organization. A colored bun around the parina's waist signifies high rank and stores the group's money. The alperes carries and waves the banner of the Santisima Tiniran. The alawasin wears a foxtail around his or her waist and sometimes carries a cane or a whip which, during Lent, is used to keep Čapayekam at a distance from sacred areas. The Santisima Tiniran paskome have definite symbolic associations. In konti and in ritual hand-shaking the alawasim move in a clockwise direction and the other two groups in a counterclockwise direction. The three *yoʔowem,* or top-ranking paskome, of each subgroup represent Itom Ačai Oʔola, Itom Ačai Usi and Espiritu Santu, who is also called Itom Aye. These three symbolize the Holy Family structure of the paskome organization. All the Banari paskome are associated with the colors red, white and gold, the colors of their flag and ribbons and of the three members of the Holy Trinity. The paskome are, specifically, a symbolic "military guard" to the Santisima Tiniran although they do not, in any actual sense, constitute a military organization. Some people believe they are associated with the body parts—the eyes, nose and mouth—the "sacred five" openings of the face. These symbolic meanings are taught to the new paskome by the maestro who holds "classes" at the church ramada on certain Sundays. The symbolism, organization, and activities of Homecarit Santa Kurus paskome are fundamentally similar except that their santo is the Santa Kurus, whose feast and prayers they sponsor, and their colors are red, white and blue.

The Tiniran paskome promise to serve for three years, but not consecutively. One must "rest" between years of service, regenerating one's financial capital and physical endurance. Paskome must formally notify the church officials in advance of the time when they wish to discharge their service. In the formal announcement of a manda, a person offers to the Santisima Tiniran red and white roses in a red pottery jar filled with river water and is acknowledged by the maestro. Years may elapse before an individual can discharge any of the paskome duties. Not all paskome groups have so much special ritual and symbolism as those connected with cults of patrons of churches and pueblos. Some paskome groups, which are formed for the purpose of house ceremonies, for example, have a much less formal and enduring organization. They concentrate chiefly on the prayer, food-giving and dancing aspects of the home pasko, depending on a network of relatives and compadres to join in the work and a Maestro to lead the prayer.

In this chapter I have discussed the structure and organization of the Mayo family, household, ceremonial kin, pueblo, saints' cults, curing, church, and paskome groups. With perhaps the exception of the shift to Spanish kin terms for distant relatives and the shift of the civil governors to church governors, the Mayo socio-political system is tightly interrelated and quite separate from that of rural or urban mestizos of the Mayo River Valley. Thus the Mayo socio-political system tends to bring into interaction persons who share common understandings, values, beliefs, and the meanings of symbols, individuals who wish to practice the Mayo way of life. Yet to be a good Mayo proves extremely demanding in terms of financial and temporal expenditures. The heads of the church ceremonial societies, including the Moʔoro and the patron saint paskome, perform in and attend ceremonies at least 200 to 250 days of the year, including home ceremonies, such as funerals, Lenten season, and San Juan home ceremonies. Many of these rituals require all-night vigils as well as daytime work. On the other hand, for traditional Mayos, understanding the meanings and organization of the sacred symbols, which the ceremonial participants manipulate, produces immense satisfaction and the prestige they acquire through participation is more than compensation for the labor and capital expended.

Lastly, the underlying structural model upon which this range of Mayo socio-political organizations is based and with which it forms a set of transformations is that of the Sagrada Familia (Holy Family), Itom Ačai Oʔola, Itom Aye, and Itom Ačai Usi or the Ili Usim. Changes in the kinship terminology, reflecting increased emphasis on the nuclear family and breakdown in large extended households, and the retention of the age-respect principle reveal the structure of the Holy Family model and become meaningful to Mayos in terms of this model. Where households, consisting of several families, continue to cooperate often they are bound together in terms of two of the elemental relations in the Holy Family model; relations between parents and children and between children themselves, who are at the same time siblings. Constructed in terms of the Holy Family metaphor, the ceremonial kinship system ritualizes the parent-child relationship and replaces the ''real'' parent with a god parent. In doing so, this ritual forms a horizontal cooperative group of co-parents who share the responsibility of raising a single child. The pueblo and church organizations simply expand and transform the Holy Family into a sacred community with God, the church, and the male and female saints coded as parents while the Mayo members of the community become the Ili Usim. As a cure for illness, parents promise children to the saints and Mayo curers supply the saints' cults with members, paskome. Often both the leaders of the church organizations become godparents of their members or their members' children and famous curers also serve in this same capacity for their patients thus utilizing a kind of double or triple transformation of the Holy Family model. Members of a sacred sodality who already are the children of the patron saint of the group become godchildren or compadres of the human leader of the sodality, too. Beyond this the patron saints also are classifed as Ili Usim of the Sagrada Familia. Lastly, the symbolism characterizing these secular and sacred Mayo social groupings reveals complex multiple combinations, recombinations, and transformations of our original extremely simple Holy Family model. For example, the three ranks of the paskome represent God the Father, God the Son, and the Holy Spirit, often called Our Mother Goddess.

In many ways it proves useful to conceive of the Mayo family and the Holy Family in terms of a triangular unity of oppositions. The triangle is inverted with the two upper angles referring to ačai and aye and the bottom angle referring to usim. This unitary triangle of the Mayo family consists of two sets of oppositions: first, parents are opposed to children as elaborated or cooked is opposed to unelaborated or raw, and second, fathers, males, are opposed to mothers, females, as culture is opposed to nature. Fathers are related to their children through a socio-cultural agreement whereas mothers are related both socio-culturally and biologically to their children having produced and fed them from their own bodies (see R. Crumrine, 1973, and Lévi-Strauss, 1966). The ceremonial kinship system, the Holy Family, and the paskome as well as other ritual sodalities transform this family triangle into a set of variations constructed upon the unity of the Mayo family and the dual set of oppositions. This model emphasizes the two sets of relations established through cultural and ritual processes: (1) the parent-child relationship mediating the generational opposition between adults and children, and (2) the marriage relationship mediating the male-female opposition. Specifically, these two sets of relationships, parent-child and husband-wife, are crucial for the maintenance of the modern Mayo way of life. Yet these two relationships are under especial challenge today as more children go to mestizo schools and lose respect for their parents and their old people and as elopements, remarriages, intermarriages, and high death rates of spouses threaten marriage stability. Since the Holy Family, a symbolically powerful elaboration of the family triangle, ritualizes, emphasizes and isolates these two relationships, this Holy Family metaphor proves extremely appropriate and highly useful in the maintenance of the Mayo way of life. Tapping an underlying structure, the Holy Family model provides a Mayo folk construct or operator for conceptualizing both the structure of their own social organization and also their means of reinforcing the special social relationships, both crucial for the continuity of an ''opposition'' Mayo culture and also most intensely under the corrosive influences of the present structure of culture contact between Mayo and mestizo societies. In order to examine the Holy Family metaphor in its most expanded and complex form, I shall turn to several additional sodalities and to the ceremonial structure which unites Mayo social groupings into a single sociopolitical system.

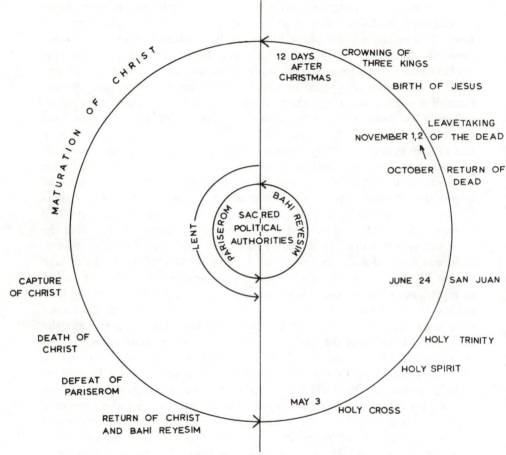

5.1 Banari Mayo ceremonial cycle

5. Ceremonialism: Mayo Pueblo and Tribal Integration

THE THREE KINGS: INTRODUCTION TO MAYO CEREMONIAL CYCLE

In the Mayo cycle of ceremonials (Fig. 5.1) this sacred myth presents the Mayo concept of a unified and divinely sanctioned pueblo government expressed in terms of yet another manifestation of the Holy Family.

> Joseph and Mary fled, out of shame it is said, because Mary was pregnant, and Joseph knew that he had nothing to do with it. But the angel appeared to Mary and told her not to be ashamed because she was going to give birth to Christ and he told her and Joseph not to be ashamed for it was the work of the Holy Spirit. He talked to Joseph alone, then, and told him not to leave Mary because of this. So Mary and Joseph came back to Belem, but there was no room for them anywhere so they had to go to a stable. And there the Child was born and the Three Kings came to see the Christ Child. The animals made special noises signaling his birth. The cock crowed, the donkey brayed, and the dog barked.
>
> Then Pontius Pilate started pursuing the Christ Child, it is said, because he was afraid. Since the Three Kings had visited Christ, Pilate thought the child must be pretty important. So the army of Pontius Pilate pursues the Christ Child every year, and kills him, but in the end He arises and He and the Three Kings triumph on the Saturday of Glory.

Mary symbolizes Itom Aye, the Mother of Itom Ačai Usi and of all Mayos (Fig. 5.2). Pontius Pilate is represented by the Parisero group, commanded by four Pilatos. The Pariserom are both symbolic of the pursuers and crucifiers of Christ and also are the repositories of a somewhat selfish and individualistic kind of religious and political power which seeks to be supreme over all law and order in the universe. "When a man wants to do something he alone wants for himself and he cares for no one else, he is like that then." During their season, which begins on the first days of Lent and ends on Saturday morning before Easter Sunday, the Parisero sodality rules the pueblo. The deterrent effect of the Pariseros on misbehavior seems very effective. Their masks and headdresses add to their physical height and the black capes, swords and weapons of the officers

5.2 Mary, Itom Aye, being carried in the final Easter procession, Banari

radiate power, natural and supernatural. The Parisero attempt to dominate and kill Itom Ačai and destroy the Holy Family proves that only God rules and that He has much greater power than they do. They are ''burned up'' by the Sun (Itom Ačai) on Holy Saturday. Then the *Bahi Reyesim* (Three Kings), represented by the pueblo governors and heads of the military societies allied with the church organization, return to power. The paskolas, who according to myth were present at the birth of Christ, participate on the side of the infant Cristo and do not appear during the Lenten season except near the end, on Easter Saturday. The other groups, including the matačinim, which continue to function, but are under the command of the Pariserom during the Lenten season, become supreme

in their spheres of power as soon as the Pariserom have been symbolically
"burned" on *Sabado de Loria* (Saturday of Glory).

Both the succession of pueblo governments and the cycle of paskos are
regulated by the re-enactment of the life of Christ and the sacred history of the
Sagrada Familia. After Lent, when the Bahi Reyesim are again in command, the
harvest and summer rains follow with the Exaltation of the Holy Cross on May
3, San Isidro on May 19, the movable feasts of the Holy Spirit, Holy Trinity,
and a number of paskos like the nativity of San Juan on June 24. In October and
November, the dead ancestors return to the villages. The year begins anew with
the feast of the crowning of the Three Kings, in the first week of January, in
which the governors are confirmed in office. The twelve days between Christmas
and the Day of the Kings represent the year in microcosm. All paskos as well as
individual and family activities fit into this general scheme of things, for the
human pattern is regulated by the divine (Fig. 5.1).

PARISEROM: THE LENTEN SODALITY

The Pariserom (Pharisees) or Hurasim (Judases) appear during the Lenten
season as a formal male religious sodality dedicated to the cult of the crucified
Christ, Corpus Christi (R. Crumrine, 1968). The organization of the group is
hierarchical and chiefly staffed through manda. Individuals with special leadership qualities, or who have served a long time, tend to rise in the ranks, being
chosen as officers by the membership. The average time of service in the
Pariserom is three years (*bahi wasuktiam*), which may be extended three more as
a gift to the saint except for officers who often serve for life.

The chain of command runs from Pilato (also called General), to Kapitan
(Fig. 5.3) to *Kabo* (corporal), to *Flautero* (flutist) (Fig. 5.4) and *Tampalero*
(drummer), to the *Tropa*. The masked Tropa carry the additional names of
Pilatota O ʔowim (men of Pilate), *Sontaom* (soldiers), Čapayeka, or *Čapakobam*
(Figs. 5.5, 5.6). Within each rank a secondary sub-rank grouping exists, such as
Pilato Yoʔowe or Pilato *Primero*, Pilato *Segundo* (second), Pilato *Tercero*
(third). Each Pilato carries a small red or black banner mounted on a long staff,
each Kapitan, a sword and each Kabo, a machete and a whip. The Flautero plays
a reed whistle on which he may render very long complicated melodies during
some rituals. The Čapayekam wear large hairy masks and carry wooden swords
and daggers made of pitahaya wood and painted with designs in red and green,
with red on the tip of each to represent the blood of Cristo Niño. In procession
the group generally proceeds in order of rank except for the Flauterom who go
first, before the Pilatom.

The Čapayeka masks cover the entire head and rest on the shoulders. Some
represent various animals, such as the *huya kowi* (javelina) or the goat. Others
have chalky white human faces and represent women, though the backs of these
masks are quite hairy. Most have long sharp noses and large pointed ears, either
to the sides or above the mask (Fig. 5.7). Many young men buy their masks from
maskmakers for ten pesos (U.S. $.80). Under the mask, a fine cotton cloth

5.3 A Parisero Kapitan,
Easter week, Banari

5.4 The Parisero Flauterom in front and the black veiled Pilatom behind

5.5   A Čapayeka with a drum

covers the neck and mouth of the wearer completely. Over his back and chest the Čapayeka wears a blanket which is cinched at the waist by a belt. He wears trousers, thonged sandals and there are cocoon rattles on his ankles. In addition, he often carries, hidden in the folds of his blanket, a wooden phallic fetish which he uses throughout the Lenten season in his rituals and "confessions." Some Čapayekam carry other props, such as violins, rattles, flowers, cap pistols, and drums, which they use in pantomimes to disrupt the ritual. All Pariserom carry rosaries, some black, some white, and adorned with pink, white, turquoise or green tassels. When the mask is over the face the Čapayeka holds the rosary cross in his mouth and silently prays. Probably the majority of Banari men have been Čapayekam at one time or another, usually in their late teens, though the officers and non-masked members are middle-aged men. Banari had just 100 men serving in the entire society in 1961, about 75 of whom were masked men; 112 in 1965, 34 of whom were Čapayekam; and 202 in 1970, 173 of whom were Čapayekam.

5.6   Several Capayekam, one with a doll

The service associated with this organization involves the repayment through penance of a debt incurred to Santo Cristo for a cure from illness. The mythico-political elements of meaning focus upon the power held by the Pariserom during the Lenten season as they pursue and murder Cristo Niño and place his remains in an *urna* (urn) which they confiscate. In the end, of course, the Pariserom are vanquished by the power of the Sun and the men are saved through baptism. This whole episode is said to demonstrate the omnipotence of Itom Ačai over all men and all things. During the Lenten season the Capayekam "confess" (*hiokot*) for the entire pueblo, which they must do almost entirely by means of pantomime since talking with the mask on is taboo. In this pantomime they act out the traditional Mayo marriage ceremony, followed by movements symbolic of sexual intercourse. Other bodily functions are imitated at various times, such as defecation and urination, often on sacred objects. They show

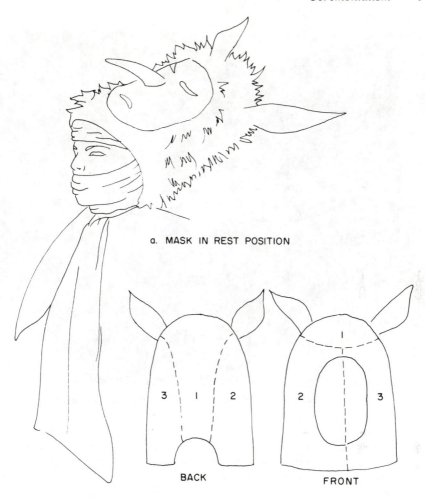

a. MASK IN REST POSITION

BACK   FRONT

b. MASK CONSTRUCTION

5.7 Čapayeka mask

disrespect to old people, especially the Oʔola (old man) who represents Jesu Nazareno in the rituals of Holy Week. Čapayekam also "confess" by doing travesties on maestros and numerous other church officials; a detailed imitation of the diagnoses of various kinds of sicknesses by hitolíom; excellent paskola and maso dancing and violin playing; pantomimes on sword or gun battles; and a large number of other rather taboo activities common to Mayo culture and society (R. Crumrine, 1969).

   Just as the Pariserom try to take over the government of the pueblo from the rightful social groups sanctioned by the supernaturals,the Čapayekam also take

5.8   A Čapayeka playing with the photographer's camera, Easter week, Banari

over the konti or "surrounding," a ceremony performed during the rest of the
year by the paskome. Instead of performing the ritual on Sundays, however, they
do it on the Fridays of Lent before the general processions. Early each Friday
afternoon of Lent they gather at the church, coming from throughout the fields
and countryside. As they arrive, small groups of Čapayekam line up in two rows
and run down the konti boʔo, which consisted of fourteen stations of the cross
and extended toward the river in the 1960s. Then they return and surround the
church by separating the two lines and each going in an opposite direction around
the church. Their officers assemble to the rear of the church while the
Čapayekam run around and perform their clowning activities (Fig. 5.8) in the
patio and before the altar of the church and the women, children, and the church
group perform rituals and prayers within the church. Finally, the Pilatom
and Flauterom lead off a procession along the konti boʔo toward the river. As
soon as the procession has passed the first station the Čapayekam run into the
church and steal the flowers that the children have offered to Cristo Niño. Then
they follow the procession, disciplining the women and children who do not kneel
properly and burlesquing the worshippers' behavior. Preceding Easter Week the
Pariserom also give home ceremonies to "rest" their image of Cristo. The sixth

Friday of Lent the crosses of the konti boʔo *batweči* (procession path toward the river) are pulled up after the procession.

On Palm Sunday the Pariserom chase an Oʔola (old man who represents Jesu Nazareno) through a mesquite forest and capture him, "like a prisoner" *(presota benasi)*. This apostle wears a white kilt and around his waist a rope, twenty to thirty feet long, of red and green colors associated with the Čapayekam and the dead. This rope is called *wikosa bwaʔe,* and is the type used to lower corpses into the grave during burial. During *Semana Santa* (Holy Week) the Pariserom take the Oʔola to homes in the area to collect funds for *Loria* pasko. For the *Tinieblas* ritual on Wednesday evening the Oʔola sits before the altar as the twelve candles representing the twelve apostles as well as the Three Marys are extinguished. With the extinguishing of each candle, the Čapayekam make a konti around their officers standing in the center of the church. After the last candle goes out, in the total darkness, they shriek loudly, terrifying the women and children representing the Three Marys and the Three Kings. Making sounds of the owl and other night creatures, this is the only time the Čapayekam may "speak." As the Maestro starts to pray, one Sacristan lights the fifth candle from the right side of the altar (male side) and the first three candles on the left (female side) representing the apostles and the Three Marys. At the instant the first spark of the fire lights the church the Pariserom thunder from the church out into the darkness of the night, then all leave for the campo santo to pray there. After the prayers, the Pariserom remain up all night in their special shelter.

Thursday of Holy Week the Pariserom capture the Oʔola from a green bower after he is betrayed by Iscariot (played by one of the Pilatom). In a formal procession they chase the Oʔola over a way of the cross which they have set up around the church and decorated with mesquite, like the crown of the old man. The old man is shielded and given mescal in gourd cups by eight *madrinas* (godmothers), while the Čapayekam try to pull him down by the wikosa bwaʔe and to knock him down with their bodies. The madrinas beat off the Čapayekam with long pieces of cane just as the godmothers of any deceased person would beat dogs and animals to keep them away from the corpse. In a real funeral these canes would later be used in the four corners of the grave to keep away anything that might wish to harm the deceased. The "running" or "tumbling" of the Oʔola, like Jesus when he fell under the cross, symbolizes death and movement to the world of the Čapayekam. In actuality, the old man was not knocked to the ground in 1961, 1965, 1970, 1971, or 1972. This "running" is followed by a second procession featuring male and female images. In the morning and early afternoon on Good Friday, the Pariserom run through the communities and rancherías felling or tumbling each family's house cross and placing it on a box. Representing a tomb, a bower of mesquite is built over the box and cross as it would be decorated had there been a death in each house (although at the time of a death in the family the cross is not pulled up or tumbled over). The church cross is tumbled in the same way by the Pariserom. Within the church they prepare a bower of cottonwood leaves in which the two crucifixes are placed, the large one and the small one. Behind this, nearer the altar, an empty coffin is surrounded by a relatively large square enclosure of smooth earth molded into long ridges representing the tomb *(tumba)*. Two paskome stand inside this area with long canes to strike dogs who dare venture near the tomb.

Late Friday afternoon all the Pilatom march into the door of the church. To re-enact the crucifixion, one of them resolutely thrusts a sword into the bower. As the candles which the congregation carries are lit and the Čapayekam carry out the cottonwood a branch at a time, apostles remove the images from the two crosses and place them in the coffin. The Mass of the Dead is performed by the maestros during the next two hours. After the mass two Pilatom mounted on horseback lead a dual procession with the coffin around the church in a counter-clockwise direction followed by two Pilatom leading the second half of the procession with an image of Mary. A later procession is actually split and symbolizes Mary's attempts to find Christ: Two mounted Pilatom with the bare crosses lead the first half of the procession around the church in a counter-clockwise direction, while two other Pilatom, also mounted, lead a procession with Mary Dolores in the opposite direction around the church. The processions meet halfway around, Mary's procession turns and joins the other, and both complete the konti by returning to the church in a counter-clockwise direction.

In the dawn hours of Saturday, twenty-four hours after the first house crosses were pulled up, the resurrection of Christ is proclaimed by ringing the church bells. The bells, the voice of the archangel, had been silenced by the Čapayekam after the fall of the old man. Homeowners raise the house crosses and place red flowers on them. During these early hours of the morning the paskola and maso dancers begin performing in the ramada in front of the church. Almost exactly at noon the Pariserom march into the church, each one accompanied by a batoaye and a batoačai who are to assist in the long and complex rituals which are interpreted as the ultimate fall of the Pariserom and the impersonators' subsequent baptism and return to the world of man. First, two paskolam, a maso, two masked Čapayekam and several alawasim run three times from the altar area of the church, which is sealed off by a white cloth, to the church patio striking the earth before the patio cross each time, shouting "Gloria" (Fig. 5.9). The *Bahi Mariam,* women and children, throw yellow and red flowers, symbolizing the triumph of Santisima Tiniran. Behind the white cloth and extending in two long lines out of the door of the church, the kneeling Pariserom are being "fanned" by their godparents as they "burn." All the Pariserom and the O?ola are immediately rebaptized by the Maestro as if new-born because they have been to the world of the dead, and the masks are thrown on a bonfire. Their duties as Pariserom are not over for on Sunday they must prepare a sacred path with cottonwood for the meeting of the risen Itom Ačai and Itom Aye who does not yet know He, Christ, has returned from the dead. Around noon, Cristo's procession comes from the Paskola dance ramada and Mary's procession from the church, with San Juan "running" as a messenger between them. At the triumphal meeting they embrace *(omom*

5.9   Group running out of the Banari church to the cross, "Gloria," on Easter Saturday

ibaktia). At this moment the Čapayekam, none of whom have worn masks since the time of their baptisms on the preceding day, again circle the church. They strike at each other with the mesquite switches, which they have carried to consecrate the sacred konti boʔo on which Itom Aye and Itom Ačai have just met. A final procession of Christ and Mary led by matačini dancers is called the "last konti." At the church door the Pariserom strike the earth patio thrice with their switches, throw them on the church roof and enter the church. A final important ritual takes place at the side of the church. As a castigation, the former Pariserom, now men, are forced to drink and to eat bread by the Bahi Mariam. "They have been on a long journey and are very hungry."

BAHI MARIAM AND BAHI REYESIM

The Bahi Mariam (Three Marys) include a group of children promised to the Marys of the Lenten season (Maria Santisima, Dolores, Magdalena), their godmothers and the women of the pueblo. They accompany the images on each of the Friday processions and after the reading of the prayers, which are given at each of the fourteen stations of the cross, throw flower petals over the procession, symbolic of the final ritual which will signal the redemption of the Pariserom. The little children represent the forces of Itom Ačai which will ultimately triumph at Gloria, but they must undergo much teasing and taunting by the Čapayekam. The batoayem always accompany the children and guide them through the processions of Lent. As a penance, women of the pueblo may walk in the procession group.

The Bahi Reyesim (Three Kings) include all the governors and the men of the pueblo, some of whom walk in Lenten processions behind the Bahi Mariam. The Bahi Reyesim symbolize the positive forces only temporarily under control of the company of Pilato, the Pariserom. They continue some of their minor duties during the Lenten season and after Loria on Easter Saturday are restored to their rightful positions as governors and rulers of the pueblo and church under the authority of the Santisima Tiniran and Cristo Niño. Thus, the major theme of the Lenten ceremonial focuses upon pueblo government while the ceremonial itself is a key ritual in pueblo social and cultural unity and integration.

To summarize, the company of Pilato and the Easter ceremonial is rich in symbolism identified with the Holy Family, the pueblo government, and supernatural power, particularly the omnipotence of Itom Ačai O?ola and Cristo Niño. Other less explicit but definite fertility associations may be found, such as the sex play of the Čapayekam and their use of phalli as fetishes, and the feeding of bread to the former Pariserom as the crowning ritual of the season. Parallels also exist between the Pariserom and the world of the dead, who control the November rains. These links exist in persistent association with the colors red and green and in the explicit belief that Čapayekam do in fact enter the world of the dead, as does Jesus, when they have killed Him. A Parisero phrases this in terms of the exact words of The Credo.

> I believe in God the Father All Powerful [Itom Ačai O?ola], creator of heaven and earth, and in Jesus Christ [Itom Ačai Usi], his only Son, Our Lord, who was conceived through the work of the Holy Spirit, and born of the Holy Virgin Mary, suffered under the power of Pontius Pilate, *was crucified, dead, and buried; descended into Hell*, and on the third day *arose* from among the dead, ascended into the heavens, and is seated at the right hand of God the Father All Powerful from which he is to come to judge the living and the dead.

At one level the Easter ceremonial re-enacts the history of the Holy Family, yet this manifestation of the past in the present is structured in terms of two opposing political forces and the supernatural power underlying their mandate to rule. Ritualization of events, which most deeply affect families, plays a basic and crucial role in the structure of the ceremonial. Human fertility through which parents produce children, the feeding of growing children by mothers, the baptism transforming non-humans into Mayos and providing one with an additional set of parents, the young people leaving the family for periods of labor or military service and their return reuniting the family, the wrath of a father whose authority has been challenged and whose wishes have been disregarded, and of course the ultimate problem of death which threatens to destroy even large extended families and is of crisis proportions to a nuclear family system like the one developing in the Mayo River Valley today—all receive consideration and a ritual solution in the dramatic structure of the Banari Easter Ceremonial. Clearly, many of the major themes of this ceremony relate directly to the Holy Family metaphor and to the kinds of problems and solutions Mayos have discovered in their attempt to adapt traditional Mayo culture and society to modern life in southern Sonora through the use of this model as a kind of mediator and logical mechanism for the generation of solutions.

THE SODALITIES OF THE DANCE RAMADA

The following sodalities supply dancers for the dance ramada and have a special relationship to sacred animals which serve as their insignia, and through whom they derive personal magical power. Four of the animal sodalities which still had active members in the Banari area in the sixties were the paskolam, the maso and maso bwikame, the goʔim (coyote society), and the wikičim (bird society). Since only the paskola and maso groups still perform regularly I will limit discussion to these two sodalities.

The Paskola Group

Separate in structure and meaning from the church sodalities, the paskolam provide essential services to almost all church activities. A large number of Mayo men and women know the sacred paskola music as well as lyrics. The professional paskola sodality is characterized by group cohesion, distinctive recruitment procedures, special costumes, ritual role, mythology, and specific Mayo symbolic values. The paskolam who dance at Banari and Homecarit usually come in groups of four with a set of musicians, though as many as seven or eight paskolam and two sets of violinists and harpists may be present for major church paskos. Paskola personnel range in age from almost senile men to boys scarcely older than toddlers.

The paskola costume (Fig. 5.10) includes bare feet, a white blanket secured at the waist and brought through the legs giving an illusion of loose pants falling below the knees, belt from which small round bells hang, and long ankle strings of cocoon rattles (*tenebarim*) which, when the feet move suddenly, make a soft distinctive rustling noise. Mayo paskolam wear a shirt and carry a *sanáhe*, a unique type of rattle with a long handle and a wooden frame in which are mounted metal disks that make a noise similar to but rather more vigorous than the sound of a tambourine. The two most characteristic parts of a paskola's costume are his hair drawn up into a top knot secured with a flower and the mask which he either wears over his face or carries on the back of his head while performing. The black, human-featured paskola mask with a zigzag border often symbolic of a mythological snake is incised and decorated with a white horsehair beard and eyebrows. The gaping mouth reveals sharp teeth and a protruding tongue, and lips painted red or a rich pink. More varying designs include spirals, lizards or horned lizards, crescent moons, and stars, all of which may be either inlaid in shell or pieces of glass mirror, or incised and painted white (Griffith, 1972). The excellent craftsmanship and designs on these masks prove highly creative.

Wearing the mask on the back of the head, the paskola dances to harp and violin music; but he wears it over his face while dancing to the drum and flute. The paskola hinabaka, explaining the meaning of the pasko and commenting facetiously on current events, are spoken with the mask on the face, causing the voice of the paskola to resound in the mask and produce a strange supernatural sound. In order to entertain the crowd, the paskolam call people by the wrong kin terms, make fun of compadres, talk in literal terms about sexual intercourse among animals, people, and the saints, pray to animals, and satirize almost all sacred institutions and features of daily life.

Although denied by individual practicing paskolam, the recruitment of pas-kolam is *said* to take place as a result of a supernatural experience in which the paskola visits a cave in the mountains and talks to an old man with a white beard. The paskola is sometimes *said* to sell his soul to the old man in exchange for the power to dance well. Some people resent the paskolam because they take money for their service and control different types of power than most people, although the power may be used for either positive or negative results. Nevertheless, paskolam, when they die, are almost universally *believed* to go and live in the mountains or forest with this old man. The paskola, closely acquainted with the animals of the forest, may see the otherwise invisible *huya ania* (sacred forest) and such sacred animals as deer, pigs, and goats. The commander of the huya ania may take the form of one of these animals who are his children. This Huya Oʔola (old man of the forest) and his wife, Huya *Hamyoʔola*, care for their children, the animals. Even in the sacred forest world, the huya ania, the Holy Family metaphor is used. The paskolam perform tricks on people and the *yoyu-maʔane* (bewitchment) can be put on another, so that the bewitched paskola is unable to dance. This harmless trick passes over quickly. The *moro yaʔut* (head advisor) of the paskola ramada not only organizes the paskolam but also guards the ramada by divining with the smoke of *yorembibam,* or native cigarettes made of homegrown tobacco (*mačuko*) wrapped in corn husks.

On the other hand, the paskolam are the best of all Mayos because they are the most characteristically Mayo in their behavior and speech, always praying and giving hinabakam in Mayo and participating in church processions. In pro-cession they invariably directly precede the images of the santo or santos. When the dancing paskolam advance they are saluted by waving of the banners of the saints carried by the alperesim who proceed in front of them. Then they turn and dance toward the rear, facing the images of the santos to whom they bow and who "bow" (are dipped) to them in turn. In this manner they slowly advance in a shuttling dance-and-salute pattern back and forth between the banners and saints, linking the paskome and images, as the total procession moves forward. After processions the paskolam are returned to the paskola ramada by the Paskome where they begin to dance their mimetic animal dances. The paskola harpist

5.10 A Paskola performer, dancing to the
music of flute and drum, Easter
Saturday

(*arpero*) and violinists (*laboliom*) and one musician who plays both a skin drum
and a whistle flute wear shirts and straw hats, on which the paskome pin colored
paper flowers. If there are deer musicians, they wear similar straw hats and
flowers. The flowers in their hats represent a Mayo kind of obligation (*yorem
obligación*) between the paskome and the paskola and maso groups. This means
they are integrated with the church ritual through flower and color symbolism.

Paskolam have additional important roles in almost all church paskos. During Loria pasko on Easter Saturday two paskolam run three times from the
church altar area to the church kurus yoʔowe bringing the news to the people that
the Pariserom are being turned and the Bahi Reyesim and Cristo Niño will rule
again.

Paskolam are impersonators of Cristo in the ritual of the first baptism in the
San Juan ceremonial and also carriers of the message to the people in the final

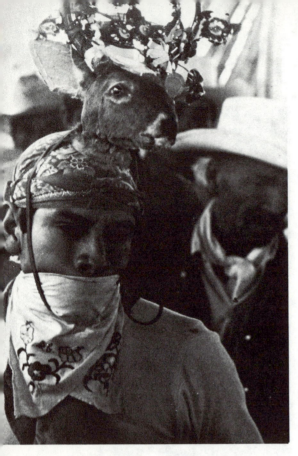

5.11 A Mayo deer dancer with special headdress in the Paskola ramada, Easter Sunday

triumph of Cristo Niño on the Sabado de Loria. Also, paskolam are linked to home rituals and formerly danced at children's funerals, funeral *cumpleaños* (the ritual marking the completion of a year's mourning), and weddings. Although all these rites of passage are said to be rarely performed, paskolam still perform in home paskos for San Juan, New Year, Lent, and other special home ceremonies, such as Liohpaskos (Damian's ceremonies for God). They are a supra-pueblo group, belonging to no particular pueblo and are hired by the paskome. Lastly, the paskola acts as a messenger and commentator on current events, and as one of the chief vehicles through which the sanctions and powers of the animal world are placed squarely behind the *kobanarom* (church governors).

Maso and Maso Bwikame

"Those who sing deer," usually four in number, play three rasps and a water drum and sing the sacred deer songs. These complex songs are invariably characterized by a cumulatively faster tempo, like the hunt which they occasion-ally portray. This rhythmic pattern always produces an exciting and powerful atmosphere. On special feast days, a long enactment of a deer hunt is portrayed by the maso and paskolam culminating at dawn. The singers, except for the flower in their palm straw hats, wear clothing much like the everyday clothing of any Mayo man, although for Banari ceremonials they generally all wear sandals.

The dancer (Fig. 5.11) with a much more elaborate costume, wears white pants, a white kilt over his trousers and usually a white shirt, though his shirt may also be of a color appropriate to the color symbolism of the particular ceremonial for which he is currently performing. Around his waist is wrapped a hand-woven belt with deer hooves on long strings which rattle against one another. Around his neck he places an abalone shell cross, and on his head a kerchief and a small stuffed deer's head, usually sensitively and realistically made, with a small moist-looking nose, wide wild eyes, ears straight up as if listening for footsteps, and real antlers from a small animal. The antlers are usually wrapped with red, white and green ribbons and white paper flowers, often daisies. In his hands he carries two large gourd rattles which sound like rattle snakes.

The maso dances close to the earth in a springy technique with his torso producing a great deal of his motion. His feet move swiftly and stay fairly close to the earth, though in his imitative movements he may kick up the dust in the face of the ''hunters'' (paskolas) who pursue him. Then he stops to flick his head in either direction, pausing as if to sniff the air for the scent of his pursuers. The odd kicks of his feet seem to convey the leaps of a running deer and the rasps speak of the sound of leaves and twigs crackling in the chase. Briefly, paskola and Maso dancing and entertainment as well as participation in the church processions and ritual are both an important diversion and an integral part of the ceremonial. Also these groups articulate with the forest world (huya ania) which is structured in terms of the Holy Family metaphor.

MAYO CEREMONIAL EXCHANGE AND TRIBAL INTEGRATION

In contrast to the Easter ceremony which functions to unify a local pueblo-ceremonial center and excludes ''strangers,'' other Mayo ceremonials unify and integrate Mayos at a supra-pueblo level, a Mayo enclaved tribal level (L. Crumrine, 1969). The municipality (*municipio*) commands some loyalty from a Mayo who is distinctly aware of its boundaries and goes to its principal city to vote, find employment, shop for certain goods, and seek the aid of the mestizo courts. Acting as both religious and civil units, the major towns of the municipios of Huatabampo, Etchojoa, and Navojoa developed and matured as Mayo mission and church centers. Villages within the municipio were related to the municipal church center and church centers themselves were related to one another. The following discussion of ceremonial exchange among Mayos in the lower Mayo River municipios of Huatabampo and Etchojoa shows, in spite of the contingencies of history, the continued existence of intra-municipio relationships, relationships maintained, re-established, reorganized, and encoded in terms of Holy Family model and its associated ritual symbols. Today Mayo ceremonial exchange patterns take many different forms, although the underlying structure represents a manifestation of the Sagrada Familia metaphor. Santos associated with certain pueblo or ranchería groups in the lower Mayo River valley visit households or church centers in an area ranging from the Guasave River, south of the Fuerte, to the Yaqui River and as far east as Cucusebora on the Mayo River. The proliferation of different types of ceremonial exchange is extreme, and the revival, adaptation and invention of new forms within the last decades attest to the continuing importance of this aspect of the organization and the associated processes in the Mayo culture of the sixties. This discussion of ceremonial exchange must be limited to the exchange of supernaturals and of the official personnel associated with them, such as church officials, paskome, and maestros (L. Crumrine, 1969, for additional discussion). The extremely formal patterns of the arrival and departure of the group from the visiting pueblo or pueblos maximize the positive union between the visitor and the host groups. Exchanges between pueblos are arranged and managed by the heads of various sodalities, for example, the lay ministers and governors, while the specific aspects of the actual processions and rituals are handled by dance sodality heads, military society officers, and heads of the patron saint cults.

Mayo ceremonial exchange means people in religious roles and religious information and paraphernalia move between churches, homes and churches, and homes (Fig. 5.12). I shall discuss two varieties of cults involved in Mayo ritual exchange, one associated with a home-based santo like the Santa Kurus of Damian and the other, with a church-based santo like the Santisima Tiniran of Banari. The home-based santos reside in a chapel near the owner's (dueño) home. The cult organization of the santo is often based on a ritual kinship or curer-clientele association with the owner of the santo. The santos of the home-based cults, whose dueños know their rituals, are exchanged between the santo's home and the paskome's home, as with the San Cayetano cult housed in a small ranchería located out in the desert away from the Mayo River itself (Chapter 7). The geographical range of the exchange may grow as the santo becomes known for an increasing number of miraculous cures. Since no formal sodality exists at the dueño's ranchería, when the saint's image is sent to another home for a pasko, the santo goes in the company of his hosts. These hosts recruit their paskome group from compadres and relatives in their own village. This pattern, in which the devotee makes a trip to the chapel of the santo and receives instructions from the dueño as he picks up the image, provides the basic structure for the more complicated Holy Cross cult of San Damian, the Mayo prophet. In this case church sodalities and santos have been brought into the exchange system through visits to Damian's sacred ramada. Called a living saint in his own right, "San Damian" occasionally is brought back to the host homes and churches to speak to the congregation assembled there. However, in general these home-based santo cults integrate households with each other, without the inclusion of a church paskome group.

Every church-based santo is associated with one or more Paskome groups. The exchange of santos between a church and homes in the territory of another and different church is rather widespread and usually this "sub-pattern"

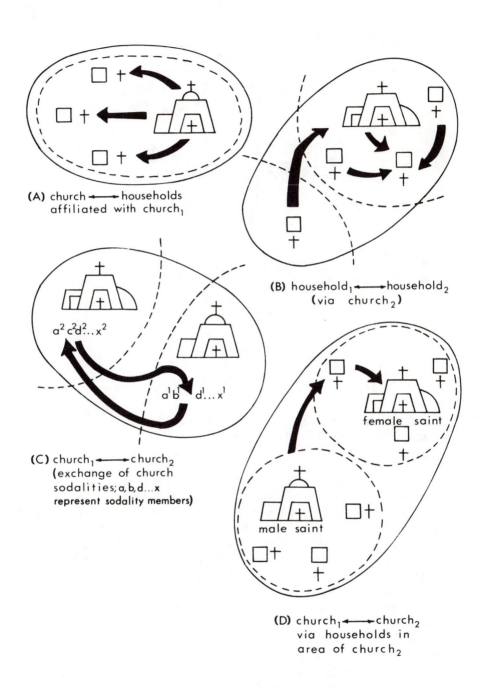

(A) church ⟷ households
affiliated with church₁

(B) household₁ ⟷ household₂
(via church₂)

(C) church₁ ⟷ church₂
(exchange of church
sodalities; a,b,d...x
represent sodality members)

(D) church₁ ⟷ church₂
via households in
area of church₂

5.12 Levels of Mayo ceremonial exchange

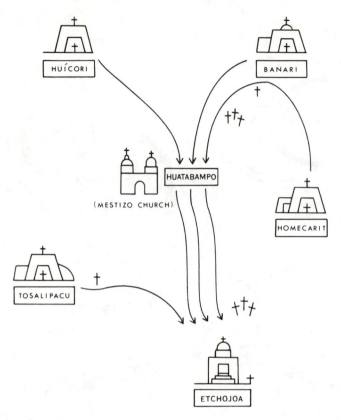

5.13   Diagram of church groups in procession to Etchojoa, Espiritu,
Santo Pasko (Adapted from L. Crumrine, 1969:15)

is part of a wider pattern of exchange between two churches. For example, in any of the several patron saint exchanges in the Huatabampo area the paskome of a host church meet the visiting image and paskome and escort them to a home in the territory of the host group where they remain for an interval to rest (*hemyori*). Therefore the cults of two different Mayo church santos are integrated through the intermediary of at least one home in the host territory. Sometimes this ritual integration involves a full home pasko, lasting at least a day and a night. Usually the hemyori lasts three or four hours and includes a brief set of rituals and prayers, before the entry of the visiting santo and his paskome into the host church proper.

To be more specific, I shall examine the relationships among six churches in the lower Mayo River area; Huatabampo—a mestizo church, and the Mayo churches of Banari, Homecarit, Huícori, Tosalipacu and Etchojoa (Figs. 5.13, 5.14). In almost every major calendrical ceremony of the year, including those of the Lenten season, the church of Banari exchanges paskome sodalities with

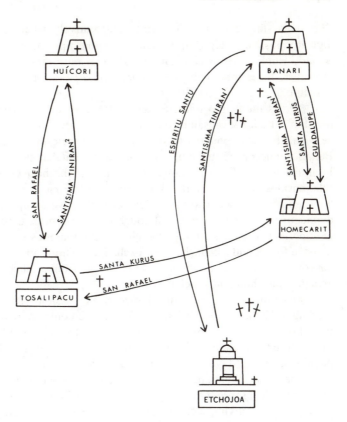

5.14   Patron saint exchanges among five Mayo pueblos
       (Adapted from L. Crumrine, 1969:15)

Homecarit whose patron saint is the Santa Kurus. These two were once one pueblo, but they split because of the founding of an ejido for a segment of the people. The cause of the split is remembered as a practical one rather than one involving ill will, so a spirit of cooperation exists between these churches. On the other hand, Banari church also split off from the same root pueblo, Huatabampo as did another small pueblo church nearby, that of Huícori, which has the same patron saint as Banari, but in this split one group violated sacred objects of the other, producing severe and unreconcilable resentment. The relationship of Banari with another Mayo pueblo in the area, Tosalipacu, is similarly charged with resentment, since Tosalipacu split from Huícori. Needless to say, no ceremonial exchange of Banari santos exists with these two pueblos. On the other hand, Homecarit, so intimately related to Banari, shares its unfriendly views in regard to Huícori, but in 1961 received Paskome from Tosalipacu for its Santa Kurus (Itom Ačai) ceremony and sent its Santa Kurus Paskome to Tosalipacu for their San Rafael (Itom Aye) ceremony in October. Established within the preceding five years, this exchange was still comparatively weak in 1961. Out of six logically possible reciprocal exchange relationships among the four churches of Banari, Huícori, Homecarit and Tosalipacu, only three have been developed. However, these three exchanges alone link all the four groups in a chain-like structure.

Across municipio lines, Banari and Etchojoa also maintain a strong relationship in their patron saint exchange, which represents a much earlier exchange between Huatabampo and Etchojoa. In spite of their differences, Huícori and the Banari-Homecarit group temporarily unite in Huatabampo and march together to Etchojoa for the Espiritu Santu ceremonial of the host church. This chain of relationships reflects several significant facts. First, better cooperation exists between friendly pueblos whose patron saints have complementary rather than duplicative functions. Second, although the oral historical rationale for the split is important, the leadership of the church communities involved often controls divisive forces and establishes new exchanges. Third, adding to tribal unity, any paskome group tends to be made up of people from a much wider geographical area than the church in which they serve.

This uniting of the Banari-Homecarit procession with Huícori before proceeding to Etchojoa for the Espiritu Santu ceremonial is explained by Mayos in the following way. The exchange between Huatabampo and Etchojoa took place long before the founding of Banari, Huícori, and Homecarit. Therefore, all these pueblos with the Mayo santos, which once constituted the church of Huatabampo, gather to the church in Huatabampo before proceeding to Etchojoa as a single procession. In a sense they are symbolically re-enacting their history as they wish to interpret it. A living sacrilege to Mayos, the old Huatabampo church in which the Mayo santos once resided is used as a market building. Nearby a modern church rises above the plaza and mestizo shops. A few rituals are performed by the priest for Mayos in the Huatabampo church, but Mayos who must go to Huatabampo to perform these rituals consider it an onerous task and are not at home in this church because the social and symbolic forms represent those of another people. Although this visit of Mayo church saints and sodalities to the mestizo church of Huatabampo represents a kind of paradox, nevertheless, in actuality it is a very different kind of relationship from those prevailing between Mayo churches, since it lacks the basic elements and symbolic values of exchange characterizing relationships between Mayo churches.

Each year, in this large procession to Etchojoa for the Espiritu Santu ceremony, a full and typical patron saint exchange is maintained. Banari goes to Etchojoa for the Espiritu Santu ceremonial the seventh Sunday after Easter, and Etchojoa comes to Banari for the ceremonial of the Santisima Tiniran the following Sunday, the first Sunday after Pentecost. The entire church community sodalities of both pueblos take part in these ritual exchanges. The heads of various sodalities arrange and manage details of the group pilgrimages, led by matačin dancers, followed by the paskome and the patron saint image. Officers of the Parisero society and the church governors often go ahead of the procession to officiate in various capacities and arrange for the arrival of the image. These processions may become enormous at times, consisting of as many as 2,000 people.

A brief description of the 1961 procession of the Banari Santisima Tiniran to Etchojoa on the eve of the Espiritu Santu ceremonial illustrates some of the integrative aspects of the church to church patron saint exchange. Nine days before the main feast day the maestros, sacristans, cantoras and paskome of the host and visiting pueblos took part in the symbolic descent of the image from heaven, *komčepte*. The local paskome prayed each morning of the nine-day period preceding the pasko days.

About 3:00 a.m. on the Saturday preceding the pasko day a procession formed in Banari, headed by a large group of boys and girls being initiated into the matačin sodality, the godmothers of the young women, and several officers of the matačin sodality. Second in the procession followed the paskola and maso dance groups, the paskome of the Santisima Tiniran and of the Santa Kurus of Homecarit, and the Santisima Tiniran image. Following the image came the church group consisting of lay ministers, sacristans, and women church sodalities. At the end of the series of sodalities appeared the church governors and other officials, and the men of the pueblo. This procession was already a composite of sodalities from two pueblos when it left Banari, for it had been joined by the paskome and the moʔoro of the Santa Kurus of Homecarit before leaving Banari. Everyone went on foot from Banari to Huatabampo, stopping several times to perform prayers and rituals at the pueblo boundary cross of Banari and at the crosses which mark the places of martyrdom of heroes of mythical significance to the Mayos of Banari and Homecarit. It arrived at the edge of the town of Huatabampo at about dawn.

At Huatabampo the composition of the Banari procession changed in one respect. A group of mestizo mariachis replaced the Mayo paskola and maso dance sodalities and the procession continued through a series of highly abbreviated salutes to various crosses and houses through the city. On arrival at the mestizo church in Huatabampo the Banari-Homecarit procession met the Huícori procession with their Santisima Tiniran image in a brief ceremony within the church. Then the combined procession moved on for a brief hemyori at a house on the side of Huatabampo nearest Etchojoa. At this time the church officials and top pueblo officials got into trucks, along with the paskolas and maso, and proceeded ahead of the rest of the procession to Etchojoa where they prepared and arranged activities for the coming events. The pilgrimage group now consisted of the young matačin sodality initiates and several officers of that society, the godmothers, the paskome (now three sets, including those of Huícori, Banari and Homecarit) and the images of the Santisima Tiniran, all under the direction of members of the parisero and paskome sodalities, appointed as assistants to the governors.

As they neared Etchojoa around nine o'clock, two women came to meet the images, one crawling and the other scattering water from side to side out of a bottle as she advanced down the path toward the images. The procession was then met by several sets of paskome who came out from Etchojoa, the Espiritu Santu paskome of Etchojoa, and the San Rafael paskome of Tosalipacu. A very important greeting had to take place at the edge of Etchojoa, where three crosses had been erected at a traditional spot, one for each of the two images of the Santisima Tiniran, and one for an additional image brought by the visitors. After speeches of greeting the enormous procession now proceeded to a house in the territory of the host church where the images were received in a series of rituals lasting about an hour and the pilgrim sodalities were offered water while the images rested on the decorated house altar. After this full hemyori the entire amalgamation of sodalities proceeded to the Etchojoa church for a further series of rituals. Upon nearing the church the host image was carried out to greet the visiting image. This meeting is invariably called the ''Meeting and Embrace of Our Father and Our Mother.'' In this case Espiritu Santu is thought of as Itom Aye and Santisima Tiniran as Itom Ačai.

By describing this one procession, during the course of one morning, I can illustrate the integration of sodalities from five ceremonial centers. Underlying this complex ritual there exists a basic structure and set of essential elements for this type of church-to-church exchange involving the patron saints of two autonomous Mayo churches. These elements include: the face-to-face encounter and salute of the host image and the visiting image on the arrival and farewell of the visiting cortege; reciprocity between the two pueblos with regard to patron saint exchange; a full pattern of hemyori for the visiting santo in a home in the host community; detailed ritual speeches and ritual routines, such as flagwaving, rosary exchange and so on, between paskome groups of the visiting santo and the host santo at the pueblo boundary cross, at the house cross where the hemyori is held, and at the church cross of the host pueblo; participation of distinctively Mayo sodalities and particularly of paskolam and masom; processions including the image and its paskome, Mayo church officials and maestros, sacristans and cantoras, and usually a variety of Mayo ceremonial dancers; fireworks and communal feasting of formal participants as well as the congregations, with the eating of traditional Mayo ceremonial foods in the Mayo church villages; and common understandings about the purpose of the whole ceremony and its many ritual segments. This type of Mayo church-to-church exchange provides one of the major mechanisms of Mayo tribal unity. Its structure involves a mechanical social combination of large numbers of sodalities together with an organic cultural combination of a male and a female saint. Forming a chain of relationships between numerous church centers, the underlying structure of this exchange system reflects the Holy Family metaphor with the meeting of Itom Ačai and Itom Aye occurring in front of the Ili Usim, members of the ceremonial centers.

In summary, the varieties of Mayo ceremonial exchange are performed in definite ways and with certain common understandings which largely exclude non-Mayo churches. On the other hand, these exchanges integrate Mayo church communities into a chain of relationships including increasingly larger groups, up to what might be called a Mayo tribal level (L. Crumrine, 1969). The exchange system, furthermore, reflects the recent local processes of splintering, regrouping, and refocusing of Mayo religious cults around santos in new locations more remote from mestizo centers. Yet the general underlying cultural structure of the system consists of the encounter and embrace between symbolic manifestations representing two sets of oppositions, Itom Ačai versus Itom Aye and the Santos versus the Ili Usim, a structure which represents an elaboration of the basic Holy Family model. These dual oppositions represent the same ones found in the Mayo family triangle, as parents versus children and males versus females, but now they have been recoded at the level of the cosmic realm and provide the symbolic structure and basis for the complex social integration pattern manifest in Mayo ceremonial exchange. Even at this cosmic level the oppositions and the mediating ceremonial ritualize, isolate, and reinforce the relationships of marriage and of enculturation which are crucial for the maintenance of an ''opposition'' culture and a Mayo way of life. Most dramatically this underlying structure, based upon the Holy Family metaphor and family triangle, is sufficiently elastic to smooth out the irregularities of the recent contingent Mayo history and reassemble a ceremonial system. This system integrates Mayos across municipal boundaries without the mediation of a political organization which in fact is at present dominated by mestizos. In a sense Mayos control an opposition political system, which is not structured and coded in terms of the dominant mestizo political symbolism but rather through sacred Mayo symbols that find their integrity in the Holy Family metaphor. The Mayo Easter ceremonial, which functions to integrate and organize Mayos at the local church-pueblo level, is also characterized by the Holy Family model as one of its major themes and organizing principles. Lastly, the paskola and maso organizations, through their participation in both these ceremonial complexes, link separate rituals into a unique Mayo ceremonial system, derive their supernatural power from the forest world which is also coded in the same Holy Family metaphors.

Clearly Mayo ritual and ceremonialism has shared meanings for Mayos and presents them as a complex set of symbols that provide both a basis for Mayo interaction with other Mayos and also a means of excluding non-Mayos. In this sense, on the basis of values, meanings, and a structure in part generated from the Holy Family model, Mayos have both re-established and created a complex behavioral system that symbolizes and reinforces a community of believers, a Mayo way of life as separate from a mestizo one.

6. The Making of the Mayo World: How and What a Mayo Must Learn

Since behaving like a Mayo is founded on certain knowledge and belief, Mayos must maintain ways and means by which a person gains this knowledge and comes to find it believable. The most important units for Mayo learning are small social groups, although only certain groups, such as families and church sodalities, are dissemination centers for a Mayo type of knowledge. Other groups, such as schoolroom and neighborhood play groups, may function as sources of non-Mayo ideas. While later experience in ceremonial sodalities proves crucial in attaining and maintaining Mayo identity and respectability, early learning within the nuclear family, a type of Holy Family, is essentially always a major necessary process in becoming Mayo. Clearly then, the Holy Family model contains direct implications for the underlying structure of Mayo learning.

THE SOCIAL UNITS AND TECHNIQUES OF ENCULTURATION

Ideally the Mayo family provides a haven for its members. Strangers, even though they are identified as Mayo, are seldom met with warmth and trust. The safety of one's own home is expressed in the Mayo saying, "You are at home. Do not fear anything." Open division between household members in front of outsiders is severely frowned upon. Numerous Mayo phrases apply to this unity, such as "*Si²ime nau mocala*" ("All together," as a group) which relates to the family as well as to the pueblo and occurs frequently in ritual speeches.

In rancherías and Mayo-dominant villages even play groups are formed largely within the household and its closely connected households, intensifying family interaction. Children are often teased by being told that their parents will give them away to yoris and on first sight of strangers some are paralyzed with fright. Even up to the ages of ten or eleven years old they will cry pitifully until the stranger passes out of sight. They often became familiar with me although

[110]

they were never very openly aggressive or talkative in contrast to mestizo children. Even one of the child's own godparents may be treated in this manner if the child has not seen the godparent for an extended period of time. Yet these same children laugh and play freely in their own household groups. On the other hand, some parents brag that their children are not afraid of strangers while the same children are teased about being given away to strangers.

In general, Mayo mothers seem patient, affectionate and respectful of their children as little individuals with minds of their own. As babies they are nursed on demand, fed coffee or other "adult" food if they want it. Usually between the ages of one and two they are gently weaned, mainly on a corn meal preparation believed to be easier for them to digest than adult food.

Owing to the secretiveness with which it is surrounded, very little was learned about toilet training of Mayo children. Measures relating to secrecy are taken very early probably as a safeguard against witchcraft on one's feces. Not going to the toilet in the house is a cardinal prescription, and Mayos were continually amazed about that custom in the United States where bathrooms are within the houses. For Mayos, to profane one's home in this manner qualifies as an extremely filthy habit. This strong taboo suggests additional evidence for the sacred nature of the Mayo family. Families either maintain small areas at some distance from the house around which carrizo mats are thrown up, or they go out in the fields. Urination is not surrounded with as much secrecy as defecation, and it is common to hear people say, "Sispea" ("I want to urinate"). Men, and often women, are not always circumspect about getting out of sight to do so.

The words for private parts and for sexual intercourse are charged with a similar secretiveness and are said to be bad words. In striking contrast, the paskola and Čapayeka burlesques present such symbolism for Mayo enjoyment. Neither sexual play nor talk of this kind was recorded from children. Sexual instruction of both men and women is provided by an older relative of the same sex. Children often sleep in the same room with their parents and in some cases even in the same bed up to ages past adolescence. Therefore, in spite of the secrecy with which intercourse is surrounded, some preadolescent opportunity for knowledge of it is available. Teenagers sometimes slip out of the house at night and meet for courting purposes. "*Hante huyapo*" ("Let's go to the bush") means let us have intercourse and is an extremely immoral thing to say.

In little arguments over playthings, which are the simplest kinds of homemade items, older children are generally expected to yield to younger. An older girl in the household shares in the care of the little children, even though she may often be no more than a couple of years older than the children themselves. In fact, she may act stricter with them than the older women of the house. If young children do not obey a request the first, second, or third time they are told, little is made of it. Appeasement of fussing children rather than letting them cry is probably related to the idea that people get sick when they are sad or ill-natured. "*Ka te siroknake*," ("Don't be sad or irritable") is a common injunction. In contrast, "Aleyate" means "Let's be happy, healthy."

Mayo men are affectionate with their children, especially younger children, and often bounce and play with them. But children are reminded that they owe respect to their fathers. Frequently the mother calls the father's attention to some matter which requires discipline. This role of the father as authoritarian increases with age, yet it varies widely with personalities. In some households old women function as authoritarians. In the category old person, sex differences become less important. Older brothers seem permissive and affectionate with younger children; where there is no older sister, they are responsible for the younger children.

Direct punishment is seldom necessary with Mayo children. I never saw a child slapped, spanked, or otherwise physically punished by a Mayo parent. Rather than by whipping, a last resort, children should be corrected verbally. Traditionally, if they disobeyed openly three times and disregarded verbal counsel, they would be made to kneel before the house cross, confess to it and "suffer" (*hiokore*). If they had been extraordinarily bad, dried chickpeas would be sprinkled on the ground underneath their knees to heighten the physical discomfort. Often one sees grown men, who have been drinking, painfully sobbing and confessing to the cross in front of the church, also known as *kurus au itom hiokore*, "cross to which we suffer."

More frequent kinds of punishment techniques involve distracting or ignoring a child. When crying or making unnecessary demands, a two- or three-year-old may be given some little chore to help the parent and keep the child busy, such as fetching pots and pans or ears of corn from one part of the house to another. If the child is being unreasonable and the distraction technique is not working he or she may simply be ignored. Ignoring unpleasant situations provides a real Mayo solution to a number of problems on the interpersonal level, from conflict among compadres and relatives to difficulties between whole pueblos. When one is not speaking to a compadre or relative, for example, one pretends not to see the other. And it may be explained, "*Ka'a taiya*" ("I don't know him," meaning, more or less, "We are not on speaking terms"). The same phrase is used if one whole pueblo has an old quarrel with another and there is little or no ceremonial exchange between them.

Teasing, which begins as early as the age of eighteen months or so and continues through adolescence, is used with most children. Čapayekam tease the five- or six-year-old children who are promised to the Bahi Maria by offering them forbidden items such as certain foods or money. The children are supposed to ignore the Čapayekam or throw flowers to dispel them. A related technique is public embarrassment or shaming, which is a popular type of teasing. While guests are present a woman may say of her ten- or eleven-year-old girl, who complains about having to grind coffee on the metate, "She doesn't know how to do anything."

Children above the age of five or six are verbally corrected for disrespect to godparents, often no worse than not rushing out to greet them properly or not speaking to them; disrespect in the church or in processions, especially not

obeying Mayo church authorities, such as Čapayekam, during the Lenten season; speaking Spanish instead of Mayo at home; jealousy of another child expressed in open aggression, though before this point little is done to control it;
sometimes open disobedience of or aggression toward a parent especially a father
or an older woman of the house; nearly always for complaining of discomfort
when working, for laziness, for becoming sleepy in public or otherwise exposing
one's health to possible supernatural dangers. Children are praised or rewarded
for helping their parents, for learning hard things well, for going to school and
for learning to endure patiently when hungry, thirsty, sleepy, or tired. In most
families young children are treated with great gentleness and their antics are
taken very lightly up to the age of four, five, or even older. Children below this
age may get by with relatively serious offenses without punishment, such as
pulling fresh flowers off the house cross. Mothers and fathers take a great delight
in young children and accept their playfulness with tolerance and unselfconscious
joy.

All children are guarded carefully from sudden frights, falls, long periods of
irritable temper, and strangers, all of which are thought to cause sickness. Bat-
like animals (čičialim) also bring sickness and the owl (*mu²u*) symbolizes death.
The child is taught to fear all of the above and to take avoidance measures. Some
Mayos claim that taking mestizo compadres endangers the health of one's child.

One of the few forms of special attention ever given to individuals as such in
Mayo society is the ceremonial promise, manda. In regard to this institution
children occupy as important a place as grown men and women. A minimal age
of a year or so is necessary before a manda contract is made. More than half of
the mandas of paskome I knew had been made for a child, to ensure its health.
Children may actually wear the rosary and go through the motions of being a
pasko persona though usually some older relative, more able to withstand the
physical rigors, performs the ceremonial labor on behalf of the child or the labor
is paid when the child matures. In the confirmation of the manda, the family's
attention is focused for the moment entirely upon the sick child. This assurance
of belonging and being of value to one's family is certainly a positive sanction
and a type of special attention to the individual which he or she can recognize
early in life.

Patient, permissive child rearing and gentle weaning coupled with secret
toilet and sex training associated with a strong emphasis on self-discipline and
intense respect for parents and older persons, produced by verbal correction and
distracting, ignoring, and teasing, characterize modern Mayo techniques of raising their children. All these methods, employed mainly in the Mayo household
but extending to the church community, bring about attitudes of carefulness,
respect, fear, and a resulting state of self-possessed tranquility so admired in the
average Mayo person. In addition, they are reflected in the structure and social
relations, which Mayos not only read into the Holy Family model but also
attempt to utilize to organize their broader patterns of social interaction both with
other Mayos and with mestizos.

ADULT LEARNING

The injunctions given to the ceremonial society members by church officials remind people of the same charges they learn as children: *"Kat em a ʔoʔoba"* ("Don't be lazy, weak"); *"ʔAčem hiapse"* ("persevere, be eager"); *"Kat em binopo taʔarula"* ("Don't get lost in wine"); *"Kate hiopnake"* ("Let's not make mistakes"); *"Katem hiusi itom beʔbare"* ("Don't shame us"); *"Katem danyota hoʔobare"* ("Do no harm [to anyone]").

The individual, by the time he reaches adulthood, ideally should be either Yoreme or yori. If he is Mayo, he should know what he "wants to do," and he should not have to be told. When one asks, *"Hitaʔapo une te enčim aniʔanake?"* ("In what way can we help you [plu.]?"), the answer is conventionally, *"? Amehiba huʔuneya enči itom aniʔabare"* ("You know how you can help"). If an individual does not do the things which are expected of him, particularly with reference to ceremonial labor, he may meet first with gossip and then with social ostracism. Another serious sanction involves scapegoating for some unfortunate event. When a horse became skittish and fell on a young man who had refused to obey the order of the Čapayekam not to ride his horse in a Lenten procession, Mayos said he deserved this slight injury as a punishment for disobedience.

The conciseness and devastating character of verbal correction directed toward a single adult contrast with the normal cultural pattern of utmost politeness in dealing with other people. Direct social controls of a normal nature appear much more often in the form of directions given by an offical to a group, for example, the hinabaka of the matačin monarca to his group of matačin performers, or of the Pilato to the Pariserom. The moʔoro takes the paskome through each ritual, and the maestro of the church lectures them on their duties and the meanings attached to each ritual and piece of paraphernalia. "If one is always taught well, then one will learn." The words with which one teaches must be well chosen and go straight to their mark. These ritual speeches have about the same general content from person to person, but talent in calling together the traditional phrases varies. The verbal instruction is highly conventionalized, yet an actual power in the words is believed to be beneficial for both adults and children.

Again and again Mayos explicitly state, "You can only learn the meaning of the ceremonies and of the lives of the supernaturals by coming to the ceremonials and seeing and performing." One cannot learn through one attendance, or two, but must come each year. Learning is a process, not an event, and involves only a word or two of highly important but relatively codified verbal instruction in an abundant context of seeing and doing. This advice was of great aid in learning something about the ceremonies themselves. When one asked about ceremonials before they occurred, Mayos had no more than a sentence to say about them and would not repeat it. But after one had carefully observed different rituals and could mention specific paraphernalia and ritual segments within the ceremonies, Mayos often elaborated at length on meanings which they would never have otherwise bothered to explain. For Mayos this represents a normal process. They will not waste explanations on non-understanding ears. Therefore, ritual participation provides an essential element in the process of community learning, which takes place even after one has become an adult. Coupled with participation, patterned ceremonial speeches reaffirm the general purposes and meanings of the rituals.

CONTENTS OF ENCULTURATION

The knowlege and beliefs of Mayo culture may be summarized as a list of postulates with their justifying proofs. The knowledge and the intensity of belief in these postulates correlates with the degree to which persons can present the justifications and "logical proofs" associated with the beliefs. Nevertheless, it can be confidently said that most Banari Mayos would agree upon the following main postulates. Although many more should be listed, space limits us to the most crucial justifying proofs of each postulate. Of course, any given ceremonial specialist would have much more extensive knowledge than this—fishermen (*kučulíom*) knowing more about the ocean lore, maestrom more about the dead, curers (hitolíom) and witches (*moriaram*) more about sickness and the associated symbolism.

1. *Yoremnok* (the Mayo language) is a sacred and powerful language because: (a) The dead cannot hear any other language. (b) The sacred speeches, hinabakam, are and must be given in eloquent Yoremnok. (c) Yoremnok, as a symbol of solidarity of Mayos, is fairly clearly stated and recognized by all. Yoremnok provides a medium of secret communication which all Mayos recognize and most value highly.
2. *Tekipanoa* (work), in the form of ceremonial labor, is performed because: (a) One will then enter heaven more easily. (b) One will gain power for health from the saints. (c) One will gain community respect in this life and have friends and compadres. (d) It is the natural heritage of most ordinary Mayos to labor on this earth.
3. One must retain the appearance of relative poverty in earthly goods because: (a) It distinguishes Mayos from the rich and unscrupulous non-Mayos who are evil. (b) By giving away one's goods in the form of food in particular one is doing a high form of tekipanoa and assuring all the good that comes from it. (c) Suffering and poverty is a natural heritage of most ordinary Mayos on this earth and must be accepted as such.
4. The Mayo earth is sacred because: (a) Mayo animan are buried in it. (b) Supernaturals have walked upon it. (c) Ritual repeated over the earth has sanctified it.
5. Respect for the manda and *tékia* (labor) derive directly from respect for the supernaturals because: (a) Tékia is binding as a contract plus the additional obligation to the pueblo which has chosen one for the office. (b) Mandas, or contracts with the saints, are binding if the saint responds to one's request

because: severe punishment in the form of sickness or instant death may await those who do not fulfill them; gossip will eventually find its way to censure those who are careless or lazy about a manda contract; it is a special kind of Mayo obligation.

6. The cross has power because: (a) The wooden cross represents a form of Itom Ačai and is sanctified by cumulation of past ritual. The cross is thought of as a place for the dead, the flags, the mortals and the saints to rest. (b) It marks the locus of meeting between a secular realm and a realm of the supernatural or the dead. (c) The sign of the cross in its unique Mayo form is a type of confession. (d) The Mayo sign of the cross, together with baptism, is one of the ritual segments which binds together compadres.

7. The water of the Mayo River is sacred because: (a) It may become a means of supernatural castigation of the people, as when all Mayos were destroyed by Itom Ačai except for Noah and his family. (b) The river, like the earth, is very old. Itom Ačai was first baptized in it by San Juan. Then most other Mayos were subsequently baptized in it.

8. The ocean is sacred because: (a) It is the home of the Bawe Hamyo?ola (Old Woman of the Sea) who owns all the fish therein. (b) A wind from the ocean may bring sickness in the spring dry season. (c) Its products, such as shells and special plants, are associated with many different curing ceremonies. (d) Its water yields salt. (e) It is customary to be baptized in the ocean as a blessing.

9. Flowers are sacred because: (a) Certain flowers are associated with specific saints and represent periods in the lives of those saints. (b) The "flowers of the saints" are to be respected (*tuisi yo?oriwa*), that is, they have power or represent the power of the saints. (c) The placing of flowers on house crosses, church crosses and altars acts as a signature on the manda contract with a saint, as a means of direct communication and a medium of exchange with the saints. (e) Flowers, together with animals, are the central symbols and subject matter of the deer songs.

10. The dead are a functioning part of the universe, and the keeping and reading of the books listing their names and dates of their deaths is necessary because: (a) They hear us pray, and require our prayers. (b) They require food and river water to drink. If they are pleased by these offerings they will let the candles on the graves burn the night of All Saints; if not, the wind will snuff out the candles. (c) When they return to the earth they may bring rains, cold weather, and sickness. (d) The Mayo earth is an inheritance from the dead.

11. The church bells are sacred and have power because: (a) They are associated with the recent destruction of the Banari church, and are one of the few items remaining in use from the old church which was destroyed. The bells represent the triumph of right over might in the restoration of the Banari church, and in the martyrdom of the saints. (b) The ringing of the bells is a signal to the angels to come down to get the soul of the dead person. (c) The bells are treated as a santo, that is, they are "flowered" with cottonwood twigs during ritual occasions. (d) The ringing of the bells, representing the voice of the archangels, is painful to the ears of the Čapayekam.

12. Most Mayo old people are respected because: (a) They are now alive due to exemplary lives, and/or solely by the will of God. (b) They are felt to be

"close to the dead" and sanctified by this proximity. (c) They are felt to be necessary in a conservative home for counseling and guidance. (d) They generally have some special kind of power accruing from a lifetime of labor.

13. If one gets sick it is because one is weak resulting from one of the following reasons: (a) One is tired, depressed, irritable, or has fallen asleep at an improper time or place. (b) One has fallen and received a blow on the head which may cause a "fallen fontanel," the cause of many illnesses. (c) One has had a sudden fright and lost his soul. (d) One has not complied with the traditional ceremonial obligations. (e) One has not completed a manda. (f) One has not taken proper precautions, such as saying prayers against witches or malevolent strangers.

Some sicknesses may be due to natural causes. These may be cured by antibiotics. Some sicknesses and deaths are caused by the will of Itom Ačai.

14. The ability to commit material to memory and the resulting knowledge and special skills are conceived to be sources of power which is both feared and respected. Detailed knowledge and skills are frequently guarded by the possessors because: (a) In the case of a hitolío, the knowledge is controlled by the person, as a cure which has been revealed to him by God in a dream or vision. (b) Specially skilled paskolas may have a similar relationship with an old man who lives in a cave in the mountains and has given them extraordinary skill in return for coming to live in the mountains after death. (c) Deer are more often alleged to have special knowledge of the ocean beaches, and the *tomi ania* (money world) than most others. Some deer, it is claimed, are lost (*ta'arula*) to the world of the church. (d) In the case of those who own popular household santos, possession of the santo and of the knowledge of his associated ritual may become a source of power to the owner, if the santo becomes widely known for its miraculous curing powers.

15. Mayos stress: (a) solidarity symbols, such as shaking hands with one's compadres, completing the traditional set of greetings, addressing the audience in speeches as a unified whole, and (b) unity rituals, such as drinking water from a single cup, a bread exchange, and the ritual smoking together by paskome for the following reasons: (i) These are the proper ways to do things, it is a sign of respect and good manners, a Yoreme way. (ii) It is regarded as dangerous to make people jealous by recognizing one above the other and dividing the pueblo within itself. (iii) One demonstrates that one is not "nervous" or guilty in one's heart by the confident and cheerful performance of these rituals, that one is of a "single heart."

CONFLICTS IN LEARNING AND KINDS OF ANTITHETICAL KNOWLEDGE

Up to this point I have not accounted for Mayo existence in a complex world of impinging mestizo values and ideas. Omissions and alterations in ceremonial life, like the period of the burning of the churches when Mayo ceremonial life was suspended for about a decade, interfere with the Mayo ritual learning process. The individual who does not properly assume ceremonial obligations has no opportunity to learn the cultural patterns associated with those ceremonies. These historical situations have produced difficulties in the normal process of becoming a Mayo: family and economic disorganization through the war periods; intermixture with mestizos; wage labor under hacendados who forbid leaving work long enough for ceremonies; and long residence by some Mayo men and women outside of Mayo country associated with wage labor, wars, and deportations. Due to these circumstances some Mayos have not had an opportunity to learn the complete patterns of rituals which reaffirm the full integration of the traditional symbol system. Nevertheless, many such Mayos still hold the traditional concepts of sickness, health, and the preservation of life through ceremonialism. Perhaps largely because these concepts and anxieties seem to outlast all other kinds of Mayo knowledge, Mayos are so capable of relearning and motivated to recreate their "traditional" culture after periods of disorganization.

Yet in the sixties many of these returning individuals formed the hard core of Mayo social continuity. Banari includes many older Mayos who took refuge in Sinaloa or even in the United States during the worst periods of the revolutionary upheaval in Sonora. After their return, these people helped rebuild the church in Banari in the late 1930s. The generation following this older one was born and raised on the Mayo River and today has reached adulthood. A larger number of the younger Mayos appear to speak Mayo as their main language than do their parents, and their children in turn may be even more deeply Mayo. A new society with a reintegrating culture may be created by this younger generation.

Due to the lower status accorded by members of the dominant society to virtually all who maintain strong Mayo identity, a Mayo is somewhat isolated from many upper-class Mexican values and kinds of knowledge. But he does come into face-to-face contact with mestizos almost every day. Thus Mayos have the opportunity to learn some mestizo basic ideas, such as the following, about the world. The basic conflict of these mestizo values with Mayo postulates is apparent.

La Castillana, or Spanish, is the true and "civilized" language (*idioma civilizada),* whereas Mayo is a tongue (lengua), hardly a language in the true sense of the word. Mayo children are penalized for speaking Mayo in school and encouraged by mestizo school teachers to speak Spanish at home. At home they are scolded by older members of the Mayo household for speaking Mayo poorly.

Money provides the all-important symbol of achievement in life. Achievement is based on successful competition with others in obtaining money, which is a pleasure-giving game with certain rules and sub-systems like bargaining. Mayos continually come out badly in money transactions with mestizos because they do not understand these rules or the premises behind them, nor do they have the same value for money.

Manual labor is to be avoided if possible. Owning a store, a *puesto,* of one's own, or a rental house or two exemplify important economic goals for middle-class mestizos. The ability to buy goods at a lower price and resell them without actually having manufactured anything oneself is a clever means of gaining money. One should aspire to making a living with one's head and not with one's hands.

One should exert every effort to extend one's social life in the direction of wealthier, more sophisticated people. This value of social mobility also has an openly competitive aspect, in contrast to the Mayo system where competition is minimized and overtly suppressed through a number of rituals. Erasmus (1961:303) characterizes this contrast beautifully by stating that Mayos stress ''equality of poverty'' while Mexicans stress ''equality of opportunity.''

One's duty involves trying to improve one's life and not to live in poverty. One must not remain within a lower social stratum longer than necessary, for one's own and one's children's dignity. Indios, or Indians, are said to live ''like dogs,'' or ''like animals.''

These main mestizo values, associated with the realm of social and economic considerations, conflict with Mayo postulates. Numerous ideas about religion and cosmogeny are also incompatible with Mayo ideas. These concepts do not meet with the head-on force of the social and economic conflict of values, however, because Mayos and mestizos do not interact as often in religious institutions, such as the church, where these ideas are discussed. Occasionally in school Mayo children learn ideas which conflict with traditional Mayo concepts. For example, the shape of the world is said to be a rotating sphere. Mayos learn at home that the world is square, flat, and suspended in space from four corners. They soon discover that it is best not to discuss most of these matters with mestizos, especially with school teachers and priests who are likely to be authoritarian in their opinions. On the other hand, non-believers are not welcome in the most intensely sacred and private Mayo ceremonies where such things are frequently discussed. These techniques, of ignoring and withdrawing, minimize conflict between divergent concepts. Lower class mestizos place a relative lack of stress on ceremonial life as compared with Mayos. They think that Mayos carry religion to an absurd extreme, while they see themselves as ''just Catholics.'' Yet some mestizos believe Mayo ceremonial life may contain significant power, but apprehension rather than reverence or piety characterizes their attitudes toward Mayo religion. For example, some lower class mestizos hold a strong superstitious value for Mayo curing knowledge and patronize Mayo curers. Briefly, less open conflict of ideas exists to the extent that economic and social class considerations are not involved, and Mayos do not discuss with mestizos the deeper meanings of their religious life and the basic premises about the structure of the universe.

In conclusion, processes of child rearing initiated in the nuclear family and types of social relations established between the members of the Mayo family reappear as the individual matures and they become part of his or her view of the world and of adult social relations in general. The nuclear family, which functions as a haven for both children and adults, provides the basic cognitive and emotive structure, which receives symbolic elaboration in the Holy Family metaphor. This unity of experience and metaphorical understanding become the basis for Mayo church center organization, ceremonial structure, and ethnic tribal integration. Patient, affectionate, respectful child rearing coupled with strong disciplinary action originating from parents and older people produce adults who are calm yet extremely sensitive about commanding or controlling others. Techniques of indirect punishment, such as confession to supernaturals or ignoring, distracting and teasing, link child learning processes with adult socialization. Indirect ritual learning becomes more and more important as one matures. Adults, who would resent instruction and direction from another individual, both respond to leaders of ritual sodalities who instruct through ceremonial speeches and learn through participation in ceremonials. Clearly, participation in Mayo ceremonialism is an integral part of becoming Mayo. In summary, a specific Mayo method of child rearing and adult enculturation communicates a set of strictly Mayo values and postulates about the world in which man lives. The Mayo nuclear family and the Holy Family become variants of basic structure upon which the world is reflected.

7. Mayo Revivalism

In this chapter I shall describe and contrast two types of Mayo home paskos, those given for San Damian's Santa Cruz and for San Cayetano. This comparison will provide the basis for a more general consideration of the questions of prophet production and of socio-cultural revival.

THE LIOHPASKO

Within two years, Damian Bohoroqui's visitation from God in October of 1957 had become an important element in the religious life of the entire Mayo valley. In light of preceding discussions, the characteristics of the movement appear strongly traditional. Itom Ačai himself had on traditional Mayo sandals (*berabočam bahi puntara*), carried a gourd for drinking water (*arókosi*), and spoke in Mayo and in hinabaka. In a broader framework, this Old Man represents Itom Ačai the head of the Holy Family. When asked if He could be the Devil instead of the Lord no one hesitated in saying He certainly could not be the Devil, because He had commanded Mayos to give paskos, and that is a good thing. The Devil would not do this. Most Mayos point out that the Lord promised a long period of rain because He was angered at the general loss of respect for the old people. The flood will be a punishment. The necessity to give paskos for the Lord in order to save the world is thought to be the main message by persons who are the most intensive participants in Mayo religious life. Damian claimed a padre added a section concerning paskos without side-attractions. In fact, Damian's Mayo version of the visitation is careful to specify that God certainly did, by all means, expect the paskolam and masom to perform, as well as matačinim, go?im and maestrom.

Subsequent to his vision, Damian became a curer of witch-caused diseases and rose in the social hierarchy within his own village, becoming a Pilato in the

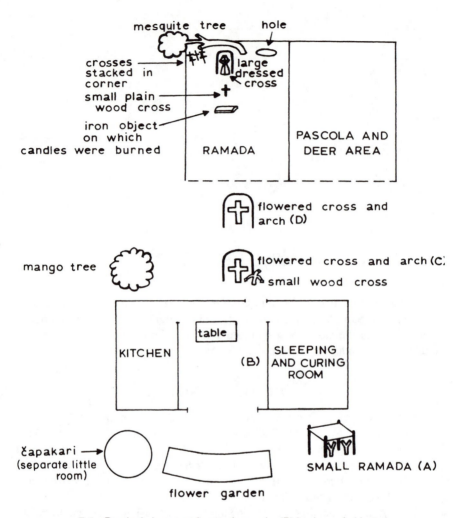

7.1   Damian's home and sacred ramada. (B) is place of objects in
Fig. 7.2. (A), (C), and (D) are shown in more detail in Figs 7.2 and 7.3

Parisero organization (Figs. 7.1–7.3). He had been monolingual in Mayo at the
time of his vision, and at first spoke with great difficulty, being naturally somewhat timid. But as a result of his powerful gift from God he became a master of
the Mayo hinabaka and also a Spanish speaker. Clearly his own personality
underwent a transformation which is characteristic of a wide variety of cult
prophets throughout the world (see Macklin and Crumrine, 1970; and Wallace,
1956, 1966).

The ceremonies (Liohpasko, God pasko) connected with the cult are made
essentially in the old pattern of house paskos. They include a procession of

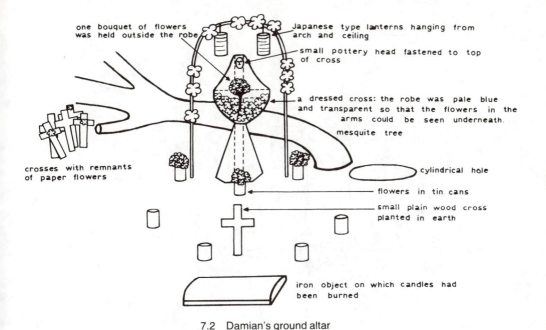

one bouquet of flowers was held outside the robe

Japanese type lanterns hanging from arch and ceiling

small pottery head fastened to top of cross

a dressed cross: the robe was pale blue and transparent so that the flowers in the arms could be seen underneath.

mesquite tree

crosses with remnants of paper flowers

cylindrical hole

flowers in tin cans

small plain wood cross planted in earth

iron object on which candles had been burned

7.2   Damian's ground altar

painted colors

red
blue

paper ribbon

about 2 feet

about 1½ feet

wood

metal tip

mat

blue slate

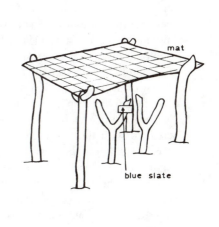

OBJECTS ON WALL AT (B) IN FIG. 7.1

SMALL RAMADA SHOWN AS (A) IN FIG. 7.1

7.3   Symbol of Damian's status as Pilato

KEY
Blue
Red
White

7.4   Liohpasko altar at El Chirrido

visiting saints to a house altar set up on the worshipper's left hand half of a household ramada. The procession is followed by a night of prayers by the maestro, cantoras and sacristans together with the formal patron saint cults of one or two churches in the area. On the worshipper's right hand side of the ramada a paskola and maso area is set up where these dancers and musicians perform all night. Charles Erasmus (1967, Figs. 14–20) has published a number of excellent photographs of Liohpaskom.

On the Liohpasko altars are placed small red and white boxes of earth with crosses on them (Fig. 7.4 and Erasmus, 1967, Figs. 19 and 20). The earth is taken from the deep hole beside the mesquite tree where Itom Ačai appeared and is generally given free to those who come to the pasko. This sacred earth is credited with the miraculous power of healing God-caused diseases. Another sacred symbol in the Mayo household pasko, the books of the dead, are also laid upon the Liohpasko altars to be consecrated. The connection between the sacred earth and the ancestors is again expressed in the Liohpasko altar cross which takes the form of a decorated wooden cross planted in the ground. It clearly represents the santo and is created in the image and symbolic idiom of the figure in Damian's visitation (Fig. 7.2). Completely wrapped in white crepe paper, Damian's crosses carry on their right arms a red flower, on their left arms a white flower (Fig. 7.5, 7.6). Although a great deal more is involved, when pressed, Mayos claim the red flower symbolizes Hell while the blue is peace and the white, hope.

The major ceremony for the Holy Cross of San Damian took place for several years on May 3 in Sinaloa at Las Flores, his sacred ramada. May 3 is also the Day of the Finding of the Holy Cross and the day of the celebration of Santa Teresa, the late nineteenth-century prophet from Mayo country. Behind Damian's home a ramada, a ground altar, and a dance area has been built. Within this sacred area the ceremony takes place. Interestingly enough, however, the majority of the Liohpaskom took place in the Mayo River valley with many in the Banari area. The Liohpasko, which I describe below as typical, was made in January of 1961 in a small ranchería, El Chirrido, only several miles from the Banari church (Figs.7.4, 7.7).

In order to make a Liohpasko a group of twelve paskome, supported by their wives or husbands, is organized by one or several of its members. This, of course, is the same as the traditional number of paskome who serve in Banari and in other Mayo churches. The group pledges to give a Liohpasko on each of eight consecutive Mondays and to repeat this cycle each year for a period of three years (Erasmus, 1961:286; 1967:102). Once the twelve individuals have elected to become Liohpasko paskome, a trip to visit San Damian and his Santa Cruz is necessary. At this time the paskome obtain the earth from beneath the sacred mesquite tree and three paper flowers, one red, one white, and one blue in color. After making the cycle of Liohpaskom the paskome return flowers to San Damian as the sign of completion of the original promise.

Liohpaskom generally begin late Sunday with the arrival of visiting santos, last through the night and terminate Monday with the return of the santos to the local church in the case of church-based santos or to the home in the case of

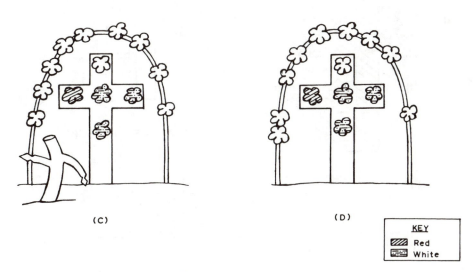

(C)   (D)

KEY
Red
White

7.5   Damian's sacred patio crosses

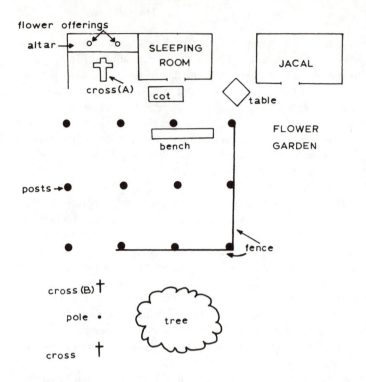

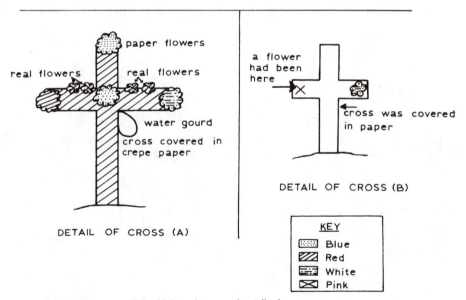

DETAIL OF CROSS (A)

DETAIL OF CROSS (B)

KEY
Blue
Red
White
Pink

7.6   Liohpasko ramada at Jiosia

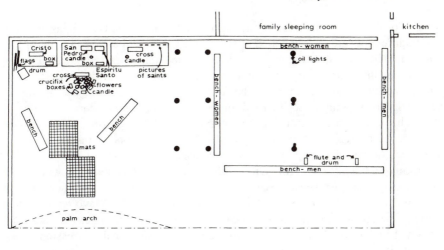

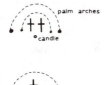

7.7   Liohpasko sacred ramada at El Chirrido

family-owned santos. It is especially important to have a church-based visiting santo present for the first and last Liohpasko in any cycle. In the Banari area the cycle is initiated and concluded with the presence of the Santisima Tiniran of the Banari church. During the week preceding the Liohpasko, the paskome have been gathering flowers and decorating the altar and three crosses at El Chirrido. A series of palm arches through which the procession will pass is set up and the services of the paskola and maso dancers are obtained. Individual families bring the decorated boxes of dirt, which they received at the initial pasko, books of their dead, and the small pictures of saints which ordinarily rest on the family altar. The image of Cristo is also placed on the altar. By late Sunday afternoon everything is prepared for the arrival of the visiting saints and the Banari church paskome. The maestro and cantoras arrive just preceding the procession from Banari and immediately kneel before the altar and begin to pray and sing. Also preceding the arrival of the procession several of the paskolam and their musicians arrive and begin dressing and doing a preliminary dance. With the arrival of the major portion of the procession the visiting santos, San Pedro and Espiritu Santo, are carried in and dipped in front of Cristo and then in front of the large flowered cross. This dipping symbolizes the introduction and greeting of the visiting santos. Then the visiting santos are placed at the back of the central portion of the altar. As the santos are placed on the altar, the Banari paskome do the traditional exercise in the area of the crosses and palm arches in front of the ramada. After this ritual the paskome come to the altar to pray and then sit down in front of the altar. During this time the paskolam begin to dance first to the violin and harp music and then to the flute and drum. The Liohpasko paskome and their wives begin to prepare food for the participants and visitors.

The paskolam dance during the night and on Monday morning—the major services are conducted at night and on Monday. During one of the visits to San Damian's home, he read part of the service used for the May 3 pasko which he sponsored in honor of the Holy Cross. The service which he read and which was recorded is in Spanish because San Damian gave the Banari maestro the books of Mayo texts. It seems likely that this maestro would use the Mayo texts for the services he conducts in the Banari area, and that this would be the service read at any Liohpasko. After the Monday service an additional procession takes place, with the images carried by the paskome and the paskolam, masom, and matačinim dancing in the procession. At some of the large Liohpaskos even go?im danced, which had not taken place for a number of years in the lower Mayo River valley. Then sometime shortly after noon the visiting saints are dipped in parting and take their leave and the Banari paskome return to the church. The Liohpasko paskome give presents, not pay, to the paskola and maso dancers and musicians, and distribute the remaining food to relatives and compadres.

The ceremonies which San Damian gave in Las Flores in honor of the Holy Cross took much this same form. On several occasions the Banari Santisima Tiniran visited San Damian's sacred ramada and was welcomed and honored by the Santa Cruz of San Damian. During the trip the Santisima Tiniran was carried in procession through the market in Navojoa causing considerable excitement and concern on the part of some of the mestizo political officials. Whether the Santisima Tiniran was present or not, a ceremony given by San Damian would be visited by other Saints and especially by *Nuestro Padre* (Our Father), an image dressed in a red robe and a crown and carrying three flowers, a red one in his right hand, a white one in his left and a blue one on the center of his chest. Nuestro Padre is one of the major saints at the small church in Rosales which is located several hundred yards from Las Flores.

The making of a major ceremony in honor of the resident saint, who then greets and entertains the visiting saint, usually of the opposite sex, is a traditional pattern found, of course, also in the large church-pueblo ceremonies. The Easter ceremonial as well as some of the other large Pueblo ceremonials also include a set of home ceremonies in which the saint is rested. Structurally, a similar relationship exists between the Liohpaskom in the Mayo River valley and the major ceremonial given by San Damian on May 3 as exists between home ceremonies to rest a visiting saint and the major church-pueblo ceremonial for the resident saint. For example, during Lent Christ is rested at home ceremonies while He is being pursued by the Pariserom, and on His return from the dead He is welcomed by Mary, Itom Aye, as a visiting saint is honored and welcomed. In summary, San Damian's Liohpasko ceremonial appears rather traditional, especially in terms of its structure and organization. Also, its symbolism is oriented around the major ritual symbol of the Holy Cross, a manifestation of Itom Ačai, the male head of the sacred Mayo Holy Family.

THE SAN CAYETANO VELACIÓN

To examine San Damian's Liohpasko from a somewhat different perspective, that of a second home-based santo, I shall briefly describe the ceremonial for San Cayetano (Fig. 4.8). His major ceremony was given by his owner (*dueño* or *apaʔateak,* watches over) on August 7, 1961, in Totoricaba, which is located in the bush away from the Mayo River itself. San Cayetano is well known as a powerful curer of diseases and especially infertility in women. He also aids persons who are lost. Women promise to dance with San Cayetano at all his velaciones while some Mayos believe the little image is equipped with male sex organs. People also say that many girls run away with young men during San Cayetano dances. When one makes a manda to San Cayetano the promise is made *al revés* (in reverse). For example, if your horse is sick, you make a bet with San Cayetano that your horse will die, then if San Cayetano cures the horse you lose the bet and have to pay the contract. If the horse dies you win, but lose the horse, and do not have to pay San Cayetano. Mayos stress that his is a very different kind of manda than one made to an ordinary saint. Nobody knows if San Cayetano originated in a visitation, as it happened so long ago. Also atypical of Mayo saints, the image of San Cayetano does not appear in any of the Mayo churches in the river valley.

The promise to San Cayetano involves a velación which includes a social dance to phonograph records or mariachi music. In 1961, one first went to Totoricaba to talk to the old man and his wife who are the dueños of San Cayetano. They have no gracia, but out of respect they are called *In Aye* (my mother) and *In Ačai* (my father) by many Mayos. The old man keeps a calendar of San Cayetano's schedule, from which the person who has promised to give a velación must select a date. After the date is set the structure of the velación takes place as follows: preparation of the home and of a neighboring home or the local church as a rest stop for San Cayetano (Fig. 7.8); obtaining and resting San Cayetano; proceeding from the rest stop to the home; praying and dancing all night at the home; and returning San Cayetano to Totoricaba. These velaciones for San Cayetano are considerably less expensive than the San Damian Liohpaskom and immensely cheaper than serving as a paskome for the Santisima Tiniran or the Santa Kurus. Depending upon the promise the individual makes, some families charge "guests" for attendance at the dance although many do not do so. A cow or goat may be purchased and killed to provide food for the persons attending, which means that an elaborate San Cayetano velación runs around 800 or 900 pesos.

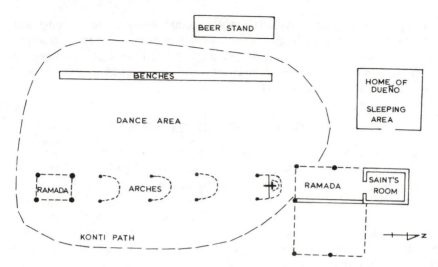

7.8   San Cayetano's sacred ramada and dance area, Totoricaba

A San Cayetano velación took place in Homecarit October 22-23, 1961 Fig. 7.9). San Cayetano's calendar was practically full and velaciones were taking place at an amazing rate. After having made an earlier trip to select a date on San Cayetano's calendar and having decorated the home, the paskome arrived in Totoricaba in mid-morning of October 22. But San Cayetano had not returned from a dance the night before. One of the paskome remarked, "He is probably *nako* (drunk)." Beside the residence for the old man and old woman there was a large dance area, a smaller adobe room which housed San Cayetano, and a ramada at the far end of the dance area (Fig. 7.8). This area was decorated with small red, white and green flags and a line of palm arches running from the saint's room out to the ramada. Within San Cayetano's small house, a travelling home for the little saint rested on a table. This travelling home consisted of a rectangular wooden box with a glass door and two little gourds. On August 7, during the time of the major ceremony for San Cayetano, couples danced in the cleared area and paskolam danced in the ramada. Also, processions took place around this dance ramada area with the paskolam doing mukti to San Cayetano.

Soon after noon San Cayetano arrived in a taxi and was carried to the old man and woman. While the old woman unwrapped, checked, and rearranged the clothing on San Cayetano, the old man counted the money from a little red box which was placed on the altar at the velación for contributions to the Saint. San Cayetano was dressed in a red flowing garment and carried red, white and blue flowers and a bit of green ribbon. The old woman returned the Saint to His small wooden travelling home and covered the box with a white cloth. After obtaining the Saint, the paskome took Him to Homecarit, disembarking from the truck or taxi several hundred feet beyond the church cross, kurus mayor. Ideally they should walk the Saint the complete way; in reality this short walk symbolically satisfied the requirement to go on foot. Before arriving at the kurus mayor the white cloth was removed from the little box, the door of the little house was opened, and *cohetes* (small rockets) were shot off. Accompanied by his or her kompañía, the individual who made the original promise carried the little box with San Cayetano to the kurus mayor where the group was met by a maestro. The individual with the Saint stood in front of the cross with his back toward the cross and his face toward the front door of the church. The others knelt and the maestro prayed and sang. Then, accompanied by more praying and singing, the Saint was taken into the church, removed from his little house and placed in the center of the altar. This ritual represented the resting of the Saint before he proceeded to the house ceremony and would have taken place in a neighboring home if a church were not available.

By this time the home had been prepared for the reception of San Cayetano. The altar was decorated and included Guadalupe (a picture) and the images of two other saints. Five palm arches stood beside the dance area and a wooden cross painted white on the face side hung on the ramada. Later in the afternoon the cross was placed in the ground under the first arch and was removed the next morning. Besides the altar, tables for food, beer, wine, and a dice game had been set up. Late in the afternoon the Santa Kurus of the Homecarit church and San Cayetano were carried to the home and placed on the home altar. The maestro,

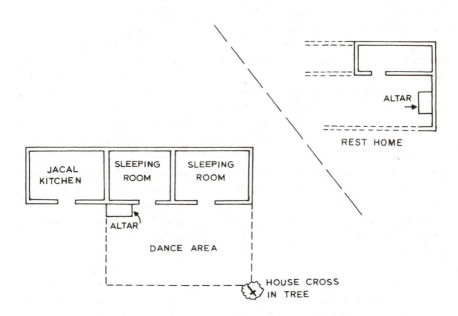

7.9   Rancheria home for San Cayetano velacion, near Homecarit

standing and kneeling before the altar, conducted a ceremony consisting of alabanzas for San Cayetano and readings from the same text about the Santa Kurus which San Damian had read. The maestro also read the text called the Five Mysteries. After each Mystery a cohete was shot off. For the remainder of the night the participants prayed, danced, gambled and drank. The following morning San Cayetano was returned to Totoricaba along with a box of flowers and the small red donation box.

The parallels in both form and structure between the San Damian Liohpasko and the San Cayetano velación are numerous. Couples dancing and gambling have replaced the paskola entertainment. Otherwise, right down to the use of red, white, and blue flowers and some of the same prayers, there exist numerous similarities. Interestingly enough, the San Cayetano velación has not been outlawed by the local or state officials and it is quite popular and open to anyone who wishes to attend. In fact, one of my bachelor Mayo friends says he prefers it because he can dance with all of the pretty girls, although his remark is as much humorous as it is serious. Evidence also indicates that social interaction exists between the two cults and that San Cayetano has "visited" Damian's Santa Kurus.

These data from the San Cayetano velaciones suggest that San Damian's velaciones are not as innovative as one might have assumed had one not considered the San Cayetano ceremonies. In fact, the San Damian Liohpasko appears rather conservative in contrast with the San Cayetano cult complex. Mestizo acceptance of the San Cayetano complex and rejection of the Liohpasko ceremonies suggests that the owner of San Cayetano has more successfully adapted the traditional Mayo small-cult complex than has Damian. Interestingly enough, the major social differences between the two cults—couple dancing, gambling, and the selling of alcoholic beverages—not only appeal to mestizos but also are meaningful in terms of their socio-cultural participation and background. In the 1960s, paskolam danced for the main velación and pasko of San Cayetano in August. Since these rituals took place in Totoricaba, at some distance from the main Mayo River valley towns, they did not attract the attention of upper class mestizo leaders or the town police. The home ceremonies for San Cayetano which take place within the towns do not involve paskola dancing and thus do not violate town regulations nor do they appear on the surface to be much different from mestizo dances. The altar is to one side of the dance area and the crowd arrives after and leaves before the major ritual takes place. Therefore, the average person is aware of mariachi music and dancing and perhaps also the drinking and gambling but not of the Mayo meanings associated with the whole velación. Unless the affair should become too noisy there is no official objection to a "dance."

I have described both of these cults in some detail because both represent a type of transformation constructed upon the Holy Family model. Damian's experience, now symbolized in his ground altar of the Santa Cruz called Itom Ačai, originally was manifest as an Old Man. This Old Man, who is referred to as Itom Ačai, complained that the younger people no longer respect nor obey their elders, a common complaint among Mayo parents. He requested that His children, the Mayos, accomplish His work. By making this new type of pasko, Mayos would show their love for Itom Ačai. Working for one's parents also is an expected part of the parent-child relationship. On the other hand, San Cayetano, also a manifestation of Itom Ačai, symbolizes the fertility and reproductive power of the Holy Family rather than the authority-love relationship between parent and child. To become fertile, women dance with San Cayetano who travels to the velaciones and *bailes* (dances) given in his honor. San Cayetano, who also protects persons travelling in the bush and mountains especially at night, is not found duplicated on Mayo church altars but lives only in the bush village of Totoricaba in the sacred ramada of his dueño. Damian's Santa Cruz, firmly planted in the earth beside the mesquite tree, does not travel to ceremonies in his honor but is symbolically represented by the sacred earth and three flowers while the Santa Cruz image is duplicated and is found in most if not all Mayo churches. In summary, the cult of San Cayetano symbolizes and enacts the fertility and reproductive function of the Holy Family. Through reproduction new individuals and their innovations are introduced. Thus the San Cayetano cult symbolically elaborates upon the innovative aspect of the Holy Family metaphor, while the cult of San Damian focuses its symbolism upon the perma-nent stable dominance between the parent and child in which children respect and aid their parents and in return receive parental support. Specifically, the Holy Cross symbolizes Itom Ačai manifest as God-man and as the archetypal curer, powerful enough to return from death. The earth, which embodies curing power and in which the Holy Cross is planted, symbolizes Itom Aye, while the flowers symbolize a contract and, in this context, the authority-love relationship which is so strong between powerful protective Mayo parents and submissive loving children. Clearly, in these two cults, different aspects of the relations constitut-ing the Holy Family are being dramatized: fertility, reproduction and change versus health, curing and continuity.

Moving to a deeper more analytical level than that of the Mayo folk model of the Holy Family, two aspects of the family triangle have been elaborated upon and acted out in these cults. The unity of the family triangle is a mediation of dual oppositions; parents versus children and fathers (males) versus mothers (females). The Liohpasko cult mediates the parent-child opposition. By follow-ing the instructions of Itom Ačai, by being obedient children, the Mayos express their love for their Father, Itom Ačai. By means of the authority-love relation-ship, ritualized in the cult, this opposition is mediated, while the San Cayetano cult mediates the male-female opposition through fertility symbols and the danc-ing of barren women with the male saint. Nevertheless, manifesting essentially identical social organization and structure of the ritual events, these two cults reveal the more general pattern of the small Mayo cult—a specific and dynamic element in the revitalization of the Mayo way of life. Such small cult groups, which share underlying structure, emphasize different symbolic aspects of the Holy Family metaphor. These differing aspects stimulate a set of cult transfor-mations on this basic model of the Holy Family.

LIOHPASKO COMMUNICATION, ORGANIZATION AND ADAPTATION

In this brief section I shall examine the history of the Liohpasko social organization in terms of the mestizo response and the resulting reduction of the cult activities. Mayos realize the Liohpasko cult of the early sixties is symbolically connected with their past religious life and with events of their ethnic history. With such intense land pressure, it is inevitable that some mestizos and Mayos believe Damian's words, "Take up your inheritance in land," mean war. Mayos know the history and danger of Mexican authorities martyrizing exponents of the cult. In the latter part of the 1800s, certainly by 1890, Mexican military officials were alerted that Mayos had been leaving their jobs on the haciendas and making mass pilgrimages to several centers on the Mayo River five to ten miles west and south of Navojoa. They were gathering to listen to people whom they called "santos." These prophets were speaking of the end of the world by flood and exhorting Mayos to prepare by gathering on certain hills and high spots in order to be saved. Mexican authorities noted that the Mayos had not been anxious to save their employers from the flood with a greater sense of humor than they faced the loss of their hacienda labor. They seemed anxious to find cause to force the peons to return to the haciendas, and to beat them to the draw if they could possibly be planning an uprising. Today, Mayos still have common understandings about the high places to which the people of each village should go in case of floods. The people downriver from Huatabampo on the wide, flat floodplain are painfully aware that they are farther from a flood refuge than the inhabitants of any other area.

Most of these "santos" had a direct relationship with Teresa de Cabora of the upper Mayo River valley, a relationship which often began in being cured by this young girl (see Macklin and Crumrine, 1973; and Spicer, 1970). Santa Teresa, the daughter of a Mayo woman and a white hacendado at Cabora, fell ill and "died" for twenty-four hours. After this she came back to life and had the power to cure blindness and stiff legs by rubbing a mixture of earth and water on the forehead and forearms of the patient. Santa Teresa is said to have cured many people in this way and held paskos which were widely attended throughout the Mayo country, and by some Yaquis and Tarahumaras as well. At one of these, a San Juan pasko in May, 1892, soldiers fell upon the group, shot many of them, and took Santa Teresa and her father. After this she fled to the United States. Her day is celebrated by Mayos on May 3, the Day of the Finding of the Holy Cross, a day traditionally associated with the Mayo military society. The house cross decoration of grain and a white ribbon, which was one of the patterns associated with the Santa Teresa cult ritual, may still be seen occasionally on a house cross here and there throughout the Mayo country. It is said that the Maestro at Banari had books which contain the ritual of the cult, and her rituals and alabanzas are also known in the lower Fuerte River area. Enthusiasm for this cult never reached the heights on the lower Mayo that it attained in the Navojoa area and the Bájima area. However, in other Mayo areas there were "living" saints, such as

San Damian Quijano, San Juan, San Luis (*La Luz*), San Irineo, Santa Camila, Santa Isabel, and Santa Agustina. By 1890 most of these local saints associated with the Santa Teresa cult had been rounded up and sent to the mines in Baja California.

Around 1928 a "live saint" called San Francisco appeared in the upper river valley and gained a large following (Erasmus, 1967:106). His sacred earth was used in curing, either being cooked in a water broth or worn in a bag around the neck. Some claimed the sacred earth was earth dampened by the Saint's urine and collected by the women. As with Santa Teresa, troops were called and San Francisco was carried off. Like the burning of the saints and the Banari church, the people of Banari have seen enough of past mestizo methods which systematically sent Mayo leaders to mines or had them executed. This entire pattern of events Mayos symbolize in the term, The Martyrs. They also mention San Damian in the same breath with The Martyrs and Bachomo, who was both a holy figure and a war leader in the 1910 Revolution. But this does not mean that San Damian is necessarily a bellicose figure. Both from the same pueblo, Damian and Bachomo were acquainted in detail with the Mayo traditional religion and culture. They were anxious to preserve this heritage and saw their collective and individual fates sealed unless there was a return to the proper ceremonial life. For Bachomo this return was prevented by the tyranny of a hacienda system, a feudal system in which poor people were land serfs working from dawn to sunset and losing their land, their independence, and even their dignity and lives. No free time existed for Mayos to give the proper ceremonies to the supernaturals and thus maintain health and well-being. In Damian's time, 1957 to 1976, there is hard work for the poor man, and progressive land modification. Land loss is far greater in terms of the sheer size of large non-Mayo farms than ever before, for enormous new areas of forest have been brought under cultivation. This not only deprives Mayos of their fields but also of their natural resources, the woods and building materials, the firewood, the herbs, the wild animals and fruits, which are necessary to Mayo existence as they conceive it. Yet the economic squeeze was not an overt Mayo rationale for the wave of religious reform. The main concern, speaking from a Mayo point of view, was an issue of sickness, death, the ancestors and the threat of cosmic cataclysm. To alleviate these problems, San Damian's supernatural visitor told him how the traditional religious participants were to take part in the special ceremonies which Damian was commanded to give.

Some various organizational problems were resolved by Damian and his close family and compadre groups. Other solutions were provided by his followers in the various pueblos, particularly in Banari, where the initial series of Liohpaskom were given. In a sense the Banari paskos validated, if not created, the cult for theirs was the first confirmation and application of the old man's directions. Banari Mayos point out that their pueblo is the source, or "root," of the 1960 Liohpaskom (liohpaskom *nawawi*) and that their leadership had the courage to risk being sent away to the mines in order to back the religion. The

Banari patron saint, Santisima Tiniran, who visited the first series of ceremonies, subsequently developed the pattern of visiting the first and the last ceremony in a series promised by local Mayos. However, intricate ceremonial innovations were nearly always based on some earlier type of usage. For example, a former paskome from Banari pointed out that Itom Ačai O?ola, the Santisima Tiniran, had said, "I am the Alpha and the Omega." Since He is the First and the Last, He should attend the first and last of a series of home ceremonies. The process of formally relating Damian's Santa Kurus and the Santisima Tiniran took place rapidly and was based on old symbols, such as sacred soil which cured God-sent illness, and three flowers, red, white, and blue. The identification between the cross and the human body, the Old Man, is fairly clear because at Damian's ramada the main altar cross is dressed in a filmy material, topped with a straw hat, and has a pottery human head (Fig. 7.2). In addition to the Santa Cruz's general male character, specifically it is said to represent Itom Ačai. These ceremonial innovations are combinations of traditional social and cultural forms.

The Mayo River exponents of the cult also command great respect from all Mayos, whether or not they are willing to participate actively in the Liohpaskom, because they are equated with the martyrs of the earlier cults. Even those Mayos who are not specifically cult members have loyalty to members and leaders, for these Mayos represent a living symbol of Mayo sacrifice and martyrdom in the past, and a symbol of Mayo cultural unity.

In the 1960s Mexican authorities in the area seemed to realize that martyrizing tends to intensify, rather than weaken, Mayo unity. The men who were the governors of Sonora and Sinaloa at the time of the appearance of Damian's Old Man, visited him within a few years after his experience, presumably to reason with him and ascertain the motives of his activities. Damian's personal freedom of movement was subsequently curtailed, particularly into Sonora where Banari is located. "San Damian spoke wonderful sermons (*etehot hinabaka*) here in Banari, but now they watch the roads and won't let him come." He is also paid a fixed monthly sum of several hundred pesos to make him a Mexican "soldier." The attempt to buy his loyalty has had its mark on him as did the visits of numerous people. Early in 1961, he received word accompanied by strong threats from a group of Yaqui governors, appointed by the Mexican authorities, that he was to keep his ceremonies out of the Yaqui country. Damian graphically and rather nervously described another visit of high ranking officers in the Mexican army. "I was at home when the generals arrived and asked for me. They said, 'Let's go and have a drink.' I said, 'Okay.' So we went to a tavern and sat down at a table. They ordered something for us to drink. Then they all got out their guns and set them on the table. One said, 'There will be no more fiestas, will there?' And they all patted their guns. I quickly said, 'No! There will be no more fiestas!' Then they brought me home again."

Mexican authorities apparently felt that there were numerous reasons to put tight controls upon the ceremonies, and in all municipalities along the Mayo

River persons had to buy permits to have Liohpaskom as they did for all house ceremonies. Pedro turned around with his back to the door after looking out to make sure nobody was there. "It was the doctor in Banari who is to blame. He told the President of Huatabampo and the President stopped the Liohpaskom. He told the President because he didn't like the curing earth part. This is why people don't talk about the paskom." In some areas paskola and maso dancers were not permitted at all and there was to be no drinking, only praying. If any kind of pasko, including a funeral, became the least bit noisy, participants were dragged off to jail. The stated bases for such tight control over the Mayo ceremonies are unclear. Besides those of the doctor above, there are probably many diffuse reasons, such as loss of native labor while ceremonies are in progress. The Catholic Church also undoubtedly wishes to regain control of the Mayos. Another Mexican rationale for the control of Mayo ceremonialism is that of fear. In Huatabampo Municipio, for example, there exists a large enough proportion of Mayos that the faint possibility of rebellion could be taken as a serious threat to the mestizo community. Even though rebellion is quite unlikely, nevertheless, it is locally deemed necessary that Mayo paskom not be held in the city. During times of community and statewide stress, the government in power does not hesitate to send in patrolling troops.

The Liohpasko cult, on the other hand, has never been proved to be militant. Just as the Santa Teresa cults were not really conclusively demonstrated to be militant before the time of the first Mexican attack upon its Mayo leaders. This original attack was based only on the intelligence report of a scout that one of these Mayos was a relative of a general who had fought beside Cajeme, a mestizoized Yaqui military leader. Therefore, the evidence indicates that originally the Mayos planned only to escape the flood which they believed was to destroy the valley. Though it had not been proven that the Santa Teresa cult had a distinctly militaristic ideology or symbolism up to this time, it apparently developed one very soon. Rebellions and small uprisings thereafter were characterized by the cries of the fighting men, *"Viva Dios y la Santa de Cabora!"* (Long live God and the Saint of Cabora," who was Teresa).

In regard to the San Damian Liohpasko cult the government's reaction has shifted away from direct military intervention to subversion and the restriction of movement of the prophet. These external as well as additional internal pressures have produced profound changes in Damian. By the spring of 1970 his manda to make paskom had been completed and he gave no pasko on May 3 at his sacred ramada in the Fuerte Valley. His curing practice required a great deal of his energy and the money earned was used for alcohol in his attempt to escape the conflict between God's request to make paskom and pressures prohibiting the ceremonies. On May 3, 1970, and in March, 1971, I drove by his sacred home-ramada altar. Since Damian was away curing and nobody was at home, I did not stop, but could observe the sacred area from my truck. The area looked almost completely stripped and even the ramada which was above the altar area was gone. The mesquite tree and three wooden crosses still stood in the center of the sacred area. A new palm curved over the third cross which must have been the Santa Kurus. Fluttering in the air, a tattered gown is still worn by the Santa Kurus and He retained his pottery head. Placed on the ground directly in front of the Santa Kurus were fresh red flowers. Besides these flowers and the palm arch there was no evidence that Damian had been at his home for some time. Thus, by May 1970, the transformation of Damian from a prophet and a cult leader to a Mayo curer was complete and by the end of 1974 Damian had died. The appearance of numerous cults led by a "living saint" in addition to the rapid spread of cult membership suggests that variables similar to those which existed in the past continue to be key aspects of life in the Mayo River valley in the sixties. Yet the spread of cults seems to have shifted from the upper river valley in the early 1900s to the lower river valley in mid-seventies. Interestingly enough, of course, this parallels the modernization process and high intensity level of culture contact moving down the river valley.

In terms of Anthony Wallace's five-stage analysis of revitalization* the Mayo data correspond to stage four, "period of revitalization," which includes six sub-stages: the formulation of a code, communication, organization, adaptation, cultural transformation, and routinization. In the cases of the San Damian Liohpasko, Santa Teresa and other north Mexican cults, these six sub-stages may be simplified and contracted into four major periods, but nevertheless, the overall pattern adheres to Wallace's general scheme (Macklin and Crumrine, 1973). The "call" or vocational struggle, Wallace's formulation of a code, certainly is clearly revealed in the San Damian and Santa Teresa cases. The second major period in Mayo small-cult revitalization involves communication of the code, transformation of a nucleus of followers, and incipient organizational developments. In this second period, Mayos accept Damian's visitation from God and some paskome initiate the first cycles of the special ceremonies. The third period is characterized by more elaborate organization, along with incipient cultural transformation and adaptation. More followers are drawn to the "saints" through sacred myths and stories concerning the powers of the leader and the cult. Some of these individuals have administrative rather than charismatic abilities and with their aid and manipulation the organization of the cult is solidified and adapted. Cultural transformation takes place among the groups of followers who, due to their rapid growth in numbers, alarm the established local and state governments. These external political power structures threaten or even deport the "saint" and in the fourth period the movement declines and the "saint" loses his prophetic leadership role and devotes himself to curing. To summarize, Mayo small-cult revitalization reflects a general four stage pattern: the prophetic experience of the "saint"; the communication and growth of a cult; solidification, adaptation and continued growth of the cult versus external political pressure and threats; and eclipse and decline of the movement and shift in the leader's role from that of saint-prophet to that of native curer.

---

*See page 6.

ESCHATOLOGY OF THE CULT

In spite of the reduced social activities of the 1960 Liohpasko ritual and its decline as a socio-religious movement, the underlying Mayo cultural pattern has not been modified. Directly connected with Damian's cult is the expectation of a great flood sent by God to kill all the wicked and purify the world, a millennial concept. The myth of Noah is often repeated, with a sense of deep significance. Mayo popular eschatology is, however, not entirely dismal. A pure and better world always arises from the slime of the cataclysmic flood. The myth symbolizes and epitomizes the hope for the perpetuation of Mayo identity and tradition, for who could the survivors be but those who have kept the commandments of Itom Ačai and Itom Aye that have been revealed through a long procession of living saints. "Those persons who have given the paskos of the red, white, and blue are God-fearing men like Noah," people say. "Very few people will be saved, for few are that good." Therefore, many wicked Mayos will be killed in the cataclysmic flood as well as mestizos, while persons who are not Mayos will be saved if they have given the ceremonies. Thus the paskom do not necessarily symbolize a race myth, for the physical identity of a person is not the main issue of salvation. The key to salvation, nevertheless, is godliness in a distinctly Mayo sense which certainly does have ethnic implications.

The fact that a long while has passed since Damian first predicted the flood does not seem to have weakened expectations of the deluge too greatly. Mayos have recent proof that the river still floods. A flood in 1914 almost wiped out the old pueblo of Navojoa while one in January, 1949 involved serious flooding and losses and required the aid of the Red Cross from Arizona (Berber, 1958:319). In September, 1957 a seven-day rain threatened the Cucusebora Dam. At that time there was extensive flooding when a large reserve of water was released from the dam. In Huatabampo the railroad warehouses and the houses of the rich, who had usurped the hill of Huatabampo, were the only refuge for thousands of poor mestizos and Mayos who were displaced from their flooded homes. There was enormous suffering and hardship associated with this inundation on the Mayo River. This occurred just before Damian's first vision, which reportedly took place the following month. Since records have been kept on the subject, the Mayo River has flooded periodically. The suffering and deprivation which result from floods often have had effects on the location and relationship of Mayo villages to one another and to mestizo centers. The mestizo commercial area of Huatabampo has gradually crowded the original Mayo occupants off the higher ground. In the heavier rainy seasons the dirt floors of the Mayo jacal houses around Huatabampo stay damp. Frequently they must be abandoned for periods in the rainy season and their timbers (*orkonim*) have to be renewed more often for they rot quickly. The split of Banari with Huícori, a bitter one, is said to have occurred during a flood in a dispute over fresh water. Banari is situated in such a low area that its drinking wells become salty when the water level in the river is even normally high in the wet season.

Although a specific date was set by Damian for the flood in the Fuerte, as the time approached, no flood appeared. While the people waited in the ramada-chapel near Damian's house a hand arose over the altar and a great wind came up and blew the paper, on which a version of the prophecy was written, away into the ocean. Some suggest this was a sign that Damian should become a curer and believe it was after this time that he began to cure.

On the other hand, Mayo farmers know that the floods enrich the soil and that the Cucusebora Dam is an attempt on the part of mestizos to control the floodwaters and utilize them for irrigation. But now they must pay for water which was formerly free to them. They can see, too, that bad drainage has accelerated the salinization of lands below Huatabampo to a fantastic rate within the last fifteen years. Mayos point out many areas near Huatabampo on which mesquite forest grew only a few years ago but which now are saline swamp. They attribute this waste to the unwise and greedy use of the river water by rich mestizos, "ricos." The idea of a flood revitalizing unusable soils is clearly understood. Some Mayos explain that the land will be more fertile after the cataclysmic flood and that the few good who survive will have a new paradise (*paraíso*).

This eschatology reflects both the guilt aspects of Mayo nativism and the essentially restorative nature of those beliefs. The millennium is characterized by idealization of past tradition rather than the future oriented type of millennialism which characterizes the cargo cults of the Pacific area, where natives make rituals to obtain European goods. The restoration includes not only a physical paradise but a newly regenerated human stock in which only the best Mayos and the few religious ones like Noah survive. Yet most people questioned about the world after the coming flood were not primarily concerned about the new world, but only about surviving the flood, for almost all were worried about their worthiness. They had not given much thought to what a world without all the material goods that came with mestizo technical culture would be like. Although some people did not believe that the mestizos would all be killed, the belief still was not in any way connected with mestizo material conveniences but rather that some mestizos might conceivably be worthy of survival. In short, the interest in mestizo material goods does not form a major interest in any part of the cult beliefs proper.

The general destruction of the irreligious was not expected to occur in any way except by the hand of God in the flood. This instance of Mayo nativism was then a "fantasy compensation" in Lucy Mair's terms (1959:119-123) rather than a militaristic solution to their followers' problems. But the massing of whole battalions in the Mayo area in 1914, a flood year, suggests that the flood and military effort on the part of the Mayos may well be mentally equatable. Even today, sorcerers are believed to be able to help control and cause floods. Thus, this "magical" means of revitalization may be partly within man's control and the distinction between a military and a "magical" reaction is not as clear as some writers have argued. In the following section I will examine other "non-magical" reasons and explanations for the existence of the 1960 Liohpasko cult and the revitalization of the Mayo way of life. Specifically the eschatology of the 1960 Liohpasko cult reveals several interesting symbolic parameters. A destructive yet fertility producing element of the natural environment, the flooding, has been selected by Mayos to symbolize an aspect of the relationship between Itom Ačai and man or Ili Usim. The flood symbolizes the punishment which a father must occasionally use to chastise his disobedient children. This metaphor acts also as a boundary creating mechanism between Mayo and mestizo societies because only those who love God and demonstrate this love through ceremonial participation will be saved from the flood. Plainly the flood eschatology provides links between a natural phenomenon, the Holy Family, the individual Mayo family, and Mayo ceremonialism and the Mayo way of life versus mestizo values and way of life.

8. Why a New Cult?

Many social scientists, anthropologists in particular, have developed systems to account for the birth of prophetic or millennarian movements. Although I cannot treat here the different types of explanations nor this kind of social movement in general, David Aberle (1966), Kenelm Burridge (1969), L. P. Mair (1959), Sylvia Thrupp (1962), and Bryan Wilson (1963) all provide general discussions of the types of explanations as well as specific information on one or several movements. Many investigators have suggested that these types of movements are the results of imbalances or of incompatibilities resulting from contact between a more powerful dominant social group or society and a subordinate group. The members of the dominated group feel anxiety, hostility, tension, and deprivation for a number of reasons. For example, they wish the material wealth of the dominant group but do not have the means to attain it, they wish to return to the precontact times when they were "free" but do not have the power to do so, or population and social group formation has changed so that the people can no longer make the rituals which they believe necessary for good health and well being. I have already mentioned David Aberle's (1966:323) discussion of relative deprivation as an important variable in the generation of prophetic movements. Very simply, people feel deprived when something which they believe is rightfully theirs is withheld from them. Mayo deprivation and tension focuses upon their inability to create the rituals and the society which they feel is rightfully and historically theirs. Due to a complex history and present Mayo-mestizo contact conditions, Mayo expectations or beliefs concerning the ideal Mayo way of life cannot be manifest in the river valley. This mismatch between cultural ideals and socio-economic reality causes individuals to feel tension. A society in this impasse tends to become prophet-producing, especially if the group or the dominant society is characterized by a prophetic or a shamanistic tradition. Prophets, who are believed to have direct access to supernatural guidance, and their cults are one of the means of initiating certain social and cultural processes.

[142]

First, they may bring the belief system in line with the changing social system, and thus effect *Cultural Realignment*. Second, they may bring the social system in line with the belief system, and thus effect *Social Realignment*. Third, they may effect some intermediate alignment of the social and cultural systems, a *Compromise Realignment*. If the prophets' solutions or those of the members of the cult are rejected by the society, prove inadequate because of a too rapidly changing economic and political situation, or are squelched by outside forces, then tension will continue.

Economic Deprivation

Much has already been said in support of a discrepancy between Mayo ideal and the actual social and physical environments which affect the economic organization in which Mayos find themselves. Within the last twenty years Mayo population has at least doubled without substantial increase of Mayo lands. In 1955 on the Mayo River there were about 5,000 ejidatarios in 35 ejidos and 2,700 private property holders with 37% of the land within the irrigation district in ejidos. Of about 65,000 hectares, 24,000 were ejidal and 41,000 were private holdings. The average size of an ejido holding was 4.7 hectares as contrasted with the average size of a private holding of about 15.7 hectares. Furthermore, new ejido assignments were not always good land nor land easily accessible to the assignees. This made it impossible for Mayos to develop and maintain the lands for financial as well as social reasons. For example, one Mayo petition asks for replacement of 600 out of 1,055 irrigable hectares alleged to be too saline for use and claims that out of its total of 4,305 hectares only 1,500 are cultivable at all.

What land has been put into ejidos within the last few years was not always parcelled with any attention to preserving community and family integrity. Since the Mayo cooperative economic unit is still a kin and compadre one, this makes it economically difficult for Mayos to develop distant wilderness land. Mayos are held in the downriver villages by family ties, the ownership of the *solar* where they live, the nearness of the campo santo where their dead are buried, and the religious and community ties of a comparatively well integrated Mayo community. In short, downriver Mayos would like their traditional lands and river water near their residential communities. Under the Agrarian Law, ejidatarios in the Mayo area are losing land which they have not used for more than two years. Even if the land itself is not lost, an ejidatario often must make a "deal" with a money lender which makes the ejidatario a peon on his own land. However, Mayos allege that splitting crops with private money lenders is often less oppressive than working with the Banco Ejidal, whose local officials are said to cheat poor farmers out of two crops while paying for only one.

That causes for economic deprivation are present cannot be denied and many appear to be getting worse. Economic distress is even greater in years when unseasonal rains and freezing ruin cotton, vegetable and fruit crops on the large private holdings near Huatabampo where Mayos work for wages. Shifts to crops like wheat, which do not require wage labor, also have serious consequences for Mayos. Yet only in the light of the ideal patterns of Mayo economic life can the extent of economic deprivation be fully appreciated. Such an ideal economy has not existed among Mayos for a very long time. But certain ideals are very strong: a self-sufficient Mayo community, each kin group with its own farming lands, adequate to its changing numbers; each community with its council to settle land disputes; each community with its own wilderness land for gathering, hunting and the provision of firewood and housebuilding materials, as well as grazing land for sheep and horses; each community with free access to salt deposits, wells, and river water; each *solar* inviolable for those who have dead there; each church sacred and central to its people; each household free to raise food crops of traditional value; and all integrated in exchange patterns in which Mexican money, goods and services figure as peripheral. All of these ideal patterns have experienced a long and intense battle for survival. In actuality, all must be modified considerably. Thus the discrepancy between real and ideal economic organization constitutes a basis for economic deprivation among Mayos. This discrepancy is partially relieved through the dual nature of the modern economic structure. Yet its very duality causes tension in the lives of Mayos who partici-pate in both Mayo and mestizo economic systems each structured and organized in terms of its own values and symbols.

Distortions in Social Organization

The traditional kinship system is in the process of rather complete transfor-mation to an entirely new system. That land use and ownership was apparently once governed through a kin unit is still important. The fundamental change which has taken place in the kinship system has, therefore, required a change in the composition of the body of men responsible to the pueblo for decisions in land ownership. Some Mayos have become increasingly sophisticated in the pattern of individual land ownership, but many have not. The recent shift in government policy away from the founding of large numbers of ejidos has in a sense confused the process of change. On the other hand, the ejido incorporates many of the unfortunate aspects of group ownership and none of the mitigating aspects, such as full judicial control by representatives of the local Mayo group.

Another item bemoaned by many Mayos, and mentioned by God in His visitation to Damian Bohoroqui, involves the loss of respect of young people for their elders. The old kinship terms made a large number of distinctions between younger and older siblings and included distinct terms for father, grandfather, great grandfather, in both mother's and father's lines. In general, the Mayo language itself involves a large number of obligatory amenities, and respect terms. Many Mayos say expressly that speaking Spanish encourages disrespect. Therefore, changes in respect patterns, accompanying the change to Spanish kinship terminology, are felt by older Mayos as a threat to their way of life.

Intermarriage with mestizos is also recognized more or less clearly as a threat to Mayo solidarity. But aside from strongly discouraging their children to marry yoris, Mayos usually do very little about intermarriage. If an offspring marries a yori, they get along as well as possible, working with their new in-laws, although in some cases the Mayo parents refuse to speak to their estranged child and new in-laws.

Much has been said about the existence of duplicate social organizations in each community. No Mayo can be certain that a dispute settled within a Mayo social unit will not be taken by a dissatisifed party to the duplicate Mexican organization. When the Mayo authorities attempt to impose sanctions on members of the group, the members not willing to accept that authority do not need to leave the community to escape but only to take refuge in the other society which lives in the same space dimension. Understandably, the focus of Mayo hostility toward yoris revueltos (Mayos turned mestizo) is one of the chief frustrations expressed from time to time in Mayo nativism. Major differences exist between the Mayo and the mestizo organizations. Mayo authority is conceived to rise from the will of the people while the Mexican organization seems to be imposed from outside. Some resulting Mayo hostility exists toward Mexican political organization, although not always necessarily toward its appointees and local officials in particular. The major sanctions available to Mayo officials in the acceptance of their decisions are ethnic and supernatural ones. In support of these sanctions, Mayos focus their hostility toward evangelistas, agnosticism, and in general any kind of deviation from traditional Mayo culture because these represent major threats to Mayo social organization and the whole Mayo way of life. The irreligiosity and ''wealth'' of yoris revueltos are their most despised characteristics, yet in fact they are not necessarily richer than many traditional Mayos. The focus of hostility toward the rich is also a complex pattern. The rich use the traditional and sacred Mayo land immorally by violating central Mayo socioeconomic traditions and keeping for themselves what should be distributed to others. The control of local political power by the ricos, who are irreligious in the Mayo sense of the term, and the alliance of many wealthier mestizos with the Catholic Church, has undermined the Mayo appeal of that institution.

The combined effects of foreign and mestizo land encroachment, floods, long periods of war and periods of more or less national political unrest have been discussed. The internecine strife of Mayo villages, manifest in factionalism and quarreling, often involves rather deep differences of opinion concerning the relationships of Mayos to various aspects of mestizo life. The extent of the seriousness of any threat to the solidarity of the pueblo social unit can only be understood in terms of what the pueblo means to Mayos. Symbolically, Mayos perceive ''The Pueblo'' as one of the major social units in their way of life. Ethnic identity centers around the concept of ''my pueblo'' every bit as much as around the Mayo River area as a whole. The fission of pueblos has probably always been a normal process of growth in Mayo settlements. But the hostile and sudden break is a different matter than the development of a daughter colony with continued ceremonial interdependence and friendly association with the mother village. The relationship between Banari and Tosalipacu is characterized by some of the most intense hostility and anxiety which Mayos show toward anyone or anything. The breakdown of pueblo unity is definitely one source of tension, especially in view of the Mayo pueblo solidarity concept.

The degree to which any social unit must be maintained through a constant struggle and process of minor adaptations, even when no continuous first-hand contact with a different society exists, is not fully known. We presume some of this kind of adaptation is normally necessary because of changes in physical environment as well as demographic changes. For example, from time to time, floods on the lower Mayo River have tended to change farmland and houseland boundaries as well as man-to-land ratios in the area. In addition to the problems produced by "natural" change and population growth, Mayo tension now pivots on the breakdown of traditional Mayo social units as a direct result of non-Mayo infiltrations, land encroachment and political and religious suppression. The interethnic threats to Mayo unity and autonomy which were characteristic of the period of the local variants of the Santa Teresa cult appear to be very similar to those which were present in the 1950s and 1960s. Yet the sources of difficulty have multiplied numerically and in intensity because of much greater population pressure and increasing damage to Mayo pueblo autonomy and to various other Mayo social units. Based upon the Holy Family metaphor, the conscious revival of "the Mayo Way of Life," which has become a sacred symbol, represents a Mayo response to these complex problems and increasing tension which threaten unity and solidarity.

In summary, Mayos experience a conflict between their concept of the ideal Mayo social structure and the existing social organization in the Mayo River valley today. Also the Mayo-mestizo contact social system ideally should recognize Mayo societal units and provide a means of linking the Mayo social system to that of the mestizos. But the structure of Mayo-mestizo social contact actually blocks gradual Mayo societal system adjustment towards the dominant system and forces Mayos either to become mestizo or to move towards a recreated "traditional" Mayo way of life. Especially when the changes in Mayo social organization affect their ability to produce the rituals and ceremonials which Mayos believe necessary for their health and the well-being of the world, Mayos feel social deprivation.

Symbolic and Religious Distortions

In addition to economic deprivation and social distortions resulting from the competition of two societies and value systems, tension exists within the Mayo social-cultural system itself. A disparity is manifest between symbolic organization and the social units available for the expression of those beliefs. Yoris revueltos have solved these problems by sacrificing the Mayo symbolic organization more or less entirely and entering mestizo society. This solution may ease their feelings of economic deprivation by opening up possiblities of new work and accumulation patterns not presently sanctioned in Mayo society. But in reality new economic vistas are also very limited for poor mestizos. This kind of resolution also possibly eases some anxieties by enabling yoris revueltos to identify, to some extent, with the dominant society. On the other hand, mestizos of the laboring and ejido classes share the political and economic frustrations of Mayos to a very large degree. The transition to mestizo life is one which is apparently made slowly, with many returns to Mayo communities on the part of individuals in the process of assimilating.

Frequently expressed Mayos' anxieties focus on the loss of or radical changes in various ceremonies felt to be necessary to the welfare of the individuals, such as the loss of certain paskos in many communities. In some areas around Navojoa individuals claim that home paskos for rites of passage, such as the pasko held for children's funerals, novenas, and the death anniversary ceremonies, were sometimes not being held. This also produces anxiety. In Banari Mayos claim these ceremonies have been held except for the people who were killed in the times of the 1910 Revolution, and they had not known when some of those people died. Since in Huatabampo paskola dancing was forbidden by municipal law in 1959-60, a child's funeral requiring such dancing could not be completed. In other words, many reasons, other than apathy or neglect, appear for the temporary or permanent loss of socio-ceremonial customs.

Mayos often mention desecration of churches and of church sites by activities which Mayos conceive to be irreligious or sacrilegious, for instance, the conversion of the old church at Huatabampo into a marketplace and the setting up of many money-making concessions and sideshows in the sacred area between the church, paskola ramada and campo santo at Banari. This evidence is cited by Mayos to show the threat the yoris pose to Mayo religious life. The opening of roads into the area below Huatabampo in the last few years increased the feelings of anxiety which individual Mayos have about their privacy. The accidental death of a child in Banari, run over by a speeding truck on the dirt highway, was proof to many of the evil roads would bring. Taxes on masks used in Lenten ceremonies and the registration of all larger ceremonies, along with many other restrictions imposed upon ceremonial life by municipal authority, are also regarded as suppressive of Mayo religious life, and an invasion of Mayo privacy. This recalls to Mayos the archetypal myths of the Martyrs, like San Juan and the Burning of the Little Children. The political suppression of the church, which appears to have dissipated somewhat since the period of the 1920s and 1930s, seems to have shifted to suppression of the home ritual, especially in the larger urban communities. Still Mayos are not completely relaxed about the security of their local churches. Some Mayo communities feel threatened by evangelistas and others by the Catholic Church organization as well as by Mexican politicians.

The erosion of ceremonial solidarity among Mayos, through the breakdown of Mayo social units, began as early as the 1880s and continues into the present. Even though this breakdown threatens the learning of Mayo symbolism, symbolic integration has shown remarkable stability. Through the crisis of the President Calles period in which church activities were almost completely suppressed, it existed only in Mayo minds. In this situation the symbolic organization provided both a rallying point as well as a guide through which a community-church center and an associated calendrical round of ceremonies were revived and creatively modified. Mayos have repeatedly reacted to the secularization of churches and images both by militance and by withdrawal and reintegration. These reactions could be interpreted as a dominant process of realigning the social organization with a strong traditional symbolic organization. In the long run the major social integrative accomplishments of all these past movements have been undone by mestizo military retaliation, gradual economic erosion, and rapid ecological change. Although each becomes ineffective, much of the realigned symbolic material, the songs, myths, and symbols, have become permanent parts of Mayo religious life. In a sense periods of intense Mayo nativism have facilitated, even while trying to limit, a rather continual collective cultural mestizoization. Both Cajeme, the war leader, and ''Santa'' Teresa had a mestizo parent. Totoriwoki, a Mayo war leader from Banari area, ''San'' Damian Quijano, and ''San'' Damian Bohoroqui had Mayo parents and were monolingual in Mayo, except Damian Bohoroqui who learned Spanish after the visitation. Thus Mayo nativistic movements include both mestizoized and conservative, both bilingual and monolingual leaders. Paskolam, curers, Pariserom, civil and church governors, and others also act as leaders in the new cults, although the central figures are quite frequently deeply native Mayo-speaking individuals who often become curers.

In summary, a mass of evidence suggests that Mayos feel deprivation and tension due to conflicts not only between Mayo social and economic organization and that of the dominant mestizo society but also between Mayo symbols, beliefs, and values and the actual Mayo social organization existing in the river valley today. Mayos have been characterized by a whole range of responses in their attempts to reduce the tension and deprivation which they feel. These responses, none of which have proved fully successful, range from military campaigns and new religions to withdrawal and re-creation of the ''traditional'' way of life. Nevertheless, one must not over-simplify the argument for there are important kinds of questions which still must be asked. Damian's new cult does present traditional Mayo symbolism in a form which involves less capital outlay and a smaller more compact social group and, therefore, is in part a *compromise realignment*. At least ideally he has opened an alternative and less costly kind of ceremonial participation which, involving fewer participants, was less likely to arouse mestizo suspicions although, of course, this latter solution failed to materialize. On the other hand, I have no neat analytic measure of the level of felt deprivation or tension among Mayos. Most, if in fact not all, societies must deal with tension-producing conflicts within and between their social and cultural systems and between the group itself and its changing cultural ecological milieu.

Conceivably other societies are characterized by unresolved conflicts and are not prophet producing, although they may in fact utilize other means of tension reduction. Until I have discovered the set of conflict resolution and tension reduction mechanisms and developed a model for the analytical comparison of tension and deprivation levels cross-culturally, my argument relies chiefly upon the analysis of the Mayo data. Without going into these more technical problems, I shall suggest a somewhat more general kind of solution to the problem of prophet production by examining the meaning of this whole process of the re-creation of the Mayo way of life.

HOW "MAYOS" REFUSE TO DIE

Maintaining Identity

The Mayo symbolization of their relationships with the social world of non-Mayos represents several categories. First, many of the ricos are feared and even hated, feelings left over from the Porfiriata and encouraged by the ricos' prodigious use of land and water. Of course, there exist exceptions where loyalty is commanded by an occasional rico who has tried to be fair with Mayo employees. A second kind of outsider is typified by the travelling and sedentary merchants and vendors. These lower class mestizos sell anything to make a profit and often take advantage of Mayos. All who capitalize on Mayo resources for unusual personal profit and who do not give some paskos are certain to arouse Mayo hostility. Enmity toward this type of mestizo is second only to that toward the evil rich. Other poor but religious mestizo farmers command the least animosity of all, for they have much in common with Mayos. Only the irreligious among them are condemned with any real hostility ostensibly not for being non-Mayos, but for lack of religious beliefs. The rancor toward the irreligious extends especially to those with Mayo ancestry who have turned away from the traditional life (yoris revueltos). Often, though not always, these people have taken up selling occupations not traditional to Mayo society and have parted with all the major demands of the Mayo religious life. They are abstractly despised as *riquitos* (little rich ones). In actuality, Mayos are very reluctant to point out any single actual real person as a yori revuelto. It is very bitter to say that a person "wants to be a yori" and even worse to claim that he actually has become one. The major foci of Mayo hostility then are the exploiting rich, with whom the organized Catholic Church is now often grouped; the yoris revueltos who have turned away from the proper traditions; and those mestizos who let the quest for money dominate their lives.

The Mayo demand for religious and political equality is an important variable in Mayo discontent and group reaction toward mestizo society. Variants of the popular myths associated with the cult of Damian, the cult of San Juan and various earlier stories of the battles of the Revolution period symbolize this demand. The stories of the Damian cult with political overtones are scattered and hard to pin down especially after the official measures had been taken against the cult. Some of these texts were collected by Erasmus (1961:286; and, quoted here, 1967:102).

> According to stories related there, God had promised much rain during the next three years in order to fill the dams so the poor as well as the rich would have sufficient irrigation water. God was said to be displeased with the administration of the Office of Water Resources because the rich were being favored through illegal means. According to some extreme versions, He even wanted to destroy the canals so no one could charge for His water.

The basic organization of the San Damian cult is neither primarily a political nor a military one, but rather that of a saint's cult, with cult leaders who arrange exchanges and decide matters of ritual. Its primary overt aims are the curing of those who are sick with God-sent diseases and the preparation of an elect to survive the flood. Although its apostles are interested in spiritual supernatural power, one must keep in mind that the very model of the Spanish church, originally presented to Mayos, was the church militant. Therefore, some of the cult's traditional symbols are connected with military organization. The Santisima Tiniran paskome are like the soldier guard of their santo. Both the goʔim and wikičim, who appeared at some 1960 Liohpaskom, were formerly full-fledged military organizations with religious and ceremonial functions. It is said that only a very few members of these societies are left, because most of them died in the battles of the 1910 Revolution. However, the Liohpasko cult tends to stimulate and reinforce traditional community organization and, therefore, functions as a symbol of Mayo identity and a means of maintaining socio-cultural integration rather than as a military symbol and cult.

Mayo eschatology of the sixties still includes the myth that in time past, Itom Ačai, who is identified with the sun, destroyed the world by fire. Mayos say that the hirelings who burned the saints of Banari will die by the hand of God in a natural catastrophe. Hurricanes, high winds, and earthquakes are all familiar phenomena in this area. Mayos express fear of such natural castastrophes which are believed to herald the end of the world. They also fear that the earth will sink into the rising sea. In the flood symbolism and the parallel myth of the Burning of the Little Children, many Mayo fears are unified and presented in a mythic and symbolic idiom: For example, the fear of natural catastrophe; alien domination; the evil rich; the loss of tradition and ceremony and the division and defeat of Mayo solidarity; the loss of resources; their own guilt at having too much love of money; starvation, suffering, and death; and the evil wills of men who control various kinds of supernatural power. The San Damian Liohpasko complex and the general revival of a Mayo way of life, constructed upon the Holy Family model, offer semi-traditional solutions to these fears and hostilities which focus upon the possible loss of Mayo traditions.

In fact, the Mayo hostilities and fears themselves have become negative symbols which characterize Yoremes as set apart from others. Mayos quite correctly realize that if their traditions and way of life disappear, then present group unity will be seriously threatened. In the discussion of Mayo enculturation I have shown how and what a Mayo learns. Part of the learning process involves seeing and participating in the ceremonials. Rooted in the metaphor of the Holy Family, the Mayo social and ceremonial organization and the ritual cycle itself reveals an extremely complex, well organized, challenging, and esthetically beautiful integration of myth and ritual. These ceremonials pull each family into a church center and relate church centers into chains of pueblos participating in ceremonial exchanges. Once an individual has learned the values and understands the meanings of the symbolism involved, participation becomes extremely compelling. Involvement, of course, is based upon the repayment of a manda made to a saint in exchange for a cure. Clearly, disease and sickness and curing and health are also an integral part of this ceremonial complex. The questions of life versus death and of Mayo-mestizo relations also receive complex treatment and answers in the Easter Ceremonial and the San Juan Ceremonial, respectively. On the other hand, in the discussion of Mayo-mestizo relations I suggest that Mayos have no real alternatives except to remain Mayo and reaffirm their way of life or to become peasant mestizos of the lowest class having lost their rich cultural traditions and having gained essentially nothing in exchange. With these facts in mind it is not surprising that at least some Mayos elect to revive in terms of the Holy Family model what they conceive of as their traditional way of life and to maintain membership and identity in a Mayo enclaved society.

The Way of Life in Mayo Revitalization

Under these conditions one would expect that Mayo hostilities and fears as well as the Mayo way of life itself would become symbols utilized by Mayos to form a kind of boundary in a socially fluid river valley. That very recent events have been incorporated into the sacred mythology and ceremonialism, e.g., the Burning of the Little Children, and the popularity of the 1960 Liohpasko cult, indicate Mayos are still creatively developing their logico-symbolic system in adjustment to contemporary changes in the river valley. Elaborating some earlier ideas of Arnold van Gennep (1909) about rites of passage, Victor Turner (1968, 1969) makes some very useful suggestions, applicable to the Mayo revival. As mentioned earlier, movement or passage from one status to another involves ritual, which aids in, or makes the novice move through, the transition period. This transitional period, a kind of limbo, "betwixt and between," is called the liminal stage, and is preceded by a preliminal stage and followed by a postliminal stage. Turner (1968:576-577) suggests that whole social groups undergoing a transition may be in a period of liminality characterized by structural impoverishment and egalitarian social relations and by symbolic enrichment. In this period of transition the secular political organization may be replaced by equality of novices and by elaboration in ritual and myth. The myths and rituals provide a dramatic and deeply exciting stimulus to persons or groups experiencing this liminal period. Providing a test case, Mayo society shows some indications of just such a liminal stage. Individual Mayos highly value equality although the structure of the Mayo family, of the Holy Family, and of many of their ceremonial sodalities is in fact hierarchical. Mayo political organization is no longer recognized by mestizos and, therefore, is in suspension while their mythology and ceremonialism shows intense and creative elaboration. Mayo ceremonialism and the Mayo way of life have become an elaborate ritual drama which is part of this liminal status that Mayos hold between an autonomous tribal society and a rural mestizo peasantry. Mayos are neither autonomous nor mestizo peasants, yet at the same time they are both, they are "betwixt and between." Solidifying this dynamic reality, Erasmus (1961, 1967) tends to see Mayos as rural peasants whereas I have emphasized their separateness and their ethnic and tribal natures. In a sense, we both have focused upon opposite poles of Mayo liminality and lost sight of the meaning of the drama and the dynamics of transition. As the drama is enacted, different solutions, such as the church paskos, San Damian paskos, or San Cayetano velaciones are created, tested, and fall into disuse or in part are absorbed by the ongoing liminal state. Clearly, variations on Mayo cermonialism and symbolism are being generated and applied by Mayos in their attempts to develop a more stable and workable adjustment between themselves as Mayos and the dominant mestizo society.

In conclusion, Damian has proposed a compromise solution to the problem of Mayo tension as well as providing a new symbolic complex, constructed upon the Holy Family metaphor, mediating one of the sets of oppositions in the family triangle and arising from the semi-liminal state of Mayo society. The cult involves some readjustment and synthesis in symbolism and cultural structure and greater shifts away from large pueblo ceremonialism toward home paskos and away from extremely expensive ceremonialism toward less costly ritual. Its rapid diffusion among Mayos indicates that the cult is innovative enough to reduce tension and provide a new set of ethnic group ritual symbols and yet traditional enough not to cause undue misfit with other Mayo symbol systems such as the Holy Family. Whether it is innovative enough to be viable in the mediation between Mayo and mestizo socio-political powers is, unfortunately, questionable. Some of the cult's elements have aroused the fears of mestizo leaders and their program of suppression would appear to have severely affected the spread of the cult. On the other hand, the San Cayetano cult, ritualizing another aspect of the Holy Family metaphor and mediating the second set of oppositions in the Mayo family triangle, appears to have successfully adjusted to the present political situation although it does not have the really deep appeal to Mayos as does the San Damian Liohpasko cult. In fact, Mayos express more concern regarding the loss of respect for parents and elders than about the fragile nature of the marriage bond. The former problem is ritualized in the Liohpasko cult whereas the latter fear is dramatized in the San Cayetano cult. One cult has sacrificed symbolic integrity for political mediation whereas the other maintaining symbolic integrity has been forced into a weak political position. In the likely event of the complete eclipse of the San Damian cult, other cults combining innovative and traditional elements likely will appear among Mayos until their liminal status is modified and Mayos gain more control over their own destinies.

Living on a reservation just north of the Mayos and still retaining a functioning political village organization, modern Yaqui Indians hold a recognized status within the nation and, therefore, should not exist in a liminal state. Yaquis, although characterized by revival of their traditional culture, have officially rejected the Liohpasko cult and have not produced recent Yaqui prophets. Edward Spicer (1970) explains this interesting difference between Yaquis and Mayos in terms of each group's history of social contact with Spanish and later mestizo societies. During the eighteenth and nineteenth centuries the Spanish and later the mestizos filtered into Mayo country in greater numbers than into Yaqui country and in doing so more seriously disorganized Mayo socio-political organization. Both Mayos and Yaquis reacted against this growing process of land loss and fighting took place until the mid-1880s when Yaqui and Mayo power was broken and mestizos occupied the river valleys. In the 1890s Mayo prophets appeared while Yaquis continued fighting as guerrilla forces in the mountains, which are more readily accessible to Yaquis than to Mayos. After the 1910 Revolution Yaquis returning to the river valley were successful both in reestablishing a number of their original mission pueblos and the pueblo political organization and in obtaining a reservation over which they maintain a degree of political autonomy. Therefore, Yaquis have achieved a level of political integration with the mestizo government, characterized by my type-4 integration in which the Yaqui political structure is recognized and respected by mestizo leadership. Mayos, no longer capable of unified political action, are characterized according to Spicer (1970:124) by a regressive response to mestizo dominance. Yaquis "did not reject the necessity for adaptation to Mexican society; they rather attempted to control the conditions for it." Turner's suggestions are verified and permit us to build upon this enigmatic difference between Yaquis and Mayos which Spicer has clearly pointed out. The Yaquis characterized by a new kind of integration between their own indigenous political system and that of the dominant society may not be conceived of as liminal. Mayos lacking this type of relationship with the dominant society are thrown into a liminal state. Although Mayos have not achieved the Yaqui level of socio-political integration with mestizo society, Mayo creativity is to be found in their dynamic ritual and mythic systems which in themselves are far from regressive. Individual Mayos admire the Yaquis' political unity and admit their own inability to explain the Mayo lack of political unification. Granting this difference in political integration and the resulting absence or presence of a state of liminality, we would predict that Mayos should be concerned with the integration of recent events into a dynamic ritual symbol system while Yaquis should lack this characteristic liminal interest. My predictions, of course, are verified by the data presented in this study. Instead of the clear political reservation boundary, Mayos substitute a dynamic symbolic ceremonial system which in its own way groups people as clearly Mayo or mestizo.

Besides acting as a boundary marking mechanism, a means of ethnic identity, a way of dealing with a liminal status, a method of explaining and bringing meaning to the world in which Mayos live and to Mayo-mestizo relations, and a mechanism for the resolution of tension resulting from relative deprivation, I shall suggest another explanation for the existence of Mayo prophetic movements and the revitalization of Mayo cultural tradition. A final general and tentative argument regarding the underlying structure of Mayo prophetic movements and revitalization will be quite briefly indicated. As contrasted with "rational" political action, revitalization movements have often been characterized as "magical" resulting from despair, disillusionment, and inability to respond in a "rational" manner. Even though the rituals and symbols are used "magically" and, in Western terms, lack referents to an ultimate reality, revitalization movements are extremely compelling and contain amazing curing and transforming powers, both at the individual and the group levels. How does one explain the source of this intense power to capture, transform, and cure individuals and social groups?

In partial answer, I postulate the existence of a similar underlying structure which ties together Mayo myth, traditional ritual, prophetic movements, and the liminal process. By presenting this embedded structure, Mayo prophetic movements, as well as other Mayo ritual and myths, provide a source of tremendous power both for the formation of socio-cultural identity and for human transformation. To type this kind of phenomenon as "magical" and "irrational" masks its very real power. This power perhaps can only be tapped through these kinds of symbols and symbolic processes, and may be required by societies and individuals confronted by certain impasses or moving through certain types of transformations or changes. My analysis suggests that Mayo society is in one such impasse. Within this type of situation and given Mayo history the present Mayo response is not irrational. Rather it represents a most reasonable set of creative adaptations synthesizing traditional Mayo culture and society with recent economic and socio-political conditions in southern Sonora. This Mayo response also provides a means of transforming individuals and maintaining their adjustment to a state of dynamic societal liminality.

A non-lineal paradigmatic formulation which resolves binary opposition through permutation represents the structure underlying this modern Mayo response. In the analysis of myths and folktales, Claude Lévi-Strauss (1963) and the Marandas (E. K. Köngäs and P. Maranda, 1962; and E. K. Maranda and P. Maranda, 1971) have developed and applied a formula which describes an underlying structure. In the resolution of opposition (a vs. b) through permutation, this structure achieves a higher level above the mediation of the opposition and beyond a simple cyclical return to the point of origin

$$f_x(a) \text{ is to } f_y(b) \text{ as } f_x(b) \text{ is to } f_a^{-1}(y).$$

It might be visualized as an ever expanding helix (Maranda and Maranda, 1971:29). In the formula, (b) represents the mediator, for example, the role of

Christ in the Easter ceremonial, and f_y, the positive function, represents Christ's living, curing and resurrection functions which characterized his life, $f_y(b)$. The negative function, f_x, in $f_x(b)$ represents the crucifixion of Christ and his death. Thus Christ's role, incorporating both the positive life and resurrection function, f_y, and the negative death function, f_x, embodies the power of a mediator. The first term (a), representing Čapayekam, unfolds or is transformed under the impact of the first function, f_x. The role of the Čapayeka has numerous negative aspects. They behave in a backwards manner and are associated with *kaifas* (an equal to and enemy of God; death) and with the dead. Mediating the life-death opposition, the role of Christ leads to the final victory $f_{a-1}(y)$, which is the transformation of Čapayekam (a) into adult men a^{-1}. From the breakup or burning of Čapayekam is produced the final victory, life (y) as adult men, a^{-1}. Thus the first three terms of the formula refer to the action: the Čapayekam appear and are defined by their negative function, $f_x(a)$; Christ, defined by a positive function, is travelling about the river valley curing the sick and ultimately after his crucifixion will return from death to life, $f_y(b)$; and Christ, also specified by the opposite and negative function, $f_x(b)$, is chased, captured, and killed by the Čapayekam, while the last member of the formula expresses the final outcome or the resolution of the mediation and represents the achievement of a new level in the expanding helix: the state of living, (y), is the positive outcome and is specified by the breakup function of the Čapayekam, (a), and their transformation function into young men, a^{-1}. "To put it metaphorically, the inverse of, say, a loss which expressed the actual impact of a negative power is not only a loss nullified or recuperation, but a gain so that $f_{a-1}(y) > f_x(b)$" (Maranda and Maranda, 1971:27). The permutation element in the formula neatly describes not only the structural power of the Mayo Easter myth but also the transformational power of the Lenten ceremonial through which boys are transformed into young men (Crumrine, 1968). Since a more technical discussion would be out of place in this book, I shall simply point out that in the transformation of Damian into a prophet and folk curer, San Damian replaces Christ as the mediator between life-health versus death-sickness in the above formulation. In other places (Crumrine, 1973; and N.D.; and Crumrine and Macklin, 1974), I have also argued that this paradigmatic formulation provides an accurate representation of the structures of other Mayo myths and rituals, of the Mayo family triangle and the Holy Family, of San Damian's transformation into a prophet, of the dynamic structure of his and other cult movements, and more generally of trance experience and of the rites of passage as formulated by Van Gennep. In other words, a structural unity underlies Mayo cultural integration and dynamics and ties individuals and their families to a distinctly Mayo system of beliefs and actions. Mayo prophetic movements, as well as Mayo myth and ritual, embody an underlying structure which appeals directly to certain Mayo individual processes involved especially in maturation and in doing so aids them in transforming themselves and maintaining their liminal status in terms of present cultural ecological conditions in the lower Mayo River valley. Even though Mayo prophetic movements appear, grow, and are transformed into small curing cults, nevertheless, individual Mayos, who are caught up in one or another cult, attain symbolic satisfaction through their participation. The Mayo prophetic movement and the whole process of cultural revitalization symbolize a people's effort to create their own destiny and to move, on their own terms, from a fluid liminal status to a more respected national status.

9. Postscript, 1988

Since the first edition of this monograph was written, I have enjoyed returning numerous times to the Mayo area to visit with my friends; yet, I always am a bit afraid of any unpleasant news which I might be told concerning the health of the Mayos. As we all age, I fear that someone close to me will have died or may be terminally ill. Fortunately, I have not had to face such bad news often, as most of my friends are still alive and healthy. In fact, one of my old friends, a critical and caustic, yet very subtle, old Mayo man, rushed up to me several years ago with a somewhat amused expression on his face and exclaimed, "My goodness! How nice to see you. I thought you had died years ago!" Of course, the more general question resulting from this concern involves the continuity or death of the Mayos as a people and of their way of life.

At least as for the present, I am pleased to note the most recent figures reveal that the Mayo population is still considerable and certainly not rapidly decreasing. Martha Muntzel and Benjamín Périz González (1987:577, 597-600), in an article in the latest "América Indígena" based on the 1980 census, place Mayo speakers at 56,387 persons with an additional 9,282 Yaqui speakers, or a total of 65,669 Cahitan speakers. In contrast to the 1950 census figure of 31,052 Mayo speakers (*see* page 15), these 1980 figures represent a considerable increase; however, the 1950 census most likely missed many persons who were bilingual in Spanish and Mayo and who did not volunteer their ability to speak Mayo to the census taker.

Interestingly, in the case of nearly all the Mayo families that I visit regularly, the children speak only Spanish, and their parents claim that they know very little Mayo and do not wish to learn the language. This is strange, because I have not heard these same adults speak Spanish except to their children. As these children mature, will they switch to Mayo speech at home or will the language and perhaps the way of life disappear as the present adult generation dies? Will the Mayos, who clearly remain in the 1980s "A People Who Refuse to Die," disappear in the latter 1990s and early years of the next century? I fear the latter, as every time

I return to southern Sonora, inflation seems worse, food is more and more expensive, and Mayos and poor rural farmers are suffering more. Yet, health services, housing and furnishings, roads and transportation, and electric and water services have improved. Despite the negative economic conditions, Mayos seem to be thriving, not only rebuilding old churches and homes, but also constructing new ones. The ultimate answer surely must depend upon the type of creative accommodation and adaptation to the modern world's culture and society which Mayos as Mayos are capable of achieving.

In publishing the findings from his 1930 field research among the Mayos and Yaquis, Ralph Beals, the expert in culture change and in the anthropology of northwest Mexico, suggested that the Mayos would soon be absorbed into mestizo society. Recently, in his concluding chapter printed in a collection of articles on northwest and west Mexico, he notes:

> . . . the enclavement of the Mayo appears unique. Many years ago I remarked that I expected the Yaqui to survive as a culturally distinct group, but that the Mayo probably soon would disappear because they had lost the boundary maintaining mechanism of the civil wing of the civil-religious hierarchy. Crumrine shows quite clearly that I was wrong, and an active complex ritual life requiring extensive participation and the maintenance of some competence in the native language are enough to permit survival of an ethnic unit without territorial boundaries or political power. Spicer often averred that the Yaqui as an ethnic group would disappear when so many individual Yaqui defected that there were too few to maintain the ritual system; it seems likely that the same is true for the Mayo (Beals 1987a, 98).

Thus, the Mayo way of life continues in 1988, in many ways, much as it was in 1973 when this book was first published.

In contrast, however, the trip to northwest Mexico has become gradually easier and the area more and more accessible, with the exception of the bankruptcy of AeroMexico. As noted earlier, Ralph Beals conducted field research in the area in the 1930s and recently wrote an account of that experience. That account, together with my description of a recent trip to northwest Mexico, was published in a monograph edited by Phil Weigand and myself which provides a graphic contrast between conditions in the 1930s and those of the 1980s. Ralph Beals (1987b,1-3) writes:

> In Sonora travel outside the settlements was extremely hazardous except with an armed party of some size. The thrice weekly trains of the Sud Pacifico de Mexico included two steel gondolas with two mounted machine guns, each manned by 20 or 30 soldiers. And near Cajeme (now Ciudad Obregón), I hid under a bush while a large mounted Yaqui war party crossed the cart track nearby. . . . The Yaqui area was under martial law during the period of my fieldwork there and access was restricted. . . .
>
> Physical conditions were also difficult. Rail travel was poor. . . . Automobile travel was possible to most places but there were no paved roads. Indeed, the only paving in towns was in older settlements still maintaining colonial cobbled streets. In Sinoloa there were some graded roads, but most roads were

simply tracks cut through the thorn forests or, in the north, the steppe or desert vegetation. Roads along the coastal plain often were deep in fine alluvial dust. All were impassible, often for days, after heavy rains.

Living accommodations were minimal. . . . Sanitation was primitive. The best hotel in Navojoa had one flush toilet, often not functioning, and a single cold shower. . . . Leslie White visited Mexico not long after returning from a long stay in China. When shortly after he visited me in 1937 in Los Angeles, he mainly wanted to know how I could do fieldwork under the appalling sanitation and food conditions, compared with those in China.

My description of current field research in the Mayo region focuses on the stark contrasts with the Beals account as follows (Crumrine 1987a,3-8):

Today, in striking contrast, even a long weekend can provide enough time for a brief visit to southern Sonora, considerable chatting with Mayos, and the observation of a traditional ritual. From as far away as Victoria, British Columbia, I can reach the Mayo area within a day. Leaving on the 7:00 A.M. flight from Victoria to Vancouver, I connect with a flight to Los Angeles, . . . to . . . the Tijuana airport. After receiving a boarding pass from AeroMexico, . . . I board the 7:00 P.M. flight for Ciudad Obregón in the Yaqui region. In the Ciudad Obregón airport, . . . a VW sedan is waiting and soon I am on the highway south to Navojoa. About an hour later I arrive in Navojoa, where there is a choice of two first class motels or several more modest one[s] nearer the highway down the Mayo River valley. Thus by 9:00 or 10:00 P.M. I am settling into a modest yet pleasant motel room with an air conditioner, hot and cold running water, and a private bath and shower.

Early the next morning, I stop by the supermarket and select a large steak packaged on a styrofoam plate and wrapped in clear plastic and several pounds of green bean coffee for my friends. . . .

After a short drive down a narrow path bordering a canal, I see an older man working in a green wheat field, wave to him, and stop several hundred meters on down the canal. Crossing a neighbor's narrow wheat field, I approach Jose's earthen roofed home, with his several hectare wheat field stretching beyond. After the traditional set of Mayo greetings with his wife, I hand her the steak, which she accepts. . . . After chatting for a few minutes, her husband arrives from his field and we greet each other again, using the formal Mayo conventions. . . .

Living at the edge of his fields and in contrast to many Mayo families, Jose and his wife do not have running water nor electricity, but the small propane range placed inside one of their substantial adobe rooms is new since my last visit. . . .

After lunch, . . . I indicate that I also wish to go to the konti and ask Jose if he is going and if they would like a ride. . . . Soon they are ready and we drive the few kilometers to (Banari). . . .

This Friday was a good choice for a visit as the crowd is large and many Pariserom as well as the church officials are participating. . . . At each of the 14 stations, . . . the procession stops, participants kneel, and the *maestrom* read a set of prayers while the masked *Pariserom* either make sure everyone within the center of the procession kneels properly or burlesque the ritual and poke fun at the men and children standing at the fringes of the ritual . . . the procession reforms and returns to the church as the sun is setting in the west. After concluding prayers in the church the participants begin to return home. . . . Jose and his family load into the car, and answer several of my questions about aspects of the ritual on the ride home. After the return drive, I arrive at the motel around 9 P.M.

The next morning I drive to the airport to Ciudad Obregón in time for the mid-morning flight to Tijuana, and reversing the route down, I arrive home around midnight after taking the late flight to Victoria. Although not really desirable in terms of the short time available for actual contact with Mayo friends, it is possible today to visit several Mayo communities and observe a complex ritual within the short period of three days. . . .

These descriptions provide dramatic contrasts and highlight the intense degrees of change and modernization, coupled with a retention of certain traditional beliefs and rituals, that have taken place in northwestern Mexico over the last thirty or forty years. These contrasts indicate that, while today, Mayos are embedded or enclosed within modern Mexico, they are able to retain, in part, their Mayo identity due to the complex and sustaining nature of Mayo ritual and ceremonialism. Having spent numerous Easter Weeks in the lower Mayo area, I continue to wonder what makes me return each year when the major outlines of the ritual are so well known, but, as strange as it may sound, on each visit I observe something unseen in former years. For example, this year on Easter Sunday morning, I followed the *Pariserom* to the cemetery for the first time where they prayed at the gravesides of several of their former members. The ritual, with the flutist and drummer playing around each of the four sides of the graves, was nearly identical to that performed around the coffin of Christ during the Good Friday wake in the church (Figures 9.1 and 9.2). Also, this Easter Sunday during the last procession around the church, I happened to be near the head of the procession beside the *Pilatom*. Suddenly, I realized that they looked quite dejected, were not wearing their hats, and were not holding their banners up but dragging them on the ground (Figure 9.4). Clearly, this represents their final submission to and defeat by the powers of the church and of God. Thus, Mayo ceremonialism is symbolically complex and socially exciting enough to keep individuals involved, interested, and participating year after year. In addition, should one tire of the well-established church-based ceremonials, the Mayos have not ceased to produce new small cults with their prophetic leaders.

As I have come to understand Mayo ritual and especially the Easter ceremonial in greater depth, the links between Mayo home ritual and church ceremonials have become clearer. The church rituals, especially the enactment of the last weeks in Jesus' life and his death and resurrection, represent a metaphorical statement of the Mayo family funeral ritual. The same *alabansas* are chanted by the *maestros* and *cantoras* at the family funeral, the eight-day ritual and the year celebration as are sung during the funeral ritual for Christ celebrated Good Friday night.

9.1 The *Pariserom* in the cemetery, Easter Sunday morning

9.2   The flutist and drummer playing at the tomb of a former *Parisero*

9.3 The *Pariserom* pulling up the church crosses at a neighboring church before "killing" Christ, Good Friday morning

9.4 Within the walled compound of the church of a new Mayo cult center

Several Mayos have told me that death did not exist before Jesus was killed; thus, his death was the origin of the funeral ritual. In contrast, birth often takes place in a modern clinic or hospital, and its ritual plays a small role in the modern Mayo ceremonial cycle. Other church ceremonials also have their family-level replicas; however, the Easter rituals represent the most highly elaborated and emotionally most engaging ones. It is apparent that Mayo ceremonialism reveals clear integration with the life cycle rituals, especially those of puberty, illness and death.

Despite the pervading nature of traditional Mayo ritualism, Mayo culture and society still provide an arena for creativity, namely the innovative and prophetical new cult rituals. Since the Mayo prophet Damian's cult, one major and fascinating messianic cult has grown into a church center (Crumrine 1975), and many families have been involved in miraculous encounters resulting in the production of *pahkom*. Some Mayos still personally experience visitations by God and the Saints, while others receive and interpret letters which appear on altars and crosses. Although today many of my long-time Mayo friends no longer participate, many helped a Mayo man and his wife build a church and produce numerous *pahkom* in order to avert the destruction of the world. This man and his wife interpreted patterns of light which appeared on a cross as letters sent from God and still fill books with their interpretations of present messages. Figure 9.5 illustrates their church today, and Figure 9.6 shows the head of the church and some of the books in which they have written the messages from God (*see* Crumrine 1975). Other such messianic impulses have also had lasting results, such as the existence of the present church in Los Arboles, which was built shortly after the Damian Bwiya or Lioh *pahko* cult declined and has been rebuilt during the last two years.

Within the last few years, the rebuilding of established Mayo churches has been a typical process. It proves simpler to note the Mayo churches which have not been rebuilt rather than to highlight those that have, because the churches in Banari, Homecarit, and Los Arboles all have been reconstructed. Only those in Etchojoa and Huícori remain unmodified. Figures 9.7 and 9.8 illustrate a new Santa Cruz church and their *pahkola* or *paskola ramada* constructed in Etchojoa *municipio* after the government moved some of the old church congregation away from the traditional church, which was destroyed by river flooding when excess water was released from the Mayo dam several years ago.

Even more intriguing, the mission pueblo of Santa Cruz in Huatabampo municipio is in the process of building a church. Santa Cruz, located very close to Banari, was one of the eight original mission villages and was abandoned by all but several families in the 1880s. In Mayo minds, this represents a partial re-establishment of the Goh Naiki Pueblo Hurasionim (the Eight Village Jurisdictions). Specifically, according to modern Mayos, the Goh Naiki Pueblo Hurasionim refers to the founding eight mission pueblo jurisdictions. Historically, the Jesuits established eight centers in both the Mayo and the Yaqui areas. Although none of my friends can actually list the specific historical eight pueblos, they accept the symbolic power of the concept and can produce lists of eight names which *are,* for them, the Goh Naiki Pueblo Hurasionim. The exchange *Pahkom* in honor of the Espiritu Santo (Etchojoa) and the Santisima Tiniran (Banari or Santa Cruz)

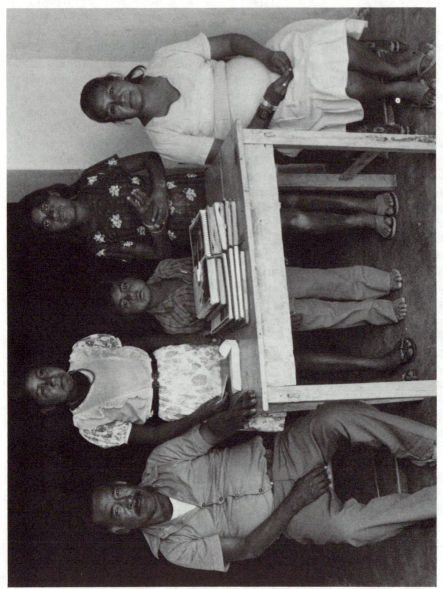

9.5 The church president and leader, his wife, and several local children with their Books of "Letters" and Explanations continue to unify Mayos at the Pueblo or intermunicipio level and contribute to the maintenance of the Goh Naiki Pueblo Hurasionim ideology. Since the original publication of this book, the number of *pahkome* groups attending the *pahko* has increased to eight. For example, in 1983, when I attended the Espiritu Santo *Pahko* in Etchojoa (*see* Crumrine nd), numerous Mayos pointed out to me that these were the "Goh Naiki Pueblo Hurasionim." Calling my attention to the eight flags of the *pahkome* groups, they argued that each flag denoted a Pueblo, which metaphorically and ideologically is very powerful, although, in reality, each flag represents a church center, all of which exist today within only two of the original eight Pueblo Hurasionim. It would seem to be a fortunate accident that the flags today total eight, an increase over the five church centers that we observed participating in the *pahko* of 1961 (Crumrine 1969). Mayos with whom I chatted in Etchojoa argued that this was a Mayo ceremony, the people attending were all Mayos, all Yoremes, and that the land was Mayo *bwiya* (land). Thus, Mayos have not overlooked the messianic implications and symbolism expressed in the Goh Naiki Pueblo Hurasionim ideology and reproduced in the ceremonials honoring the Espiritu Santo and the Santisima Tiniran.

Since the rains were not adequate last summer (1987), and the Mayo area received very little winter rains, the water situation in Spring 1988 is extremely crucial. The Mayo dam is essentially dry, except for a little water which is being retained to keep the fish stocks alive. Local farmers are relying upon wells to draw up underground water for irrigation. Below Banari, many of the wells are salty because the ocean water seeps up the valley, replacing the fresh water drawn out of the wells. With our knowledge of Mayos, we would predict that such a tense situation would increase religious and cult activity. When I arrived in the Mayo region Easter Week, 1988, I approached one of my *Paskola* friends hoping that he would be dancing for a *velaroa* for Christ before Good Friday, which I could attend. I was disapointed to learn that he had not been employed, but I agreed to give him a ride up the river valley where he was dancing for a *pahko* to honor Guadalupe on Monday of Easter Week.

Guadalupe is popular in the Mayo region, and occasionally families promise to have a *pahko* in her honor, which would not be unusual nor new. It seemed a bit peculiar during Easter week but not worth breaking a promise to take Juan and his wife to bathe in the ocean, a typical Easter week custom they said. Had I thought much about this event, I would have realized that a *pahko* for Guadalupe was completely out of season during Easter week. I solved the difficulty by offering to take the *Paskola* to the fiesta home in the morning and return and go to the ocean with Juan and his wife in the afternoon. After an hour's drive up the river valley, we arrived at the *pahko* home. I asked permission to *mukti* (pray) at the altar and entered the side door of the house. After going to both altar tables, I began chatting with a young man who was decorating the second one. Later, I was told that he and the father of the home owner observed Guadalupe and the other saints on the wall above the present altars during one of the few rains last summer, 1987. The old man, who lives in a neighboring village, was extremely frightened and has not returned since, but his son, this young man, and a group

9.6 A new Santa Cruz church in Etchojoa Municipio with several *pahkome* and the *comisario*

9.7　The *paskola ramada* in front of the new Santa Cruz church

which gathered around them had realized that Guadalupe and the saints wanted a series of *pahkom* which the group had given each month on the anniversary date of her visitation. At first, not realizing the role this young man was playing in the development of this *pahkom* series, I was complimenting him on the paper flowers which he was making and asking where he lived, etc. Turning away from the altar, I noticed a line of decorated crosses extending out from the house door, considerably more than the typical three. Immediately, I moved out the door, listening much more acutely to the typical Mayo chatting going on between my *Paskola* friend, the home owner, and his neighbor. In an attempt to keep the conversation from moving to other subjects, I asked about the crosses and the *pahkom*. They then related the events of the visitation and took me back into the house to point out the place on the wall where Guadalupe appeared. They explained that there would be prayers and *paskola* dancing all night until early the next morning when the *pahko* would conclude.

Although Guadalupe appeared during one of the only rains last summer, the Mayos pointed out their concern regarding the lack of rain. More specifically stimulated by the drought conditions in northern Sinaloa, the daughter of one of my friends who is attending a business school in that area returned to Banari for her Easter holidays with the following account. An old Mayo woman of San Miguel in the Fuerte River valley of Sinaloa had been visited by Guadalupe, the latter having requested prayers and ceremonies. The old woman had begun to organize a *pahko*, which people were saying would please Guadalupe and resolve the drought. Thus, one of the typical Mayo responses to stress is again being employed to reduce their anxiety concerning the present negative climatic conditions. In conclusion, although Mexico is undergoing intense change and extremely serious inflationary conditions, and poor rural farmers are especially facing profound challenges, Mayos continue to endure and to adapt creatively their traditional means of coping with personal, familial, and societal dilemmas to modern Mexico, to world crises and to modernization in general.

References, 1988

Beals, Ralph L.
   1987a   "The Renaissance of Anthropological Studies in Northwest Mexico." In *Ejidos and Regions of Refuge in Northwestern Mexico,* edited by N. Ross Crumrine and Phil C. Weigand. *Anthropological Papers of the University of Arizona,* Number 46:95-102. Tucson: University of Arizona Press.
   1987b   "Reflections, Contrasts, and Directions, by Ralph L. Beals and N. Ross Crumrine." In *Ejidos and Regions of Refuge in Northwestern Mexico,* edited by N. Ross Crumrine and Phil C. Weigand. *Anthropological Papers of the University of Arizona,* Number 46:1-10. Tucson: University of Arizona Press.
Carlos, Manuel L.
   1974   *Politics and Development in Rural Mexico: A Study of Socio-Economic Modernization.* New York: Praeger Publishers.
   1987   "Enclavement Processes, State Policies, and Cultural Identity among the Mayo Indians of Sinaloa, Mexico." In *Ejidos and Regions of Refuge in Northwestern*

Mexico, edited by N. Ross Crumrine and Phil C. Weigand. *Anthropological Papers of the University of Arizona,* Number 46:33-38. Tucson: University of Arizona Press.

Crumrine, N. Ross
1975   "A New Mayo Indian Religious Movement in Northwest Mexico." *Journal of Latin American Lore* 1(2):127-145.
1976   "Mediating Roles in Ritual and Symbolism: Northwest Mexico and the Pacific Northwest." *Anthropologica* 18(2):131-152.
1978   "A Transformational Analysis of Mayo Ceremonialism and Myth." *Journal of Latin American Lore* 4(2):231-242.
1981   "The Mayo of Southern Sonora: Socio-economic Assimilation and Ritual-symbolic Syncretism — Split Acculturation." In *Themes of Indigenous Acculturation in Northwest Mexico,* edited by Thomas B. Hinton and Phil C. Weigand. *Anthropological Papers of the University of Arizona,* Number 38:22-35. Tucson: The University of Arizona Press.
1981   "The Ritual of the Cultural Enclave Process: The Dramatization of Oppositions among the Mayo Indians of Northwest Mexico." In *Persistent Peoples,* edited by George P. Castile and Gilbert Kushner, pp. 109-131. Tucson: University of Arizona Press.
1982   "Transformational Processes and Models: With Special Reference to Mayo Indian Myth and Ritual." In *The Logic of Culture,* edited by Ino Rossi, pp. 68-87. South Hadley, MA: Bergin & Garvey Publishers Inc.
1983   "Symbolic Structure and Ritual Symbolism in Northwest and West Mexico." In *Heritage of Conquest: Thirty Years Later,* edited by Carl Kendall, John Hawkins, and Laurel Bossen. Albuquerque, New Mexico: University of New Mexico Press.
1983   "Mayo." in *Southwest,* Vol. 10 of *Handbook of North American Indians,* edited by William C. Sturtevant (volume editor, Alfonso Ortiz), pp. 264-275. Washington: Smithsonian Institution.
1983   "Mask Use and Meaning in Easter Ceremonialism: The Mayo Parisero." In *The Power of Symbols,* edited by N. Ross Crumrine and Marjorie Halpin, pp. 93-101. Vancouver: University of British Columbia Press.
1986   "Drama Folklórico en Latino América: Estructura y significado del ritual y simbolismo de Cuaresma y de la Semana Santa." *Folklore Americano* 41/42:5-31.
1987a   "Reflections, Contrasts, and Directions," by Ralph L. Beals and N. Ross Crumrine. In *Ejidos and Regions of Refuge in Northwestern Mexico,* edited by N. Ross Crumrine and Phil C. Weigand. *Anthropological Papers of the University of Arizona,* Number 46:1-10. Tucson: University of Arizona Press.
1987b   "Mechanisms of Enclavement Maintenance and Sociocultural Blocking of Modernization among the Mayo of Southern Sonora." In *Ejidos and Regions of Refuge in Northwestern Mexico,* edited by N. Ross Crumrine and Phil C. Weigand. *Anthropological Papers of the University of Arizona,* Number 46:21-30. Tucson: University of Arizona Press.
N.D.   "The Yorem Pahko and Goh Naiki Pueblo Ideology: Fiestas and Exchange Pilgrimages in Mayo Indian Identity, Sonora, Northwest Mexico." In *La Peregrinación: Pilgrimage in Latin America,* edited by N. Ross Crumrine and Alan Morinis. In press, New York: Greenwood Press.

Crumrine, N. Ross and M. Louise Crumrine
1977   "Ritual Symbolism in Folk and Ritual Drama: The Mayo Indian Cayetano Velación, Sonora, Mexico." *Journal of American Folklore* 90(355):8-28.

Lutes, Steven V.
1983   "The Mask and Magic of the Yaqui Paskola Clowns." In *The Power of Symbols: Masks and Masquerade in the Americas,* edited by N. Ross Crumrine and

Marjorie Halpin, pp. 81-92. Vancouver: University of British Columbia Press.
1987   "Yaqui Indian Enclavement: The Effects of an Experimental Indian Policy in Northwestern Mexico." In *Ejidos and Regions of Refuge in Northwestern Mexico,* edited by N. Ross Crumrine and Phil C. Weigand. *Anthropological Papers of the University of Arizona,* Number 46:11-20. Tucson: University of Arizona Press.

Muntzel, Martha C. and Benjamín Pérez González
1987   "Panorama general de las lenguas indígenas." *América Indígena* 47(4):571-605.

O'Connor, Mary I.
1979   "Two Kinds of Religious Movements." *Journal for the Scientific Study of Religion* 18(3):260-268.
1980   "Ethnicity and Economics: The Mayos of Sonora, Mexico." Ph.D. dissertation, University of California at Santa Barbara. Revised and in press.

Glossary

NOTE: With the possible exception of *dueño, mestizo,* and *ranchería,* all the following words are used by Mayos when speaking Mayo. Some are obviously Spanish loan words, such as *Alawasin, Alperes, ejido,* or *kurus mayor,* but many are strictly Mayo terms, such as *abaso sewam, goʔim,* or *maso.* Other terms represent combinations, such as *Bahi Mariam* (Three, a Mayo word, and Marys) or *Bahi Reyesim* (Three Kings). Since the loaning is not always completely clear, I have refrained from marking each word as either Spanish or Mayo.

* * *

abaso sewam   green leaves of the cottonwood tree

Alawasin   "sheriff"; lowest ranking member of the Paskome

Alperes   flagbearer; second-ranking member of the Paskome

Bahi Mariam   women and children having certain roles in the Lenten ceremonial

Bahi Reyesim   Three Kings; the governors and men of the pueblo

batoačai   male ceremonial sponsor or godfather

batoaye   female ceremonial sponsor or godmother

Compadre   co-parent

Čapakoba
      or Čapayeka   masked members of the Pariserom

Dueño   owner or guardian especially of a saint's image

ejido   a communal land-holding unit which may either be divided into separate land assignments or be farmed communally by the members of the association to whom the land is assigned by federal authority. It includes common village forest as well as cultivated fields.

Espiritu Santu   Holy Spirit. In Etchojoa, the patron saint, Espiritu Santu, is known as Itom Aye, Our Mother.

goʔim   coyotes; members of a division of the Mayo military society

hemyori   literally "to rest"; also applied to the ritual pause or recess in a procession at the altar of a household before proceeding to the pasko-giving household or church.

hinabaka   a sermon or ritual speech in the Mayo language

hitolío   herbal doctor, believed to possess supernatural power to diagnose causes of illness and cure witchcraft-caused diseases. Shamanlike curer.

Huya Anía   the sacred forest world

Ili Usim   children of God

Itom Ačai   any form of Our Father, Jesus, Christ, Christ Crucified; the Father of God (Itom Ačai O?ola), San Isidro, Santisima Tiniran, the church-yard cemetery cross and other crosses or any other manifestation of male divinity.

Itom Ačai O?ola   Old Man God, God the Father

Itom Ačai Usi   Our Father Son, Jesus, The Infant Christ

Itom Aye   any form of Our Mother, any of the Three Marys, the Holy Mother, Mary Magdalene, Mary Dolorosa, Santa Teresa, the earth, the church, some crosses, or any manifestation of female divinity.

Kabo   corporal in the Parisero society

kalbário   The Way of the Cross

kobanárom   church or pueblo officials

Kompañia   the co-operative group of persons related to a single individual through ceremonial or ritual kin (co-parent, godparent, or godchild) ties

konti   a regular Sunday service at the church, the service of the Way of the Cross each Friday of Lent except Good Friday, and other services involving processions surrounding the church.

konti bo?o   "surrounding road," the way or road of a procession

kurus yo?owe   "great cross." A generic term applied to the pueblo boundary cross, the churchyard cross, the dance ramada cross, and several other crosses central to Mayo ceremonial life and treated as saints or *kurus mayor*, "major cross".

Liohpasko   a "gift" Pasko or ceremony for God

Maestro   lay minister. Mayo church maestros form a sodality with internal rankings and organization.

Maestro Mo?oro   assistant to the maestro, a very active role in which guidance of the Paskome through rituals is the chief task. The ritual insignia of this role is a thin drum, often beaten while leading the Paskome.

Maestro Yo?owe   head lay minister of a Mayo church, who reads prayers, plays an important part not only in the performance of home and church ritual but also in all important religious and community decisions apart from and through the council

manda   ritual promise made by a family or individual to a saint to give a ceremony for the saint in the event that a severe sickness is cured or a personal crisis is passed safely

Maso (pl. masom) deer, or deer dancer; ritual dance specialist who performs at Paskos and is associated with a body of myth and sacred literature.

Maso Bwikame deer singers

Matačin a member of a dance society closely associated with the church organization, whose mature male members dance at almost every major household and church event outside the Lenten season, and into which the adolescent boys and girls of the downriver Mayo area are initiated during the ceremonies of the Santisima Tiniran and Espiritu Santu in the spring.

mestizo a technical term, used here to refer to any non-Mayo Mexican

Monarka dance leader of the matacin society

Mo?oro helper assistant, as maestro mo?oro, assistant maestro. Man who directs, or leads the ceremonial hosts (Paskome) in the performance of rituals.

mukti to pray or worship in the church

Parina highest ranking Paskome

Parisero men's Lenten sodality acting out the part of the army pursuing, capturing, and crucifying Jesus for a period of seven weeks between Ash Wednesday and Easter. A Parisero may be assigned community tasks at any time in the year.

Pasko refers particularly to the paskola and deer dance and song aspects of a Mayo ceremony and feast days climaxing a Mayo ceremonial; also spelled *pahko*

Paskola a costumed ritual dance specialist, performing animal dances to the flute and drum or harp and violins at house and pueblo ceremonies, whose activities are associated with a body of sacred literature and mythology

Paskome ceremonial hosts, or those who give the ceremonial. Being a host implies having made a manda to a saint and having been cured. The duties of the host involve ceremonial labor, and food giving.

Pasko Personasim ritual hosts who donate goods and services, organize the ceremony, and take the responsibility for its actualization in payment of a promise made to the supernatural whose ceremony they are giving. Or *Paskome*.

Pilato pilate, top-ranking officers of the parisero sodality, felt by Mayos to be wise in ritual knowledge

ranchería rural cluster of several often related households; may run up to 200-300 persons or in exceptional cases perhaps 1,000, usually removed in geographical distance from other settlements. For Mayos the unit is often exogamous.

Santa Kurus Holy Cross. A white flowered cross generally made of wood, often with flowers or a palm arch from arm to arm. Known to Mayos as Itom Ačai.

San Rafael   Saint Raphael, patron of Tosalipaku, called Itom Aye, or Our Mother by Mayos in the villages downriver.

Santisima Tiniran   Holy Trinity. Patron saint of Banari. The Santisima Tiniran image of a nearby village, Huicori, where it is also patron, differs considerably. Or *Tiniran* or *Itom Ačai*.

Sagrada Familia   Holy Family

sibo   to bewitch

solar   the ancestral land upon which a Mayo's house is located

tebátpo kurus   house cross; from *tebat*, patio

tekiame   those who have pueblo and church offices validated by the people through council approval

tiopo   Mayo church

Utes Yoʔoria   very sacred, used in reference to the ''Holy Family''

velación   a ritual involving prayer and vigil

wakabaki   beef stew, a fiesta food

wawari   bilateral relative or bilateral kin unit

wikičim   (*wikit*, sing.) birds, members of a segment of the Mayo military society

Yoreme   no precise English equivalent; means a person identified as a member of the Mayo ethnic group; either refers specifically to a Mayo or in a general sense to any Indian in either Mexico or the United States

Yori   uncomplimentary Mayo name for non-Mayo Spanish speaker

References

Aberle, David F.
  1959   The Prophet Dance and Reactions to White Contact. *Southwestern Journal of Anthropology* 15:74–83.
  1962   A Note on Relative Deprivation Theory as Applied to Millennarian and other Cult Movements. In *Millennarian Dreams in Action,* edited by Silvia Thrupp. Comparative Studies in Society and History, Supplement II:209–214.
  1966   The Peyote Religion Among the Navaho. *Viking Fund Publications in Anthropology,* 42.

Barnett, Homer G.
  1957   *Indian Shakers: A Messianic Cult of the Pacific Northwest.* Carbondale: Southern Illinois University Press.

Beals, Ralph L.
  1945   *The Contemporary Culture of the Cahita Indians.* U.S. Bureau of American Ethnology, Bulletin No. 142.

Berber, Laureano Calvo
  1958   *Nociones de Historia de Sonora.* Mexico, D. F.: Librería de M. Porrua.

Burridge, Kenelm
  1969   *New Heaven, New Earth: A Study of Millennarian Activities.* Oxford: Basil Blackwell.

Crumrine, Lynne S. and N. Ross Crumrine
  1967   Ancient and Modern Mayo Fishing Practices. *The Kiva* 33:25–33.

Crumrine, N. Ross
  1964   The House Cross of the Mayo Indians of Sonora, Mexico: A Symbol of Ethnic Identity. *Anthropological Papers of the University of Arizona,* Number 8. Tucson: University of Arizona Press.
  1968   The Easter Ceremonial in the Socio-Cultural Identity of Mayos, Sonora, Mexico. Ph.D. dissertation, University of Arizona, Tucson.
  1969   Čapakoba, The Mayo Easter Ceremonial Impersonator: Explanations of Ritual Clowning. *Journal for the Scientific Study of Religion* 8 (1):1–22.
  1970   Ritual Drama and Culture Change. *Comparative Studies in Society and History* 12 (4): 361–372.
  1973   'The Earth Will Eat You Up': A Structural Analysis of Mayo Indian Myths. *América Indígena.* 33(4): 1119–1150.
  N.D.   Transformational Processes and Models: with Special Reference to Mayo Indian Myth and Ritual. For publication in *New Trends in Structural Anthropology,* edited by Ino Rossi.

Crumrine, N. Ross and Lynne S. Crumrine
    1969   Where Mayos Meet Mestizos: A Model for the Social Structure of Culture Contact. *Human Organization* 28 (1): 50–57.
Crumrine, N. Ross and B. June Macklin
    1974   Sacred Ritual vs. The Unconscious: The Efficacy of Symbols and Structure in North Mexican Folk Saints' Cults and General Ceremonialism. In *The Unconscious in Culture*, edited by Ino Rossi. New York: E. P. Dutton & Co.
Erasmus, Charles J.
    1952   The Leader vs. Tradition: A Case Study. *American Anthropologist* 54: 168–178.
    1961   *Man Takes Control: Cultural Development and American Aid*. Minneapolis: University of Minnesota Press.
    1967   Culture Change in Northwest Mexico. In *Contemporary Change in Traditional Societies Volume 3: Mexican and Peruvian Communities*, edited by J. H. Steward. Urbana: University of Illinois Press.
Flores, Anselmo Marino
    1967   Indian Population and Its Identification. In *Handbook of Middle American Indians, Social Anthropology.*, edited by Manning Nash, vol. 6, pp. 12–25. Austin: University of Texas Press.
Geertz, Clifford
    1957   Ritual and Social Change: A Javanese Example. *American Anthropologist* 59: 32–54.
Gennep, A. van
    1909   *Rites de Passage*. London: Routledge and Kegan Paul. Also 1960 *The Rites of Passage*. (Translation of the French edition). Chicago: Phoenix Books, University of Chicago Press.
Gentry, Howard S.
    1942   *Rio Mayo Plants*. Carnegie Institute Publication, No. 527.
    1963   *The Warihio Indians of Sonora-Chihuahua: An Ethnographic Survey*. U.S. Bureau of American Ethnology, Bulletin No. 186.
Griffith, James S.
    1972   Cáhitan Pascola Masks. *The Kiva* 37 (4): 185–198.
Guariglia, Guglielmo
    1959   Prophetismus und Heilserwartungs-Bewegungen als volkerkundliches und religionsgeschichtliches Problem. *Wiener Beiträge zur Kulturgeschichte und Linguistik, Band XIII*. Horn, Wien: Verlag Ferdinand Berger.
Gunther, Erna
    1949   The Shaker Religion of the Northwest. In *Indians of the Urban Northwest*, edited by Marian W. Smith, pp. 37–76. New York: Columbia University Press.
Köngäs [Maranda], Elli Kaija and Pierre Maranda
    1962   Structural Models in Folklore. *Midwest Folklore* 12:133–192.
Lanternari, Vittorio
    1963   *The Religions of the Oppressed: A Study of Modern Messianic Cults*. London: Macgibbon & Kee.
Lévi-Strauss, Claude
    1963   *Structural Anthropology*. New York: Basic Books Inc.
    1966   The Culinary Triangle. *New Society* Dec. 22:937–940. Translated from Le Triangle Culinaire in *L'Arc* 26:19–29.
Macklin, B. June and N. Ross Crumrine
    1973   Three North Mexican Folk Saint Movements. *Comparative Studies in Society and History* 15 (1): 89–105.

Mair, Lucy P.
1959   Independent Religious Movements in Three Continents. *Comparative Studies in Society and History* 1:113–136.

Maranda, Elli Köngäs and Pierre Maranda
1971   *Structural Models in Folklore and Transformational Essays.* The Hague: Mouton and Co.

Nolasco Armas, Margarita
1969   *Notas para la Antropología Social Del Noroeste de México.* Mexico: Instituto Nacional de Antropologia e Historia.

Peacock, James L.
1967   Comedy and Centralization in Java: the *Ludruk* Plays. *Journal of American Folklore* 80(318):345–356.

Perez de Ribas, A.
1645   *Historia de los triunfos de nuestra santa fe entre gentes las mas barbaras y fieras del nuevo orbe.* Madrid: 1944, a Mexican edition.

Proyecto
1957   *Proyecto de Programa de Gobierno del Estado de Sonora.* Mexico: Impresiones Modernas.

Redfield, Robert
1941   *The Folk Culture of Yucatan.* Chicago: University of Chicago Press.

Spicer, Edward H.
1940   *Pascua, A Yaqui Village in Arizona.* Chicago: University of Chicago Press.
1961   Yaqui. In *Perspectives in American Indian Culture Change,* edited by E. H. Spicer. Chicago: University of Chicago Press.
1962   *Cycles of Conquest: The Impact of Spain, Mexico and the United States on the Indians of the Southwest, 1533–1960.* Tucson: University of Arizona Press.
1969   Northwest Mexico: Introduction, (and) The Yaqui and Mayo. In *Handbook of Middle American Indians,* edited by Evon Vogt, 8:777–791, 830–845. Austin: University of Texas Press.
1970   Contrasting Forms of Nativism Among the Mayos and Yaquis of Sonora, Mexico. In *The Social Anthropology of Latin America,* edited by Walter Goldschmidt and Harry Hoijer, pp. 104–125. Los Angles: University of California Press.

Turner, Victor W.
1964   Betwixt and Between: The Liminal Period of Rites of Passage. In *Proceedings of the 1964 Annual Spring Meeting of the American Ethnological Society,* pp. 4–20.
1968   Myth and Symbol. In the *International Encyclopedia of the Social Sciences.* New York: The Macmillan Company and The Free Press.
1969   *The Ritual Process: Structure and Anti-Structure.* Chicago: Aldine Publishing Company.

Wallace, Anthony F. C.
1956   Revitalization Movements. *American Anthropologist* 58:264–281.
1966   *Religion: An Anthropological View.* New York: Random House Inc.

Wilson, Bryan A.
1963   Millennialism in Comparative Perspective. *Comparative Studies in Society and History* 6 (1): 93–114.

Worsley, Peter
1968   *The Trumpet Shall Sound: A Study of "Cargo" Cults in Melanesia.* New York: Schocken Books.

Index